A Goushā Weekend Guide

American Wilderness

Where to go in the nation's Wilderness, on the Wild and
Scenic Rivers and along the Scenic Trails

by Charles Jones and Klaus Knab

GOUSHĀ
TIMES MIRROR

GOUSHĀ PUBLICATIONS
San Jose, California

Editor: **Charles Jones**
Writers: Parts I and II, **Charles Jones**
 Parts III and IV, **Klaus Knab**
Designer: **Roger J. Waterman**
Cover Artist: **Masami Miyamoto**
Copy Editor: **Diana Yee**
Photographs: Ed Sherman, pages 37, 91, 207; Dick Smith, pages 2, 16, 160, 202; all others courtesy of U.S. Forest Service

With thanks for invaluable help from the following:

Forest Service; National Park Service; Forest History Society, University of California, Santa Cruz; Forestry Library, University of California Berkeley; Wilderness Society; Appalachian Trail Conference; Pacific Crest Club; various departments and commissions in state governments.

Copyright © 1973 by The H. M. Gousha Co., P.O. Box 6227, San Jose, California 95150 A subsidiary of The Times Mirror Company.

Library of Congress Catalog Card Number: 72–98729
ISBN Number: 0–913040–21–5

All information in this book was correct to the best of the publisher's knowledge at the time of publication. Readers are invited to suggest changes and corrections.

Contents

Wilderness and Primitive Areas, Wild and Scenic Rivers and Scenic Trails in National Systems

Hikers look out into the Selway-Bitterroot.

1. Absaroka, MT
2. Agua Tibia, CA
3. Allagash Waterway, ME
4. Anaconda-Pintlar, MT
5. Appalachian Trail, ME-GA
6. Beartooth, MT
7. Black Range, NM
8. Blue Range, AZ
9. Bob Marshall, MT
10. Boundary Waters Canoe Area, MN
11. Bridger, WY
12. Cabinet Mountains, MT
13. Caribou, CA
14. Chiricahua, AZ
15. Clearwater River Middle Fork, ID
16. Cloud Peak, WY
17. Cucamonga, CA
18. Desolation, CA
19. Diamond Peak, OR
20. Dome Land, CA
21. Eagle Cap, OR
22. Eleven Point River, MO
23. Emigrant Basin, CA
24. Feather River Middle Fork, CA
25. Flat Tops, CO
26. Galiuro, AZ
27. Gates of the Mountains, MT
28. Gearhart Mountain, OR
29. Gila Primitive Area, NM
30. Gila Wilderness, NM
31. Glacier, WY
32. Glacier Peak, WA
33. Goat Rocks, WA
34. Gore Range-Eagles Nest, CO

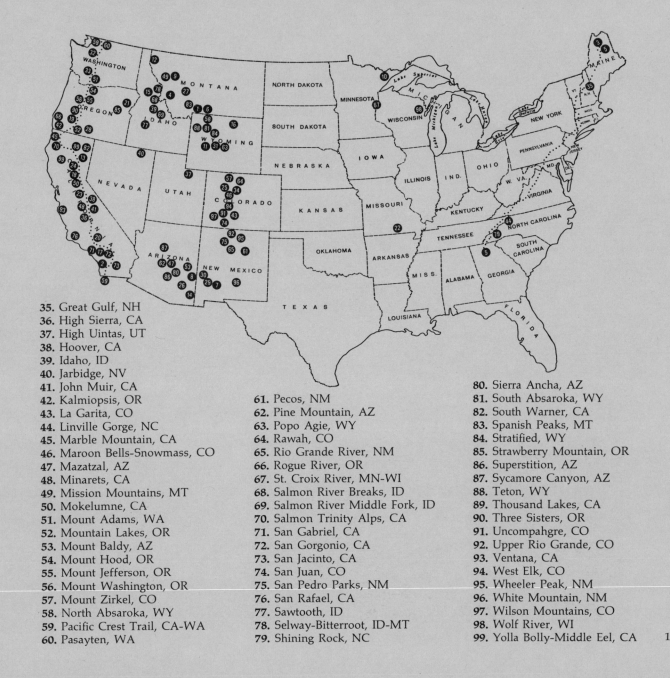

High above the clouds on Mt. Washington, a hiker pauses to look at Mt. Adams far away.

I Wilderness Touring

4   *Pearl Basin is seen from the Continental Divide in the Bob Marshall Wilderness.*

Wilderness Touring

Many of the basic backpacking books, like those listed on page 11, contain all hikers need to know about what to take, how to go and all kinds of tips on backcountry travel. Though there are a few pages here on those basic points, this is a guide to where to go, not how to go, out on the trails.

Using This Book

The list of information at the top of each Wilderness and Primitive Area is helpful by keeping in mind the following points:

1. Season. The best season to go, the seasons when the area is open and/or the peak (when used most) and slow seasons are given as often as possible. Most areas are open year round, but either difficult at some times or have some portions closed because of overuse or fire danger. Hikers should always write to the administrator of the area before going, and the seasonal conditions are an important subject to inquire about locally.

2. Access. Because many roads near the backcountry are subject to changes, both in route and condition, usually only the main roads to the area are given. Local inquiry *on the spot* is very important. If federal or state agencies are closed, the county sheriff's office is a good place to ask.

3. Camping. Various terms are used across the country in each vicinity to describe conditions.

To try to give some uniformity, three terms are used here. "Primitive camping" means that there is no specified spot for camping. "Primitive campsites" means that there are sites used for camping, but with no "improvements." Rarely found in the wildlands, "Improved campsites" means that an established spot has water, toilet or other constructed facilities.

4. Problems. The beginner's problem may be the veteran's passion. "Snow in winter" means "Stay out" to some and "That's the place" to others. Some problems, like lack of water, are universal cautions. Listed in this category are the known conditions that could be a problem, especially to beginners and those not in the best of physical condition. One serious and increasing problem is that of the overuse of wildlands. That, too, has been indicated where such conditions are known to exist.

5. Address. Usually the address of the Forest Supervisor is given. In some cases, a district station address is given. Even where a district isn't given, hikers should find out which district has the most information or most informed person for the area in question. In the case of states without nationally designated wildlands, the address given for Forest Service and National Park Service areas is the regional address, so readers may write to inquire about all possible backcountry in a region, rather than to one area at a time.

5

The maps with each Wilderness and Primitive Area are not intended to be trail maps, but rather to give some idea of size, shape, landmarks, major trails and surrounding towns and roads. The best maps to use as trail maps are the ones sold by the U.S.G.S. (United States Geological Survey; see page 10). The scale of each map used in this book should be carefully noted for a guide to size and distance; and the maps are not all to the same scale, but scale is indicated on each map.

Many additions to the National Wilderness Preservation System, Wild and Scenic Rivers System and Scenic Trails System are under consideration. Some of the areas are in national forests, some in national parks, others in national wildlife refuges. Most of them will be acted upon by Congress by 1974 and were still in the study or selection process at the date of publication of this book. Their exclusion here only indicates that designation is pending, or information is unavailable for mapping.

The Wilderness Background

Where can we go to get away from the noise of our cities, the trash of some of our parks and beaches and the flab of our own muscles? All of us have an idea that there is an America out there still full of lakes and mountains, stands of perpetual trees and the distant peaks we could look at, even if not climb.

And there is such an America. To some it is now more a legal battlefield than a wilderness. To others it is still a place to be tamed and put to service. To yet others it is space for the friendship of solitude, the heft of a pack and the footloose feeling of legs well used.

American attitudes toward wilderness were not always so complicated. In early America, the frontier progressed westward by means of cleared trees, plowed lands and new orchards. The feeling of the pioneer was not devoted to the magnificence of the wilderness he found. It was the promise of the product that lured him on. What a harvest of crops and animals there was in the hills of the East, the streams of the middle continent, the mountains of the West.

It seems odd now to think that appreciation of the wilderness itself—not just as a resource—began in the cities, but it did, with such men as Thoreau and Emerson and others who saw, even if they didn't always experience, the saving grace of wildness in the land. If there is any American writing and painting that has been mightier than the axe, it was the pens and brushes of the early men who went out from the cities and brought back the character of the wilderness spread before them.

A century after the first romantics of the

wilderness, the American mind had gone through several changes of attitude. In 1924, the Gila Wilderness was established. It was not just the first one. It was the first area set aside to be preserved, on a national scale, as wilderness for its own sake. Earlier, the rationale of preservation had gone from saving wilderness for its watershed potential to an attempt to save it for its intrinsic sake in small areas, such as in New York's efforts in the Adirondacks.

Aldo Leopold sits with his dog Flip in 1911.

Aldo Leopold and others were responsible for the setting aside of the Gila Wilderness. After Leopold came the other great Forest Service influence, Bob Marshall, whose leadership established most of the Wilderness in the United States. After his death in 1939, the pace of preservation at the federal level slowed dramatically.

Naturally, there were other people involved in saving land as wilderness. John Muir was foremost among them for the West. Benton MacKaye had a vision for the Appalachian Trail, Clinton Clarke for the Pacific Crest Trail.

Today, the battle rages. Preservation groups accuse the federal government, especially the Forest Service, of being on the side of timber, mining and cattle interests. The officials answer that they are only following their policy of "multiple use," or using wilderness lands for commercial purposes as well as recreational ones. It is a confrontation, on a larger scale than ever before, between the frontier attitude toward wilderness and the appreciation of it for is own sake. Both sides have deep historical roots.

To Western man, the forest has been a foreboding place full of evil gods to be tamed and used. In Asian societies, a copse was a peaceful place where the trees themselves were sacred. (Longer explorations into the history of man's attitude toward wilderness can be found in *Wilderness and the American Mind* by Roderick Nash,

Yale University Press, 1967, and *Roadless Area* by Paul Brooks, Alfred A. Knopf, 1964.)

To a large extent, the users of this book and others like it will determine the blend of attitudes which shape our remaining wildlands. Including vast acreage in the National Wilderness Preservation System is only one step. The proper use of the land after declaring it protected is all that will preserve it. Hopefully, the informed user will be more responsive to the environmental quality of his wilderness.

Getting on the Trail

In response to a questionnaire about whether his area was overused or underused, a forest ranger pointed out that a Wilderness cannot be underused. But they can be, and many are, overused. More and more, restrictions on use are being put on hikers in order to preserve the wild nature of these lands. Accepting such provisions for the sake of the backcountry is just one example of the fact that wilderness touring is as much a matter of attitude as it is of conditioning and equipment.

Preservation of our wild environments depends almost entirely on how people use them. And that use depends on one simple idea being practiced: Leave no trace. It is not an easy task at first because it requires new skills, but they are easily learned. The hardest part of learning to leave no trace is that it takes what to most people is a new kind of habit, one akin to the stealthy tactics of traveling in secret.

Most of the basic backpacking books listed on pages 11-12 give some information on what to do to leave no trace. It involves such things as not cutting across trail switchbacks, replacing rocks used for a fire ring, cutting *no* wood and returning human wastes to the soil. A good pamphlet on trackless camping is "How to Camp and Leave No Trace," available from the Gerry Division of Outdoor Sports Corporation, P.O. Box 5544, Denver, Colorado 80217.

The Wilderness Act and Other Trail Rules

Under the terms of the Wilderness Act of 1964, certain restrictions were placed on the use of the Wildernesses created by the Act. One of the most important for the hiker is that no motorized equipment of any kind—cars, outboards, *any* motor—may be used within the boundaries of these protected lands. The hiker's solitude will be a quiet one, especially in some areas where air routes have been changed so they do not pass over a remote piece of backcountry.

No commercial enterprises, roads, structures or other installations are allowed. Logging has been eliminated, mining greatly restricted and grazing may continue only where it is already a practice.

Specific regulations from one Wilderness to another vary. And the agency which administers one area has a set of rules different from the administrator of another area. For example, hunting is allowed in most places on national forests, but not in most national parks. Such information is available from each area.

Almost all backcountry travel now requires a permit. This is for the safety of the hiker and the use of the land in such a way that it will not be damaged. Almost all such permits are free.

What To Take

Lists accompany just about every book published on backpacking. They cover every kind of equipment possible, and most of them say that beyond the necessary things, what goes along is a matter of taste. And it is true that beyond the necessities *what* goes in the pack is a matter of taste.

But for everything carried on the structure of man's back, *what kind* is the key question. Weight is the most important factor, along with durability. Paring off the ounces makes it possible not to worry about the pounds. So every kind of equipment should be as light as possible and still stand the rigors of the trail and the weather.

Probably the most important items to con-

sider are the sleeping bag, packframe and boots. In all three, the combination of being very light in weight and very sturdy means, in general, that the more expensive kinds are the better ones. At the present time, lightweight and durable equipment costs more to make than heavier and durable equipment. In clothes, food and cooking utensils, the same rules apply.

Beyond the simple consideration of weight and toughness, the choices get very complicated.

Equipment was bulky and heavy in 1919.

9

They depend on weather, kind of terrain, length of stay and many other factors, including, again, personal taste.

Where to buy the equipment is just as complicated. Wilderness and mountaineering shops have the most advanced designs and materials, but often department stores and "surplus" stores have adequate and sometimes excellent equipment in some items. But even beginners—especially beginners—should get the lightest and most durable sleeping bags, pack assemblies and boots they can afford.

Maps and Directions

The best maps—the only adequate ones—for use on the trail are available from the United States Geological Survey. They show the trails, all structures, waterways and bodies of water, as well as the contour of the land, which is very important to know, especially for going cross-country if necessary. The maps can be ordered from the United States Geological Survey, Distribution Section, 1200 Eads St., Arlington, VA 22202. A free index of maps, with costs, is available for each state.

All maps should be used with a few cautions in mind. The date on the map is important because time brings changes in roads, buildings and even contours, which maps cannot keep up with unless they are frequently revised. Precision is another variable factor.

Safety

The dangers of backcountry travel should be neither feared nor taken lightly. Knowledge of the dangers and preparation for them takes the place of unfounded fear and lighthearted ignorance.

The most common dangers to backpackers are overestimates of endurance, getting lost, acci-

A lucky fisherman poses at a 1907 fish camp.

10

dents, lack of preparation for weather and other natural conditions and the greatest leveler of them all—fear and its panic. Books listed in the Backcountry Bookshelf discuss these problems, and experience short of disaster helps overcome them.

Other safety considerations include what people can do to make the land and its inhabitants safe. Among the primary concerns is fire safety. The best rules are to follow local instructions with great care, learn the various ways to build fires and the signals of fire danger, such as dry weather and flammable soil cover, and how to put a fire dead out.

Trail Health

For the apparently simple task of getting in and out of the backcountry, foot care has top priority. The basic backpacking books go into this extensively, but there are two important things to remember. Boots should be of the best possible quality (socks too), and breaking in shakedown hikes of short distances are *vital*. The same shakedown trips go for the pack and frame—and for the legs and back and wind.

Local conditions and personal situations will dictate much of the safety precautions necessary. Such things as water, insect, weather and animal problems to be encountered determine what special care needs to be taken in collecting the first aid kit beyond the basic one which is carried everywhere in any case.

And one of the best techniques any backpacker can learn in order to leave no trace is how to take care of human waste so the soil can use it.

Two Final Words

The key to starting a successful wilderness trip is preparation—reading, asking, conditioning.

The only way to leave the wilderness there for everyone is to leave no trace.

Backcountry Bookshelf

Books

Angier, Bradford. *Home In Your Pack*, Stackpole Books.

Brower, David, ed. *Going Light—With Backpack or Burro*, Sierra Club. (Paperback version: *Sierra Club Wilderness Handbook*, Ballantine Press.)

Brower, David, ed. *Manual of Ski Mountaineering*, Sierra Club.

Bunnelle, Hasse. *Food for Knapsackers*, Sierra Club.

Caldwell, John. *The New Cross-Country Ski Book*, The Stephen Greene Press.

Colwell, Robert. *Introduction to Backpacking*, Stackpole Books, 1970

Farquhar, Francis P. *History of the Sierra Nevada*,

University of California Press.

Fear, Eugene H. *Outdoor Living: Problems, Solutions, Guidelines*, Tacoma Unit of Mountain Rescue Council.

Fletcher, Colin. *The Complete Walker*, Alfred A. Knopf.

Manning, Harvey. *Backpacking: One Step at a Time*, REI Press.

Mendenhall, Ruth Dyer. *Backpack Cookery*, La Siesta Press.

Mendenhall, Ruth Dyer. *Backpack Techniques*, La Siesta Press.

Merrill, W. K. *The Hiker's and Backpacker's Handbook*, Winchester Press.

The Mountaineers. *Mountaineering: The Freedom of the Hills*, The Mountaineers.

Osgood, William, and Lesley Hurley. *The Snowshoe Book*, The Stephen Greene Press.

Riviere, Bill. *Backcountry Camping*, Doubleday and Company.

Starr, Walter A., Jr. *Starr's Guide to the John Muir Trail* (now part of the Pacific Crest Trail), Sierra Club.

Thomas, Winnie and Hasse Bunnelle. *Food for Knapsackers and Other Trail Travelers*, Sierra Club.

Voge, Harvey, ed. *A Climber's Guide to the High Sierra*, Sierra Club.

Watters, Jim, ed. *Knapsacking Equipment*, Sierra Club.

Wheelock, Walt. *Ropes, Knots and Slings for Climbers*, La Siesta Press.

Wilkerson, James A. *Medicine for Mountaineering*, The Mountaineers.

Wood, Robert S. *Pleasure Packing*, Condor.

Pamphlets

Bureau of Land Management. "Room to Roam," Government Printing Office, Washington, D.C. 20402, 75¢.

Forest Service. "Backpacking in the National Forest Wilderness," Government Printing Office, Washington, D.C. 20402, 25¢

Forest Service. "Explore!" Government Printing Office, Washington, D.C. 20402, 35¢.

Forest Service. "National Forest Vacations," Government Printing office, Washington, D.C. 20402, 55¢.

Forest Service. "Wildlife for Tomorrow," Government Printing Office, Washington, D.C. 20402, 60¢.

Magazines

The Living Wilderness. Published by The Wilderness Society, 729 Fifteenth St., NW, Washington, D.C. 20005.

Summit Magazine. Box 46, Bear Lake, CA 92315

Wilderness Camping. Fitzgerald Communications, Inc., Box 1186, Scotia, NY 12302

Backpacker's Organizations and Agencies

Adirondack Mountain Club
Gabriels, NY 12939

American River Touring Association
1016 Jackson St.
Oakland, CA 94607

Appalachian Trail Conference
P.O. Box 236
Harpers Ferry, WV 25425

Bureau of Land Management
Washington, D.C. 20240

Bureau of Sport Fisheries and Wildlife
Washington, D.C. 20240

Florida Trail Association
33 S.W. 18th Terrace
Miami, FL 33129

Forest Service

Federal Building
Missoula, MT 59801

630 Sansome St.
San Francisco, CA 94111

P.O. Box 3623
Portland, OR 97208

633 West Wisconsin Avenue
Milwaukee, WI 53203

Federal Office Building
P.O. Box 1628
Juneau, AK 99801

517 Gold Avenue, SW
Albuquerque, NM 87101

324 25th St.
Ogden, UT 84401

Federal Center, Bldg. 85
Denver, CO 80225

Trail clothes have changed a lot since 1909.

13

WILDERNESS TOURING

1720 Peachtree Road, N.W.
Atlanta, GA 30309

Green Mountain Club
108 Merchants Row
Rutland, VT 05701

Mazamas
909 N.W. 19th Ave.
Portland, OR 97220

The National Audubon Society
1130 Fifth Ave.
New York, NY 10028

National Park Service

Federal Building
P.O. Box 10008
Richmond, VA 23240

1709 Jackson St.
Omaha, NB 68102

P.O. Box 728
Santa Fe, NM 87501

450 Golden Gate Ave.
P.O. Box 36063
San Francisco, CA 94102

143 South Third St.
Philadelphia, PA 19106

Pacific Crest Club
P.O. Box 1907
Santa Ana, CA 92702

The Sierra Club
1050 Mills Tower
San Francisco, CA 94104

U.S. Geological Survey
Washington, D.C. 20242

Western River Guides Association
994 Denver St.
Salt Lake City, UT 84111

Wilderness Society
729 Fifteenth St., N.W.
Washington, D.C. 20005

II Wilderness Lands

Hikers look out over the Great Gulf Wilderness in New Hampshire's White Mountains.

Wilderness Lands

ALABAMA

There are four National Forests in Alabama, the Bankhead, Conecuh, Talladega and Tuskegee. Some of Bankhead may become a designated wild area. It is located in the Bee Branch Scenic Area-Black Warrior Area near Haleyville.

Bankhead National Forest

There are several canoe trips, good in the wet season, on Bankhead. One is down the Clifty Fork of Brushy Creek from Capsey Creek to Lewis Smith Lake. Of the three best trips, this one is least disturbed by man; an 18-mile trip, one or two days will do it with leisure.

The trip on the Sipsey is one of the easiest at 10 miles, with nine miles on the backwater. There are wildflowers along the bank in spring on this one-day or half-day jaunt.

Clear Creek is another one-day run which can be shortened or lengthened. It is about 12 miles, with a portage for a dam at Camp McDowell. Along the way are beaver slides and high bluffs below the dam. Begins at County Route 25 and goes to Falls City on Lewis Smith Lake.

State Parks

Near Groveoak, Bucks Pocket is 2,000 acres of mountains, but with powerboating possible, it is not truly a wilderness. Peak use is in summer, but winters are the slow season.

Almost 5,000 acres, DeSoto State Park is a suitable area for hiking, camping, canoeing, and there is some white water. The slow season is winter.

For more Alabama information, write:

**State of Alabama
Department of Conservation and
Natural Resources**
*64 North Union Street
Montgomery, AL 36104*

Forest Service
*P.O. Box 40
Montgomery, AL 36101*

ALASKA

The possibilities of wilderness experience in Alaska are as huge and varied as the state itself. There are, for instance, over a million acres of State Parks alone, Mount McKinley National Park contains almost two million acres and the National Forests cover over 20 million acres. Even a National Monument in Alaska reaches giant proportions, such as the 4,400 square miles of Glacier Bay.

Many of these areas, as well as others, are being considered for inclusion in the National Wilderness Preservation System, in addition to 15 candidates for status as Wild and Scenic Rivers.

Hikers in Alaska in the spring and summer should always take large amounts of mosquito repellent.

Chugach National Forest

This Kenai stretch of over 4.5 million acres is mostly a hunting and fishing area. As is the case in much of Alaska, it is extensively serviced by charter and commercial airlines. There is fishing for trout, salmon and other fish; hunters go for moose, sheep, mountain goats, Alaska brown bear and elk.

But there is also unexcelled scenery and much land of a wilderness nature. Fiords, glaciers, lakes and rivers cover the area. The Nellie Juan Wilderness Study Area, 600,000 acres of wildlands, is being considered for Wilderness designation, including mountains, ocean shore, virgin forests, islands, lakes and rivers.

Glacier Bay National Monument

This is the largest area in the entire National Park System, and though it has only 11 miles of trail, there are many off-trail opportunities, since the Monument covers 4,400 square miles. Of that, 30 percent is either ocean, lake, stream or river.

Glacier Bay, as far as white men were concerned, was discovered by John Muir in 1879. Here there are mountains up to 15,300 feet, both bare and vegetated lowlands, steep fiords and inlets, headlands and open ocean. Glacial activity covers five areas of biological succession, from recent to prehistoric.

Hiking, fishing, winter sports and climbing are available. The weather can be wet in any season, and visitors should be wary of both brown and black bears as well as the insect population. No supplies or equipment are available locally.

Katmai National Monument

Long range backcountry trips are possible on Katmai, with much of its 4,362 square miles offering rugged country. Hikers should always carry rain gear and mosquito repellent, in addition to other equipment, and bring lightweight foods and stove fuel from Anchorage.

There are few trails, so Park Rangers urge that hikers check in to get the most current information before starting on any trip. It is also wise to get instructions on the safest places and methods to hike and to ford streams. Most trips begin at Brooks Camp.

Firearms are not permitted, and backpackers should beware of brown bears and moose, especially with young. The best time of year for hikers is the last two weeks in August and the first week of September.

Mount McKinley National Park

This National Park around the foot of the Alaska Range has an incredible variety, from the hotel-parking lot-guided tour complex all the way to the solitude of the highest mountain challenge in North America.

Mount McKinley, 20,320 feet, is strictly for the most experienced of mountaineers, with expeditions to its peak lasting as long as 30 days. But there are other climbing slopes down to the 5,000-foot level and thousands of acres of trailless backcountry, with much of it suitable for families with children. Hikes of a day or a few weeks are possible.

Winter weather can be severe, but it is still country for snowshoeing, skiing and dog sledding (October to April), or for hiking and wildlife viewing and photography (May to September).

Tongass National Forest

In this huge, 16 million-acre area there are islands, fiords, lakes, inland waterways, Alaskan coast sections, snow-capped mountains and wilderness trails. Three Wilderness Study Areas are under consideration for inclusion in the National Wilderness Preservation System.

The Russell Fiord Area is 227,000 acres of geologically young, rugged, scenic land. It is difficult to get to, but the wildlife rewards are many.

Tracy Arm is a cascade of natural sights, wildlife and mountain hikes. As a Wilderness, it would be 283,000 acres of fiords, glaciers, lakes and mountains. It is accessible by land and sea.

Northeast of Ketchikan, Granite Fiords Wilderness Study Area is living evidence of massive glacial action with fiords, mountains and valleys along the Behm Canal. There are open meadows, stands of willow, cottonwood and an array of mosses and lichens to go with a crowning ice field in this 500,000 acres of remote wildlands.

State Parks

Alaska's state parks offer much the same kinds of terrain and activities as the same types of federal lands. Glaciers, lakes and rivers predominate, with the peak season in summer and the slow one around Christmas.

Chugach State Park is open to winter use, with mountain and glacier terrain and a partially visable old mail route. There are some avalanche and slide areas.

Kachemak Bay State Park and Wilderness Area is also open year round, with beaches and inlets as well as mountains.

Denali State Park is extremely cold in winter, but has outstanding views of Mount McKinley, 30 miles away. Here there are low mountain lakes and heavy flora of small variety.

Two State Recreation Areas, Chena and Nancy Lake, offer limited wilderness opportunities but are more extensively used and have more motorized visitors.

For more Alaska information write:

Forest Service
Federal Office Bldg.
Box 1628
Juneau, AK 99801

National Park Service
c/o Alaska Group
P.O. Box 2252
Anchorage, AK 99501

State of Alaska
Department of Natural Resources
323 E. 4th Avenue
Anchorage, AK 99501

U.S. Bureau of Land Management
555 Cordova Street
Anchorage, AK 99501
(for map of 12 Alaska canoe trails)

Alaska has changed little; packs have.

Blue Range

Season: *Summer and fall are best.*

Size: *216,737 acres*

Access: *From the west by roads off U.S. 666; on the east by roads off U.S. 180*

Camping: *Primitive camping*

Problems: *Severe rain and lightning storms in summer, especially in the north; flooding in the lower canyons; rugged terrain*

Location: *Apache National Forest*

Address: *Blue Range Primitive Area*
Apache National Forest
Springerville, AZ 85938

Known locally as "the Blue," this Primitive Area was probably on the route of Coronado as he searched for the Seven Cities of Cibola. Pablo de Castaneda, who chronicled the journey, described the area with its many pine nuts and acorns.

This is the southern edge of the Colorado Plateau, and the land is as rugged as it is beautiful, with timbered ridges and deep canyons. The Mogollon Rim, made famous as the "Tonto Rim" in Zane Grey's books, crosses from west to east. The change in elevation, from 9,100 feet on the Rim in the north, to 4,500 feet in the southern section, creates unusual geological and ecological conditions, as well as different types of weather. The Rim receives twice as much rainfall—30 inches—as the south portion.

The Blue River and its canyon are scenically spectacular, sprinkled with ponderosa pine and cutting through colorful rocks. Fishing is good only on the upper tributaries to the Blue. The Apache trout once inhabited these waters but have now crossed with planted trout; an effort is being made to re-establish the pure strain.

Wildlife that hikers encounter include deer elk, bear, mountain lion and bobcat. The area around the Blue Range is inhabited by hunters in the fall.

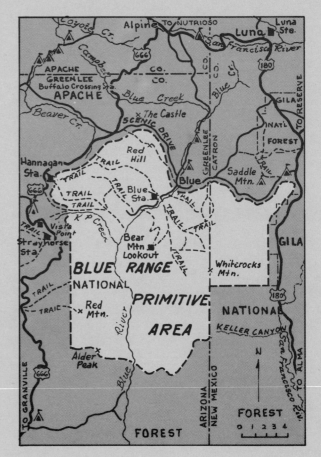

21

Chiricahua

Season: *All year except when closed by heavy snow; summer is peak season, winter slow.*

Size: *18,000 acres*

Access: *From the east off U.S. 80 by Forest Service road from Portal; from the west by several roads off State Route 181*

Camping: *Primitive camping*

Problems: *Extra water should be carried in late spring and early summer.*

Location: *Coronado National Forest*

Address: *Chiricahua Wilderness*
Coronado National Forest
130 South Scott
Tucson, AZ 85702

The Chiricahua Mountains contain this small, surprising Wilderness. Like an island in the desert, it is a pine- and fir-shaded series of very rugged peaks, visited mostly by Forest Service rangers and a few ardent hikers. The Chiricahua Mountains rise up sharply off the desert floor in the southeast corner of Arizona.

With the surrounding desert, the conifer cover, variations in elevation, exposure, slope and moisture, the plant and animal life has an unusual range. One species, the Chiricahua squirrel, is found only here.

Trails in this Wilderness are well maintained and signed, and there are many to choose from, some probably used by Cochise and Geronimo for hunting. Cochise's "stronghold" is nearby, as is Old Fort Bowie.

22 *Before protection, many wildlands were cut.*

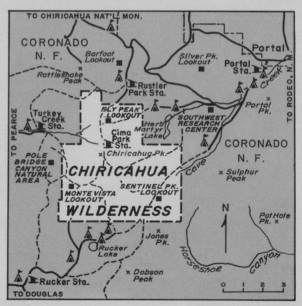

Galiuro

Season: *All year; no winter snow; spring, fall and winter slow*
Size: *52,717 acres*
Access: *From the northeast by two roads off the Arivaipa Valley road and one road from Bonita on State Route 266*
Camping: *Primitive camping*
Problems: *Very hot in summer; dangerous flash floods*
Location: *Coronado National Forest*
Address: *Galiuro Wilderness*
Coronado National Forest
130 South Scott
Tucson, AZ 85702

This is one of the roughest desert terrains in the Wilderness Preservation System, as well as being exceptionally scenic—and all but inaccessible.

Desert shrubs and grasses cover most of the area, except for scattered pines at higher elevations. The flanks of the Galiuros form a series of spectacular cliffs and benches cut by deep canyons. The terrain and brush make hiking very tough going in many areas, especially off the trails.

The trails themselves are well maintained and signed, but a good map is important. Rangers should be asked about current water sources.

There are many outstanding rock formations in the Galiuros. Rockhounds will find good lessons in desert geology, and the center of the area, as well as some canyons, is dotted with old mines.

Common desert animals are found here, and the animal types of the 8,000-foot variety inhabit the upper slopes. They are deer and bear, mountain lion and javelina, or wild pig.

Water is generally very scarce, so extra supplies of it should be carried. Summer temperatures make that season best for confirmed desert rats only.

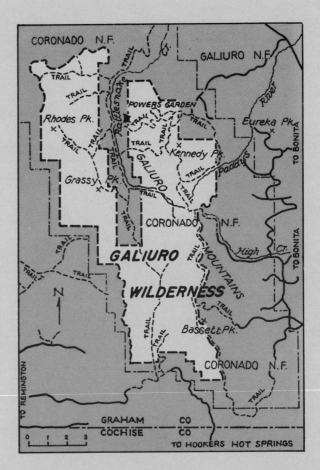

Mazatzal

Season: *Most attractive in spring and fall; difficult from November to February because of snow and ice*

Size: *205,137 acres*

Access: *From the east off State Route 87 on dirt roads; from the west on Forest Service Road 269 off U.S. 17 and on Forest Service Roads 24 then 205 from Cave Creek*

Camping: *Primitive camping*

Problems: *Very rugged terrain; springs and permanent water supplies not plentiful*

Location: *Tonto National Forest*

Address: *Mazatzal Wilderness*
Tonto National Forest
711 West Main Street
Payson, AZ 85541

The "Matazal" Wilderness, as it is called locally, is an extremely rough and remote area on the north end of the Mazatzal Range. These are mostly desert mountains with narrow-walled canyons. From the east, most of the area is inaccessible except for constructed-trails. The very colorful canyons and cliffs are a main feature of this spectacularly scenic range.

While there are approximately 180 miles of trails in the Wilderness, they are primitive and often quite difficult to follow. Only experienced hikers should try backpacking here and only veteran mountaineers should attempt the peaks. The mountain tops and high plateaus offer a reward in addition to the climb itself. Evidence of ancient Indian use is abundant and situated in places all but inaccessible. These areas made good defensive positions and are still seen by only a few determined climbers.

Wildlife and vegetation are abundant and varied. The deer is the most common creature, along with bear, javelina, mountain lion, coyote, lynx, bobcat and fox. Quail are numerous.

Plant life is surprisingly varied, including pine, fir, juniper, oak, cypress and laurel, along with semi-desert types, including cactus.

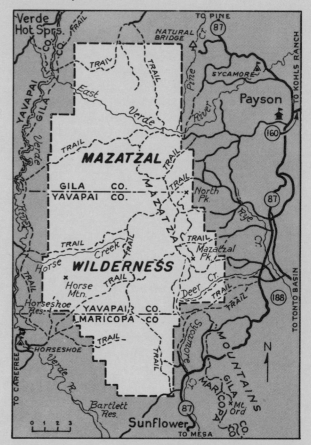

Mount Baldy

ARIZONA

Season: *All year; snow in winter*
Size: *7,106 acres*
Access: *From State Route 73*
Camping: *Primitive camping*
Problems: *Some rough terrain; overused*
Location: *Apache National Forest*
Address: *Mount Baldy Wilderness*
Apache National Forest
Springerville, AZ 85938

The only wilderness-type land in Arizona with a subalpine vegetation zone, Mount Baldy's climate is a sharp contrast to the hot, dry deserts of the state. The headwaters of the West Fork of the Little Colorado River rise here, and fishing is good, wild game abundant.

From 8,700 feet to 11,000 feet, the terrain varies from gently sloping timbered benches to extremely steep, rockstrewn mountainsides cut by deep canyons.

Problems of overuse on this small Wilderness have prompted the Forest Service to make some regulations governing its use. Among the most important to backpackers are these:

1. Fifty people at one time will be established as the carrying capacity, with adjustments made pending yearly evaluations of impact studies.
2. Camping will be limited to groups of no more than five, while hiking and riding groups may be no more than 25.
3. Commercial packers will be limited to groups of 25.
4. During summer months, a Wilderness Guard will regulate use and encourage visitors to remove litter. Garbage disposal containers will be placed at each entrance point.
5. A rotation grazing system with proper stocking levels will be used within the Wilderness.
6. Active erosion scars caused by man's disturbance will be rehabilitated.
7. Natural barriers will restrict travel off trails, and the Wilderness Guard will discourage hikers from leaving the trails.
8. A program of information and education will be established to acquaint hikers with these conditions.

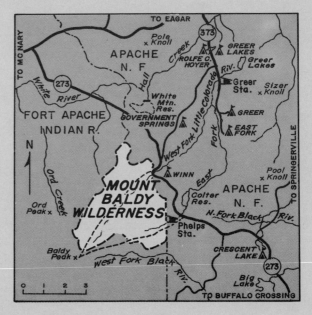

Pine Mountain

Season: *All year; summer is best.*

Size: *19,569 acres*

Access: *By roads off Interstate 17*

Camping: *Primitive camping*

Problems: *Unstable water supply; rain in July and August; very rugged*

Location: *Prescott and Tonto National Forests*

Address: *Pine Mountain Wilderness*
Prescott National Forest
Prescott, AZ 86301

The eastern section of this relatively small Wilderness is rough, rocky country of brush thickets with turbinella oak, coenothus and mountain mahogany. Stands of virgin ponderosa pine predominate in the west, which has a gentler slope than the eastern section.

The Verde River Rim separates the two sections and the river lies at the base of the eastern slope. Escarpments are common here, and though game is abundant, the thick cover and steep canyons make hunting very difficult. Wildlife to be seen are deer, quail, javelina and an occasional turkey among the pines at the heads of the canyons.

Climbing up through the Wilderness, hikers pass through several different life zones on the way to the top of Pine Mountain, 6,827 feet. Turret Peak and Skeleton Ridge are other points of scenic interest.

Relative remoteness, an unpredictable water supply and limited trail development give this area a true sense of wilderness. Signs of man are few and include some Indian ruins along the Verde Rim. There are only 18 miles of trail, most of them in the western sector. Hikers should be prepared to bring their own water supply, and care should be taken for flash floods. Camping in drainage bottoms is dangerous because the floods strike unannounced.

Much of the land surrounding Pine Mountain is possible backpacking country, but is also rough and with undependable water supplies. Just six miles southeast of Pine Mountain Wilderness is the Mazatzal Wilderness, with country so rough and remote that few people ever experience it. It is the largest in Arizona, containing 206,137 acres (see page 24).

Sierra Ancha

ARIZONA

Season: *All year; frost at upper elevations even in May and June*

Size: *20,850 acres*

Access: *From State Route 288, Forest Service Road 203 goes to the east side, 487 to the west side and 203 to the north.*

Camping: *Primitive camping*

Problems: *Unstable water supply*

Location: *Tonto National Forest*

Address: *Sierra Ancha Wilderness*
Roosevelt Ranger District
Tonto National Forest
Roosevelt, AZ 85545

One of the three or four roughest, most inaccessible of the Southwest's Wildernesses, Sierra Ancha is made of high desert mountains and precipitous box canyons. Its high vertical cliffs create unusual rock formations and shelter prehistoric cliff dwellings.

There is much evidence of early Indian life. Some interesting and unusual remains are located near Workman Falls just outside the Wilderness. The Pueblo Canyon cliff dwelling on the slope of Cherry Creek is one of the best preserved and most interesting in the region. All Indian ruins and artifacts are protected by the Antiquities Law. No digging or removal of anything is permitted without approval of the Smithsonian Institution and the Forest Service.

The extremely rough topography limits and in some places prohibits cross-country travel. Even so, hiking, horseback riding and hunting are popular in the Sierra Ancha. Big game is abundant. There are no trails classed as important recreation trails in the area.

Next to the Wilderness on the southwest side is Sierra Ancha Experimental Forest where many wildland research programs are done.

Vegetation found in Sierra Ancha includes many different types, from raspberry and honeysuckle to pine, aspen and oak, with several different kinds of wild berries.

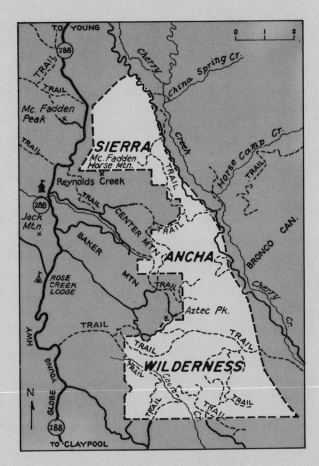

27

Superstition

Season: *All year; very hot in summer and cold in winter*

Size: *124,117 acres*

Access: *From the north and west off State Route 88; from the south off U.S. 80-89*

Camping: *Primitive camping*

Problems: *Extreme temperatures; water very scarce; dangerous flash floods; easy to get lost off trails*

Location: *Tonto National Forest*

Address: *Superstition Wilderness*
Tonto National Forest
230 North 1st Avenue, Room 6208
Phoenix, AZ 85025

What is perhaps the hottest, driest Wilderness in the nation is also the one closest to a major city. Phoenix is only forty miles from Superstition, water must be packed in except in winter and summer temperatures often reach 120 degrees.

Yet, for its harshness and rugged, rocky desert terrain, the Superstitions abound with both the history and legends of man's passage through it. Early day Indian civilizations are evident in Hieroglyphic Canyon, the cliff dwellings in Rogers Canyon, Indian Terrace near Reavis Ranch and the Indian Fort in Pine Creek.

Spaniards came early to look for ore, and the crude figure of a miner carved by the Peralta brothers can still be dimly seen. Other mines were found and lost, with the famous Lost Dutchman still eluding treasure hunters. Jacob Walz, the Dutchman of the story, was said to have taken thousands from his mine, but he never told where it was. He did hint enough to lure searchers, many of whom, even in recent times, have died mysteriously in the quest.

Steep canyons cut among the sharp peaks of the Superstitions, most famous of which—and most photographed—is Weavers Needle, a focal point in the Lost Dutchman search. This desert can be very inhospitable, not only in summer, but in winter's bitter cold, torrential rains and snowstorms.

For such a harsh land, there is much life in the Wilderness. The great saguaro cactus, the century plant, grasses and flowers are just a few of the many kinds of vegetation. Deer, javelina, rabbits and rattlesnakes live with wrens, roadrunners and hawks.

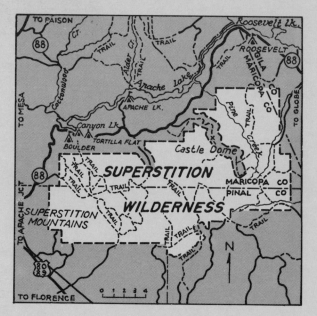

Sycamore Canyon

Season: *All year; spring and fall are the peak season.*

Size: *46,542 acres*

Access: *From the north on a dirt road near Parks on U.S. 66-89; from the east by several roads off U.S. 89A; from the west by Forest Service Road 318 from Jerome*

Camping: *Primitive camping*

Problems: *Unreliable water sources; hot in summer; flash floods in spring and in rains of July and August*

Location: *Coconino, Kaibab and Prescott National Forests*

Address: *Sycamore Canyon Wilderness*
Coconino National Forest
P.O. Box 1268
114 N. San Francisco
Flagstaff, AZ 86002

This is a unique canyonland environment cutting through the Colorado Plateau, the Mogollon Rim and then winding 20 miles along Sycamore Creek. In the upper section, the canyon walls seem almost to touch, while in other places it is as much as seven miles from rim to rim.

Ranging in elevation from 3,600 feet to 7,000 feet, the canyon has walls as high as 2,000 feet. Seven different geological eras have been exposed by wind and water.

The colors in Sycamore Canyon are a spectacular combination of stone and vegetation. Red sandstone mixes with white limestone and brown lava, all of which make a marked contrast to the different greens of chaparral and woodland species. Higher elevations support ponderosa pine and stringers of Douglas fir.

A long history of prehistoric use is in evidence, with ruins of a vanished Indian culture. Later history has seen grazing over the years, and the unique Taylor Cabin is a reminder of the stock tenders' life.

Offering an abundance of browse species, this is an essential winter range for deer, elk and turkey, and some of these animals never leave the canyon. There are also quail, dove and the Albert squirrel.

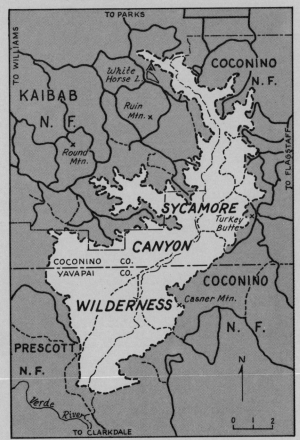

Other Wilderness Lands

Backcountry in Arizona extends from the desert heat of 125 degrees to snow-topped mountains, from desert lakes to ski touring high country. Hikers should always check in with Rangers and carry plenty of water.

National Forests

Every national forest except one in Arizona has one or more areas of designated Wilderness. The exception is Sitgreaves, which is stretched along the Mogollon Rim and does have within its borders areas suitable for wildland hiking.

The Bureau of Land Management administers two Primitive Areas, Paria Canyon and Aravaipa Canyon. Paria Canyon is the more remote and primitive of the two; it is partly in Utah. The canyon is subject to sudden, deadly flooding, but careful hikers enjoy the steep walls, the river and many Indian petroglyphs. Aravaipa has 1,000-foot cliffs above Aravaipa Creek, one of the few perennial-flowing desert streams.

National Parks

Taken together, Grand Canyon National Park, Grand Canyon National Monument and Marble Canyon National Monument string along and around the Colorado River for about 184 miles.

This is high plateau country with deep, arid canyons, and is carry-your-own-water land just about anywhere in the wild portions, and can be extremely rugged going. Most of this justly famed desert is open all year (and parts overused), except that Grand Canyon National Park's North Rim can be inaccessible from November to April. Grand Canyon National Monument is difficult to get to, as is Marble Canyon, which is only reached by river.

Petrified Forest National Park has two areas which are now designated Wildernesses, totaling 50,260 acres. Painted Desert Wilderness, the larger of the two, is in the northern section of the Park, and Rainbow Forest Wilderness is in the south. Both are in terrain of mesas and badlands with limited fauna and some pinyon, juniper, sage and saltbush. These are very colorful areas of highly eroded bentonite clay. In both Wildernesses, hikers are required to bring their own water and fuel for cooking.

State Parks

The Bill Williams River in Alamo Lake State Park is one of the better areas for wilderness experience in Arizona State Parks. It is rolling to mountainous desert with a 500-acre lake and 1-1/2 miles of the river.

Picacho Peak State Park is more mountainous desert, with a springtime desert floral display which has been called the most spectacular in the state. The peak itself has been a landmark to travelers for hundreds and possibly thousands of years.

For more Arizona information, write:

Forest Service
517 Gold Avenue S. W.
Albuquerque, NM 87101

National Park Service
450 Golden Gate Avenue
P.O. Box 36063
San Francisco, CA 94102

Arizona State Parks
1688 West Adams
Phoenix, AZ 85007

ARKANSAS

Of the two large National Forests in Arkansas—Ouachita and Ozark—the Caney Creek Back Country area on Ouachita is the only sizable wildland in the state. It is 10,236 acres of mountainous topography with a year round season, and sheltered by oak, hickory and shortleaf pine. Deer and wild turkey, quail and black bear, as well as wild hogs roam this hill country where no motorized vehicles are allowed.

Rock outcroppings and sharp ridges afford far views and the splendor of solitude. Plant life has been practically undisturbed in recent years, and it grows now in profusion, from the tiny to the mighty.

Streams in the area give up good catches of bass, sunfish and chub. All drinking water here should be treated before drinking, though, even in the clear streams.

Slow season is from October to December, the peak season between June and August.

A few rivers in Arkansas are suitable for boating, and vary from gentle floats to some white water.

For more Arkansas information, write:

Forest Service
1720 Peachtree Road N.W.
Atlanta, GA 30309

Arkansas State Parks
412 State Capitol
Little Rock, AK 72201

Agua Tibia

Season: *November to June*

Size: *25,995 acres*

Access: *From the north on Forest Service roads off State Route 79; from the west on roads off State Route 76 near Pala*

Camping: *Primitive camping*

Problems: *Variable water supply*

Location: *Cleveland National Forest*

Address: *Agua Tibia Primitive Area*
Cleveland National Forest
3211 Fifth Avenue
San Diego, CA 92103

Almost half of this relatively small Primitive Area is the Mission Indian Reserve. The Missions were the early dwellers of this land, and artifacts are still found.

Agua Tibia is limited to winter use only because of fire closure from July to October every year. But even with a shortened season of use, there is much of interest in this region, especially for those with an interest in botany or birds.

Plants range from those of desert types at 1,500 feet to the timber of over 5,000 feet. Because over half the area has not had large fires for over 100 years, it is rich in specimens of native plants at their peak, and in examples of ecological systems in climax condition. It is a natural laboratory for the study of this type of mountainous southern California terrain.

Of special interest is the chaparral belt, with ceonothus, manzanita and redshank, which have reached what is considered maximum growth for these species. Plants 14 to 16 feet high are common, with manzanita growing in tree-like proportions of 8- to 10-inch base diameters.

A number of tree species grow in Agua Tibia, including the white fir, incense cedar, bigcone Douglas fir, and Coulter and Jeffrey pine. The oak-conifer type of tree cover provides a habitat for many kinds of birds.

There is a large population of bandtailed pigeons, for which Palomar (pigeon roost) Mountain was named.

There are not very many trails in the area, and not many hikers, so deer, mountain lions, bobcats and coyotes may occasionally be seen.

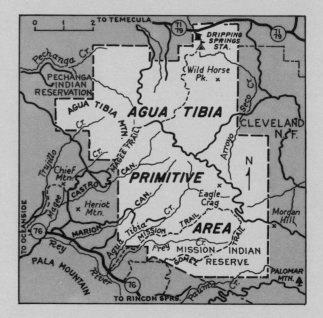

Caribou

Season: *Summer*

Size: *19,080 acres*

Access: *From California State Routes 44 or 36, take County A21 to Silver Lake, the east trailhead entrance; Forest Service road 31N10 goes to the north trailhead entrance.*

Camping: *Primitive campsites*

Problems: *Be prepared for rain.*

Location: *Lassen National Forest*

Address: *Caribou Wilderness*
Mt. Lassen National Forest
Forest Supervisor's Headquarters
Susanville, CA 96130

Its easy access, many lakes for base camps and small size make Caribou an ideal Wilderness for family backpackers. Most of the trails cover gentle slopes, with very few steep pitches. Leisure packing in solitude is the keynote of this rolling, forested plateau. There are three trailheads to start from, with Silver Lake a good place to enter.

The land at higher elevations is rough and broken, but the volcanic and glacial origins are obvious and welcome at the numerous lakes, which are tree-lined depressions of many sizes. Eastern brook trout, rainbow trout and Eagle Lake rainbows are planted in the larger, deeper lakes.

While this is not a land of high mountains and majestic views, it does have its own special character. The forest cover is mostly Jeffrey and lodgepole pine, and in early summer, wildflowers brighten the trail, water lilies cluster in the ponds.

There are no major peaks in the area, but crater peaks and cinder cones, such as Red Cinder at 8,370 feet, give Caribou its ancient character. Like the rest of Lassen National Forest, this area is a natural laboratory of volcanic history.

Several species of animals may be seen, ranging in size from the many squirrels and chipmunks to the large and shy deer and black bear. Once in a while, the lucky, quiet or observant hiker can catch a fleeting glimpse of a pine marten. The rare pine marten was a much hunted prize of early trappers, but is now protected and doing well in the more remote sections of Caribou Wilderness.

Hikers in this wilderness should be aware of the geology of volcanos and glaciers, and should wear clothing which can be adjusted to varying temperatures.

CALIFORNIA

Cucamonga

Season: *Year round, except the Middle Fork of Lytle Creek is closed in summer after about June 20*

Size: *9,022 acres*

Access: *From U.S. 66 on the west, to Mt. Baldy; from Lytle Creek road on the east*

Camping: *Primitive campsites*

Problems: *Only the Middle Fork of Lytle Creek has water all year; fire danger great.*

Location: *San Bernardino National Forest*

Address: *Cucamonga Wilderness*
Lytle Creek Ranger Station
Star Route, Box 100
Fontana, CA 92335

San Bernardino National Forest, where the Cucamonga Wilderness is located, was the first "Forest Reserve," designated in 1893, and renamed a National Forest in 1925. Today, the land around it, and some land which the forest surrounds, is heavily developed in housing and recreation sites.

The Wilderness itself has, of course, no development and is a very rough land of sharp peaks and steep mountainsides. Elevations range from 5,000 to 9,000 feet, with the mountain peaks—Telegraph, Cucamonga, Big Horn and Timber Mountain—lined along the western perimeter.

Pines predominate in Cucamonga, with Jeffrey, lodgepole and sugar pines all represented. There is an occasional meadow, or "cienega," as they are called locally.

The Middle Fork of Lytle Creek is the only fishing stream. It can be reached from Lytle Creek Ranger Station. It is the only year-round stream in the Wilderness. The fishing season is limited, however, because fire closures restrict public use along the stream both inside and outside the Wilderness after about June 20.

This is one of the few places in southern California where bighorn sheep can still be seen. Scattered small bands live in these mountains, where they are protected by law. Difficult to get close to, the bighorns are very wary of humans. Binoculars are necessary to spot them, and a tele-

photo lens a must to photograph them. Watch the mountainsides where the steep pitches seem to have no footing at all.

Hikers should be especially aware of the high fire danger in Cucamonga Wilderness. Always get the most current information from a ranger station before going in.

34

Desolation

CALIFORNIA

Season: *July 15 to October 1; lighter use in September*

Size: *63,469 acres*

Access: *From the east via State Route 89; from the south via U.S. 50.*

Camping: *Primitive camping; fires and camping prohibited around some heavily used lakes.*

Problems: *Heavily overused (see below)*

Location: *Eldorado National Forest*

Address: *Desolation Wilderness*
Eldorado National Forest
100 Forni Road
Placerville, CA 95667

This may be the most overused Wilderness in the United States. On an *average* summer day there are 3,400 people hiking, camping and riding within Desolation's boundaries. Concentrated in a few areas, this use has severely damaged campsites, vegetation and soil. At one time, it was thought that a few improvements, such as toilets, at some campsites would help protect the environment, but it has turned out that the improved campsites got even more concentrated use.

Now, a determined staff on the Eldorado National Forest has proposed some innovative steps to repair what was beginning to be irreversible damage. If these steps are adopted, they will control individual use, group size and length of stay by strict regulation, introduce a wilderness manners education program and possibly use a Wilderness test. Some trailheads will be closed, camping will be restricted, horse use will be regulated and firearms will be prohibited between January 1 and September 15.

A five year fish planting moratorium will be declared to give biologists a chance to evaluate the capacity of Desolation's lakes to sustain a natural fishery versus a put-and-take, artificial one.

In addition to an education program to alert the public to the dangers of overuse, the staff at Eldorado plans to "depublicize" Desolation in an attempt to save it from destruction.

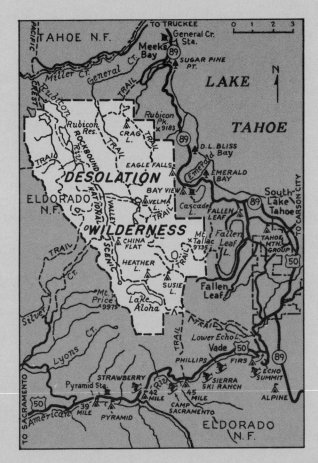

Dome Land

Season: *All year*

Size: *62,121 acres*

Access: *From the west via State Route 190 to Forest Service Roads 22S05, 22S01 and 23S07; from the east off State Route 178 on a dirt road about 30 miles east of Kernville to Chimney Meadow.*

Camping: *Primitive camping*

Problems: *Rugged terrain*

Location: *Sequoia National Forest*

Address: *Dome Land Wilderness*
Cannell Meadow Ranger District
P.O. Box 6
Kernville, CA 93238

This rugged land gets its name from monolithic outcroppings with strange shapes and sizes caused by erosion and weathering. Elevations range from 3,000 to 9,000 feet, with light vegetation on the lower slopes. There is some mixed conifer, but mostly the area is covered by pinyon pine, sagebrush and rabbit brush.

Deer stay in the area all year and are especially concentrated in the winter. The northern and western portions are still open to cattle grazing.

A large portion of this granite-domed terrain is referred to as the "roughs" of the South Fork of the Kern River. South of Rockhouse Meadow down to State Route 178, the roughs are inaccessible to all but the most dedicated hikers. The land around the South Kern here is steep, rocky and broken. Hikers make their own trails.

In contrast to the roughs is Manter Meadow, in the middle western section of the Wilderness. It is described as "outstanding high quality meadow," and is accessible by two trails from Big Meadow, just outside the Wilderness on the west. Manter Meadow is on private land, as is Rockhouse Meadow just above the roughs.

Campers in the wilderness can expect warm days and cool nights.

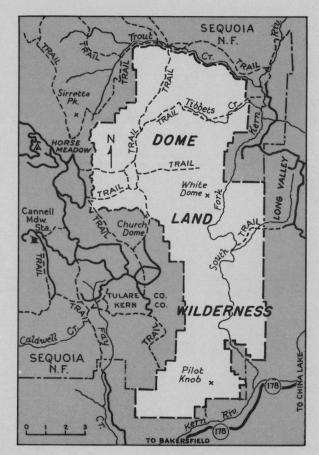

Emigrant Basin

CALIFORNIA

Season: *August is the season of peak use, late September is the slow month.*

Size: *97,020 acres*

Access: *From the north and west off State Route 108*

Camping: *Primitive campsites*

Problems: *Overused*

Location: *Stanislaus National Forest*

Address: *Emigrant Basin Primitive Area
Stanislaus National Forest
175 S. Fairview Lane
Sonora, CA 95370*

Another of the Primitive Areas under consideration as a Wilderness, Emigrant Basin is a place of broad expanses of glaciated granite, lava capped peaks, alpine lakes and meadows and deep-walled canyons. The headwaters of the Cherry and Stanislaus River rise here, and there are many lakes, some of them unnamed.

Elevation at the Cherry River is 6,000 feet, and at Leavitt Peak, on the crest of the Sierra, 11,575 feet. There are timbered areas of pine, juniper, fir and hemlock.

Yosemite National Park lies to the south, with popular pack trips from there into Emigrant Basin, where settlers passed through in the 1850's.

Like many other California wildlands, and some in other states, too, Emigrant Basin suffers from overuse because it is in such a popular and populated area.

Too many of these travel Emigrant Basin.

High Sierra

Season: *All year*

Size: *10,247 acres*

Access: *The best way in is from Cedar Grove in Kings Canyon National Park.*

Camping: *Primitive camping*

Problems: *Heat in summer; undependable water supply; rattlesnakes*

Location: *Sierra and Sequoia National Forests*

Address: *High Sierra Primitive Area*
Sierra National Forest
1130 "O" Street
Fresno, CA 93721

This southern Sierra country has been proposed as the Monarch Wilderness with an area of some 36,000 acres. The Monarch Divide here is very rough terrain with few travel routes of any kind.

Rising from the Middle and South Forks of the Kings River, at over 2,000 feet, to 11,000 feet, the land here is very steep and possibly the wildest in California. There are few trails, very little flat land and only two small lakes. Half of the area is hot and dry with many rattlesnakes, and the moister river canyons are almost inaccessible.

Grand Dike offers many climbing challenges, and the Tehipite Valley approaches the scenic scale of Yosemite, but the going is extremely rough. In this entire wildland, there are only 20 miles of trails. This is truly a back-country area and is best visited by experienced hikers.

Pack trips were too populated even in 1925.

38

Hoover

Season: *July and August only at higher elevations*

Size: *42,779 acres*

Access: *From the east off U.S. 395 by way of Twin Lakes, Green Creek, Virginia Creek and Lundy Lake; from the south by Saddlebag Lake; from the north via Opal-Obsidian Campsite south of Sonora Junction*

Camping: *Primitive camping*

Problems: *Possible inclement weather all year; steep trails*

Location: *Toiyabe and Inyo National Forests*

Address: *Hoover Wilderness*
Toiyabe National Forest
111 N. Virginia Street, Room 601
Reno, NV 89501

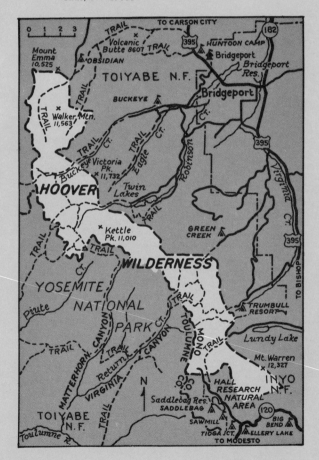

High and extremely rugged Hoover Wilderness is best suited to experienced backpackers and mountain climbers, and is not a good area for horse travel. The eastern fringes of the Wilderness, however, offer striking scenery, pleasant camping, trails and better than average fishing, with a number of lakes, streams and meadows.

Elevations within the boundary vary from 8,000 feet to almost 13,000. Even in the middle of summer, hikers should expect rain, summer blizzards, extreme cold and heavy winds.

Most of the area is alpine-type country, with few trees. The lower portions, though, have lakes, flats and meadows with stands of lodgepole pine and aspen, and good fishing in the lakes.

In addition to luxuriant plant life at lower elevations, mule deer, bears, bobcats and coyotes are seen, with an occasional mountain lion. Sage grouse inhabit the lower areas, mountain quail the higher levels. Commercial packers are available by writing to the Forest Service (see address above).

Established in 1931, the Wilderness was named in honor of President Herbert Hoover, who spent boyhood vacations in the area and was later superintendent at the nearby Bodie mines. A lake in the Wilderness also bears his name.

39

John Muir

Season: *Early June to mid-October below 10,000 feet; high country and passes, July 1*

Size: *503,258 acres*

Access: *From the east via roads off U.S. 395 between Lone Pine and Mammoth Lakes; from the west at Mono Hot Springs, Lake Edison, Florence Lake, Courtright Reservoir and Wishon Reservoir*

Camping: *Improved campsites, primitive camping*

Problems: *Overused; afternoon thunderstorms July to September; no trail maintainence until the end of June*

Location: *Sierra and Inyo National Forests*

Address: *John Muir Wilderness   Inyo National Forest*
Sierra National Forest   2957 Birch Street
1130 "O" Street   Bishop, CA 93514
Fresno, CA 93721

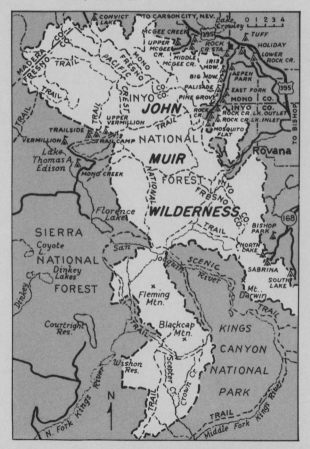

This Wilderness, though the largest in California and seventh in the nation, is being "loved to death," in the words of one Forest Service official. Use restrictions will probably have to be imposed in the near future.

The overcrowded condition is no puzzle. John Muir Wilderness is probably the area most often thought of as the ideal backcountry. Here, Mount Whitney, 14,495 feet, is the highest peak in the contiguous 48 states, and may be the highest peak in the world with summer traffic jams of hikers. Many peaks are over 12,000 feet, and offer strolls, hikes and climbs for all ages and conditions and for burro and horse. A 200-mile stretch of trail from north to south is the longest in the United States not crossed by a road.

Seekers of solitude should select other areas between mid-July and Labor Day, or take side trails. Another possibility in John Muir, for experienced and conditioned hikers, is to travel cross country from drainage to drainage—with map and compass. During this peak season, walkers should avoid the Pacific Crest Trail and spots within a day's hike from trailheads. In September and October, crowds are thinner.

John Muir, naturalist, "Thoreau of the West," a man obsessed by the Sierra, made this

40

country famous. For a long while it was very near-ly his own, for he knew it better than anyone. These trails were among his favorites. Even today, the farther reaches of the Wilderness remain as he saw them, with the rare bighorn sheep and golden eagle, the coyotes, martens, hawks and owls. It is still the summer range of some 50,000 mule deer.

The land is rough and steep for the most part, with deep canyons. But there are many beautiful meadows and great stands of pine, fir, cedar and hemlock. Elevations vary over a range of 10,000 feet, from 4,000 to almost 15,000. Precipitation ranges as broadly—from 15 to 50 inches—and summer temperatures begin at 25 degrees and go up to 85. There is usually a six-week, frost-free period from July 15 to August 31.

Carved by ancient glaciers and eroded by the winds, these mountains let loose the head-waters of the South and Middle Forks of the San Joaquin River and the North Fork of Kings River.

Here, in addition to Mount Whitney, are some of the main points of interest: Fish Creek, Cascade Valley, Mono Recesses, Seven Gables Peak, French Canyon, Humphrey Basin, Glacier Divide, the Palisades and their glaciers, Red Mountain Basin, Blackcap Basin and, for more leisurely hikes, all the western slope and its lakes.

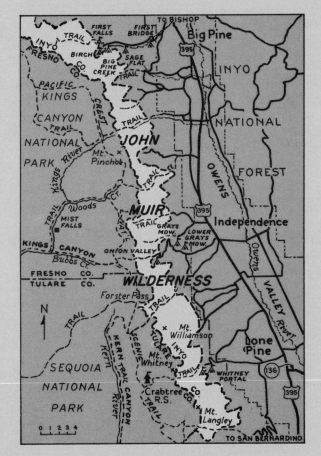

41

CALIFORNIA

Marble Mountain

Season: *June 15 to October 15; peak July 4, slow September to first snow*

Size: *213,363 acres*

Access: *The Wilderness is practically surrounded by good roads. Closest points of entry are on the north, south and west.*

Camping: *Primitive campsites; base camps on or near boundary*

Problems: *Occasional cool periods and thunderstorms*

Location: *Klamath National Forest*

Address: *Marble Mountain Wilderness*
Klamath National Forest
1215 S. Main Street
Yreka, CA 96097

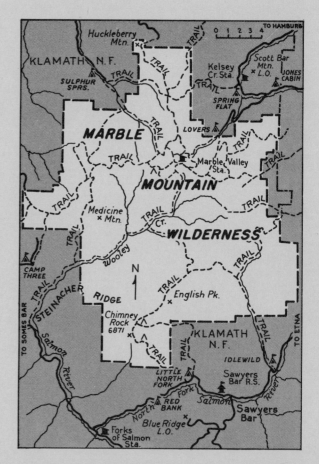

Although there are some steep trails here, Marble Mountain is not only "mild and mellow" country, it is one of the richest in variety for the backpacker. The area is heavily forested and easily traveled over shaded trails. Glacial activity has formed lakes with adjacent meadows for ideal camping. The lakes—over 80 of them—are abundantly stocked, and there are ocean runs of steelhead and salmon in the lower, larger streams, such as Wooley Creek.

Over 400 species of flora grow in the Wilderness, with some, such as the weeping spruce, which occur very rarely. Wildlife is plentiful, but fortunately the area is relatively free of insects. The Columbia black tail deer here are among the finest and largest in California.

The mountains were once the floor of a large shallow ocean where, later, deep pressures and volcanic activity raised the submarine deposits above the ocean. Marble Mountain itself is composed mostly of marine organisms, which were eventually crystalized into a white marble. The color gives the impression of perpetual snow.

One of the main features of this Wilderness is its ease of travel by foot or by horse, and the long trips that are possible. With proper planning, a whole summer could be spent in Marble Mountain Wilderness.

42

Minarets

CALIFORNIA

Season: *Lower elevations, June to mid-October; higher elevations and passes, July 1*

Size: *109,484 acres*

Access: *From the north off of State Route 120; from the east through Mammoth Lakes via Forest Service Road 3511; from the west at Clover Meadow*

Camping: *Primitive and improved campsites*

Problems: *Overused; little firewood; sudden summer thunderstorms*

Location: *Sierra and Inyo National Forests*

Address: *Minarets Wilderness Inyo National Forest*
Sierra National Forest 2957 Birch Street
1130 "O" Street Bishop, CA 93514
Fresno, CA 93721

Its southern neighbor, John Muir Wilderness, shares at least one problem with the Minarets. Both are plagued by periods of hiker jams—backpacking and camping traffic so heavy that no wilderness experience is in sight. It is not unusual to arrive at a nice quiet little lake at midday and then be joined by a party of 100 by afternoon.

And like John Muir Wilderness, the western slopes here are less crowded—and less accessible. Between mid-July and Labor Day, it is advisable to stay west of the Sierra Nevada crest.

This whole area offers excellent opportunities for experienced mountaineers, with glaciers, barren faces and peaks. Almost a dozen peaks reach over 12,000 feet, including Mount Dana (13,053 feet), Mount Gibbs (12,764 feet) and Mount Lewis (12,296 feet). Walter A. "Peter" Starr, Jr. was still compiling his famous guide to the Sierra when he was killed in the mountains around Ediza Lake, site of his last camp.

Although the greater part of the Minarets Wilderness is barren, there are stands of pine, fir, hemlock and aspen. Most of the trees grow around the upper reaches of the San Joaquin River.

A large number of creeks, streams and lakes are on trails in the area. They afford good fishing for rainbow, golden and eastern brook trout.

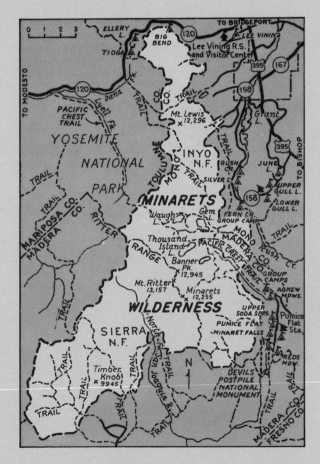

Mokelumne

Season: *Summer*

Size: *50,400 acres*

Access: *From the north, via California State Route 88, south to Plasse Trading Station on a four-wheel drive road to the boundary; from the east via Blue Lakes; trails from the south on State Route 4 are very primitive.*

Camping: *Primitive and improved campsites*

Problems: *Some areas, such as the Summit City Creek trail to the Mokelumne River, are for hardy backpackers only.*

Location: *Stanislaus and Eldorado National Forests*

Address: *Mokelumne Wilderness*
Forest Service
Jackson, CA 95642

In this rugged and primitive land, the forces of nature are many and obvious. The sculpture of swift streams, the wind blown granite formations and the abundant wildflowers are constant reminders that man has seldom been here.

Rocky, barren Mokelumne Peak dominates the heights of the Wilderness as the canyon of the Mokelumne River dominates the deeper land. It is along this river in the south and around the lakes in other parts of the area that camping is best. Fishing is good at Blue Hole near Salt Springs.

The forest cover is scattered, with firs the prominent tree, mixed with pine, cedar, hemlock and many varieties of shrubs. Wildflowers are on display much of the year.

Hikers can see many small rodents and fur bearers and possibly black bears. Two kinds of deer, the California mule deer and the Columbian black tail, graze the alpine meadows. At the higher levels and harder to see are a few mountain lions.

Adventurous hikers and fishermen may come across a hand-hewn log cabin deep in the North Fork of the Mokelumne. Monte Wolfe, the hermit of the Mokelumne, had a claim there and fished and hunted for twenty years before he disappeared. One spring, his partner discovered an uneaten meal on the table, but Monte had vanished forever.

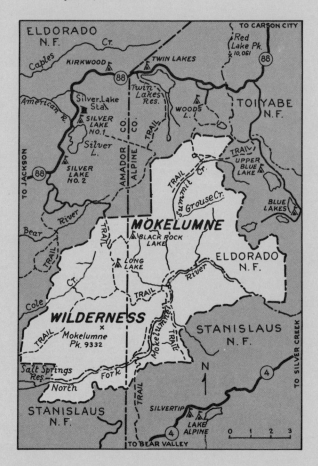

Salmon Trinity Alps

CALIFORNIA

Season: *June 1 to October 1 is the snow-free season; July and August peak season.*

Size: *223,340 acres*

Access: *From State Route 3 at Coffee Creek Ranger Station on the east; from the south off State Route 299 at Hawkins Bar, Helena and Junction City*

Camping: *Primitive and improved campsites*

Problems: *Steep, rocky terrain; severe summer thunderstorms; occasional rattlesnakes*

Location: *Klamath and Shasta-Trinity National Forests*

Address: *Salmon Trinity Alps Primitive Area*
1215 S. Main St.
Yreka, CA 96097

California's Coast Range is almost overlooked in comparison to the famous high mountains of the Sierra. Here, the highest point is Thompson Peak, at a mere 8,936 feet—low in comparison to the 14,000-footers of the Sierra.

But the crest of the Coast Range along the Salmon-Trinity Divide is as rough and wild as any country on the eastern slope of the Sierra. Sharp, jagged peaks and glaciated canyons create a sawtooth range of barren alpine country at higher elevations. Below are timbered and grassy meadows on many lakes and streams. Some of the best trails in the area wind along the ridges.

Fishing is excellent, including silver salmon and steelhead trout in the lower reaches of the major streams. The profusion of creeks, rivers and lakes offers constant surprises to anglers touring these headwaters of several major streams. Access trails are numerous at both high and low elevations.

Gold was discovered along the Trinity River in 1848. Though today mining is almost nonexistent, the Klamath Mountains became the second richest area in California. Old mines and shacks in some places remain, and it is still possible to pan a little gold here and there.

45

San Gabriel

Season: *All year, with fire closures*
Size: *36,137 acres*
Access: *Good highways offer easy access on all sides except the south.*
Camping: *A few improved campsites; mostly primitive camping*
Problems: *Lack of water; heat; overused*
Location: *Angeles National Forest*
Address: *San Gabriel Wilderness*
Angeles National Forest
150 S. Los Robles
Pasadena, CA 91101

Surrounded by the cities and recreation areas of southern California, this Wilderness has preserved in it some of southern California's most scenic country. Unfortunately, like much of the wilderness in this area, San Gabriel is overused in summer, especially early summer, and well traveled in winter, though slower.

The country is broken and steep, hot and dry in summer, with snow in the high country in winter. Most of the Wilderness is covered with chaparral from 1,600 feet to 5,000 feet. Up to 8,200 feet stand mixed pine and fir along the ridgetops.

Trails are few here, only about 12 miles in the entire Wilderness. The off-trail section is broken, steep, brush-covered terrain.

San Gabriel is a Wilderness which offers a challenge to backpackers and horsemen alike; it is suited to those who like its type of environment.

San Gabriel has some rugged, barren trails.

San Gorgonio

CALIFORNIA

Season: *All year at lower elevations; summer in the higher altitudes*

Size: *34,644 acres*

Access: *From the north and west at Barton Flats and Camp Angelus, on California State Route 38; from the south on Forest Road 1S03*

Camping: *Primitive campsites*

Problems: *Fire danger*

Location: *San Bernardino National Forest*

Address: *San Gorgonio Wilderness*
Civic Center Building
175 W. 5th Street
San Bernardino, CA 92401

Hikers with an interest in zoology and botany have an opportunity here to observe and study life forms from desert zones to an alpine environment. Located in the summit region of the San Gorgonio Mountains, the Wilderness sits on the highest range in southern California, with San Gorgonio Mountain on top at 11,502 feet. San Bernardino Peak, at 10,624 feet, is the initial point for the San Bernardino meridian. From the peaks, there are expansive desert and mountain views. Below timberline stand pines and some unusually fine white firs and black oaks. Small meadows and lakes dot the area, in contrast to barren rock.

Off the trails, water is scarce and the hiking is rough enough for inexperienced backpackers to stick to the maintained routes. For more solitude than in the rest of the Wilderness, the eastern section offers fewer trails, with good camps at Dry Lake, Dollar Lake and on the North Fork of the Whitewater River. Access is difficult, though, over long trails.

Fishing is only fair in most of the lakes, and hunting, too, is limited. On the east side of the Wilderness, there are a few bighorn sheep, but they are hard to find and to see and are protected by law against hunting in any season.

47

San Jacinto

Season: *June to October*

Size: *20,564 acres*

Access: *From the north off U.S. 10 and State Route 111; from the west off State Route 243*

Camping: *Primitive camping*

Problems: *Winter snow*

Location: *San Bernardino National Forest*

Address: *San Jacinto Wilderness*
Idyllwild Ranger Station
Idyllwild, CA 92349

This is one of the most curiously contrasting areas in the Wilderness Preservation System. Divided into two small sections, the San Jacinto is separated by Mount San Jacinto State Park. Among other highlights, the northern portion has some incredibly beautiful scenery, but is not visited nearly as often as the southern part.

Views go from the Salton Sea on the east to the coastal islands in the west, over 100 miles away. Sights range from the Mojave desert to San Gorgonio Mountain, while life zones travel the same extremes, from Sonoran, or desert, to the Arctic-Alpine.

One of those rare bits of wildland, the north section has never yielded any evidence of habitation by man. There are no trails (except a small piece of Pacific Crest Trail) and no campsites. It is, though, well watered country. Looking down on San Gorgonio Pass, it covers all the drainage of Snow Creek. Fishing is good below the falls of Snow Creek on all its main branches. Only experienced backpackers should attempt to penetrate this area to any extent, and then only with map and compass.

South of the State Park, San Jacinto is somewhat different. There are trails, including the Pacific Crest, and spur trails for hikers and pack and saddle travelers. A good loop hike begins in Idyllwild, goes 5 miles to Tahquitz Peak Lookout past meadows, streams, trees and wildflowers.

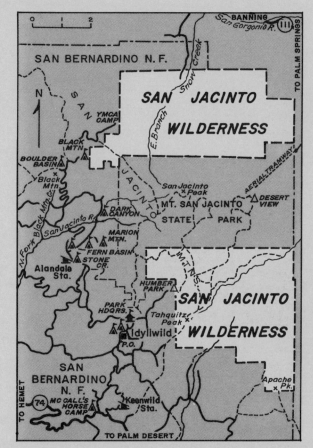

San Rafael

CALIFORNIA

Season: *November 1 to June 1, with fire closures*

Size: *142,722 acres*

Access: *On the north, many roads lead from State Route 166, and on the south from State Route 154.*

Camping: *Many improved campsites*

Problems: *Sudden snowstorms and flooding possible; overused*

Location: *Los Padres National Forest*

Address: *San Rafael Wilderness*
District Ranger
U.S. Forest Service
Star Route
Santa Barbara, CA 93105

Like many of the places in southern California where the wilderness experience is possible, this area is overused and in danger of losing its wild nature. It is just north of Santa Barbara, and its low elevations (1,166 to 6,596 feet) make it attractive in winter and spring, but hot and dry in summer and fall. Fire closures restrict entry in the summer, and every season carries a constant danger of fire.

Low areas are brush covered, but the high ridges are pine, fir and cedar forests. These forested ridges contrast sharply to the surrounding brush-covered slopes.

Within the Wilderness, a 1,200-acre sanctuary is maintained for the California condor. Sisquoc Condor Sanctuary is closed to all and no trails go into it. Only scientific research purposes may gain entry.

A pack train threads Mission Pine Basin.

49

South Warner

Season: *Spring through fall*

Size: *68,507 acres*

Access: *From the north and west from Alturas, on U.S. 395; from the southwest at Likely on U.S. 395; from the west on roads north and south of Eagleville; all access roads are gravel.*

Camping: *Primitive campsites*

Problems: *Sudden thunderstorms; possible late and early snows*

Location: *Modoc National Forest*

Address: *South Warner Wilderness*
Warner Mtn. Ranger District
P.O. Box 220
Cedarville, CA 96104

For alpine enthusiasts seeking backpacking with some ease, South Warner is the spot. Its Summit Trail traverses the area from north to south for 27 miles. Fifteen of those miles run along at 9,000 feet, with easy grades and alpine and high peak scenery. At the south, the trail begins at Patterson Meadow, and ends at the north end at Porter Reservoir.

For breaks in the alpine scenery, there are numerous spur trails leading down to glacial lakes and lush mountain meadows. Patterson Lake, on the north flank of Warren Peak (9,722 feet), is backed by 800-foot cliffs which rise to the summit. Other landmark mountains in the area are Eagle Peak, the tallest at 9,906 feet, and Squaw Peak, 8,650 feet.

The views here are spectacular and varied. Not only are the Wilderness peaks there to see, but also all of Modoc County and much of Lassen, along with northeastern Nevada, peaks in Oregon and Mounts Shasta and Lassen.

Variety of view is matched by the topography, with lakes, springs and canyons, aspen, conifer and grassy slopes.

Patterson Lake and Clear Lake, as well as most of the streams, have excellent fishing for trout. Deer inhabit the area, but no hunting of any kind is allowed on State Game Refuge 1-C, a portion of which lies in the Wilderness.

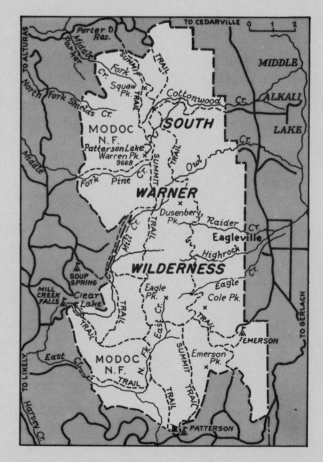

Thousand Lakes

CALIFORNIA

Season: *About June 1 to early October*

Size: *15,695 acres*

Access: *From the southwest, 14 miles from California State Route 89; from the south, 6 miles from State Route 89; from the east, 6 miles from State Route 89; from the north, 10 miles from State Route 89*

Camping: *Primitive campsites*

Problems: *Variable temperatures; no running water*

Location: *Lassen National Forest*

Address: *Thousand Lakes Wilderness*
Lassen National Forest
707 Nevada Street
Susanville, CA 96130

The many lakes here give the Wilderness its name. Magee Peak, an extinct volcano, formed numbers of lava pot holes in an ancient eruption, and the pot holes are now lakes. The top of 8,676-foot Magee is accessible by trail, but the main attraction is Thousand Lakes Valley, in the north section. It is an expanse of level ground which covers 500 acres. Short trips are good here.

The larger lakes contain rainbow trout, with fishing good throughout the season. Hunting is not good because of poor forage.

Elevations range from 5,000 to 9,000 feet. The portion above timberline is typical Sierra Nevada country, with open and barren mountainsides and ravines. There are formations of lava and granite and dense stands of lodgepole pines, with some open and brushy areas.

Campers can expect cold temperatures at night and warm daytime temperatures. Visits to the Wilderness should be confined to the period of about June 1 to the first snowfall, usually early October. Running water is not available, and lake water should be boiled before drinking.

Pack animal trips into Thousand Lakes are not advisable because neither the transport roads nor the forage can be depended on.

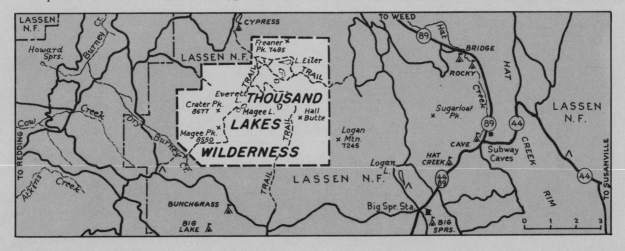

Ventana

Season: *All year, with fire closures*

Size: *95,152 acres*

Access: *From the west along State Route 1, especially at Big Sur Station; from the east via Forest Service Road 18S02*

Camping: *Improved campsites used because of fire danger*

Problems: *Fire danger; sudden flooding; overused*

Location: *Los Padres National Forest*

Address: *Ventana Wilderness*
District Ranger
U.S. Forest Service
406 South Mildred
King City, CA 93930

Although characterized as a hiker's paradise, Ventana is experiencing the difficulty of too many hikers on its trails. Mid-winter is the slow season. For the sake of the wilderness, that is the best time to go, though it is the time of rain and floods. During the summer and fall, use is restricted because of extreme fire danger.

Covered with dense chaparral, the lower slopes begin at 1,200 feet and rise to oak, madrone and pine on 4,833-foot Ventana Peak. The southernmost natural old growth redwoods occur here, too, in Little Sur and Big Sur Canyons. And unique to the area is the bristlecone, or Santa Lucia, fir.

Bird life is abundant in the summer; almost all streams are stocked with fish. Ventana is the habitat of the exotic wild boar, deer, wild pigeon and quail.

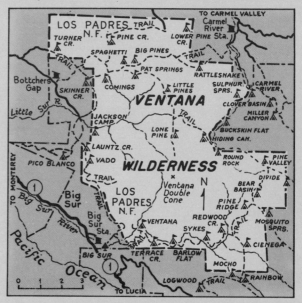

Ventana Wilderness lies along the Pacific.

Yolla Bolly-Middle Eel

CALIFORNIA

Season: *May to November; deer hunting, September-October*

Size: *111,091 acres*

Access: *From the east through Orland, 80 miles; Corning, 65 miles; Red Bluff, 50 miles; from the west through Covelo*

Camping: *Primitive campsites*

Problems: *Water is very scarce in summer. Ask rangers for current sources, and be prepared to carry your own.*

Location: *Mendocino and Shasta-Trinity National Forests*

Address: *Yolla Bolly-Middle Eel Wilderness*
Mendocino National Forest
Willows, CA 95988

Local people refer to the area as "the Yolla Bollys," which is a name of Wintun Indian origin, and means "high, snow-covered peak." Snow in winter does cover the peaks, which range from 6,000 feet up to 8,083 feet at the South Yolla Bolly Mountains. During the season, from May to November, extreme temperatures may reach as low as 20 and as high as 90 degrees.

This Wilderness, established in 1931, has no roads at all, only narrow foot trails. Most of them are easy trails with gradual slopes, even though they may cover wide ranges in elevation. Signs of deer and black bear are not uncommon along the trails, which wander through fir, pine, cedar, brush and grassy meadows.

From the peaks and ridges, views are magnificent, both near and far. Other portions of the Coast Range spread out to the west, and the Sierra Nevada rises far to the east.

Though far from a town of any size (the northeast section is 50 miles from Red Bluff), the Yolla Bollys are not difficult to get to by road. Tomhead Saddle, on the northeast boundary of the Wilderness, is accessible in summer even in the family car. There are campsites at Tomhead, but no water. Many trails start from the Saddle, one of the best being Syd Cabin Trail to the South Fork of the Cottonwood River ($4\frac{1}{4}$ miles from Tomhead Saddle). Fishing is good in the Cottonwood, as well as in the Middle Eel, Thomes Creek and Buck Creek.

Pack trips are available in the Yolla Bollys, but feed is scarce toward the end of the summer. The U.S. Forest Service has a list of packers. (See address above.)

The remoteness of the area has helped keep it in almost virgin condition; very good for solitude. The weather is moderate in summer.

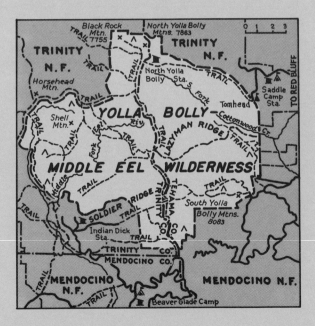

53

Other Wilderness Lands

California's gifts from nature are not exactly unsung. They are so well sung, in fact, that most of the backcountry is suffering from overuse, especially in the Sierra and in southern California. But there are still some areas outside the Wilderness Preservation System which have the room and character for wilderness experience.

National Forests

On the Klamath National Forest, there is one area of 171,000 acres around Preston Peak. It is not a designated wildland and is rough, rocky and dry, but it does offer hiking and climbing on 80 miles of trail. The area is open from June to October.

Mount Shasta Recreation Area on Shasta Trinity National Forest is 25,000 acres of rugged volcanic mountain terrain. It is open all year, but snow free only between June and October. As the Ranger there said, "A few hardy souls climb during winter months," but it is very rugged, steep country. There are snowfields all year, can be vicious storms all year and no water is available.

On Sierra National Forest, in addition to John Muir and the Minarets Wildernesses and the High Sierra Primitive Area, there are two fairly large roadless wildlands. The Dinkey Lakes area has moderate to gentle terrain with a few jagged peaks and granite domes, some of which are similar to those at Yosemite. Heavy forest is interspersed with meadows and lakes. The slow season is in June, September and October. Weekends can be crowded and some lakes are overused. Like Dinkey Lakes, Kaiser Crest, a roadless area, is open from mid-June to late October. Kaiser Peak, at 10,320 feet, is not a difficult climb, and some trails in the region are classified as easy. There are some outstanding views of the Sierra Nevada crest. Thunderstorms are common in the afternoons from July to September, and the Twin Lakes area is overused, especially on weekends.

Just west of Marble Mountain Wilderness, Salmon Trinity Alps Primitive Area and the Yolla Bolly-Middle Eel Wilderness are some fine river trips on Six Rivers National Forest. The six rivers which originate or flow through the Forest are, from north to south, the Smith, Klamath, Trinity, Mad, Van Duzen and Eel North Fork. For six miles a trail follows the South Fork of the Smith River, with an additional 12 miles of rugged river and no trail above Gunbarrel Camp. The trail is at river grade in a steep, rough canyon, and hikers may have to wade or swim above Gunbarrel Camp. Bear may be plentiful and poison oak always is. The peak season is July and August, with good fishing for trout in spring and summer, salmon and steelhead in fall. Rafting is also good. Rafting, kayaking and canoeing are good on one of the other rivers, the Klamath, with about 13 miles of river within the Forest. Floaters can drift on to Requa near the Pacific Ocean. Only tributary waters should be used for drinking without being treated.

National Parks

At the southern tip of the Cascades, Mount Lassen Volcanic Park has 150 miles of trails looked over by 10,457-foot Mount Lassen, a plug-dome volcano. In addition to thermal areas, lava flows and old volcanoes, hikers find lakes, streams, waterfalls and meadows. Autumn brings the mixed colors of conifers and broadleafs like aspen and cottonwood, and summer colors give an array of wildflower hues. Part of the Park is now in the Wilderness Preservation System.

Redwood National Park, near Crescent City, California has some wilderness land, but can be crowded from June to August. The Redwood Creek Trail is over eight miles long, paralleling the creek with high ridges on both sides. In the Tall Trees Grove the highest tree known stands over the second, third and sixth tallest. The giant of them all is 367.8 feet tall.

World famous Yosemite National Park is jammed with the hustle and bustle of tourists in some sections, but other places exist where the grandeur has the added pleasures of solitude. Over 700 miles of trails wind through the Park, mostly in the north and southwest. The western border is along the Sierra Crest, and trails lead into several Wildernesses. The Pacific Crest Trail (see page 180) runs along the Sierra here too.

There are many other wilderness lands in California, including a State of California Wilderness Park, the Mount San Jacinto Wilderness in southern California, the desert solitude of Death Valley and many acres of national forests.

For more California information, write:

Forest Service
630 Sansome Street
San Francisco, CA 94111

National Park Service
450 Golden Gate Avenue
P.O. Box 36063
San Francisco, CA 94102

State of California
Department of Parks and Recreation
P.O. Box 2390
Sacramento, CA 95811

Flat Tops

Season: *All year except no hikers in winter*

Size: *102,124 acres*

Access: *From the north via State Route 132; from the south on Forest Service roads at Dotsero; from the west on dirt roads at Buford*

Camping: *Primitive camping*

Problems: *Snow anytime; low temperatures*

Location: *White River National Forest*

Address: *Flat Tops Primitive Area*
White River National Forest
Glenwood Springs, CO 81601

This is a strange land of many sharp contrasts. In it, the visitor finds rolling lands, steep cliffs, jagged rocks, mountain peaks, open grassland parks and densely timbered valleys.

Interesting ecologically is the fact that grasslands now cover 40 percent of this plateau, dead timber another 46 percent. An almost solid stand of Engelmann spruce once covered 68,000 acres. Now, green trees in small clusters stand on about 4 percent, while young trees form an understory within a forest of dead, silver-gray snags. This dying and rebirth is the result of an extensive spruce bark beetle epidemic in the early 1940's.

The abrupt, irregular border of Flat Tops is formed by lava rocks which rise in long walls, like the so-called Chinese Wall and the Devil's Causeway. These sheer escarpments are the most prominent feature of the White River Plateau.

The plateau, alpine peaks and open grass parks create distant horizons with exquisite scenery, solitude, tranquil lakes, rushing streams, abundant wildlife and virtually no evidence of man's intrusion.

The famous White River big game herd of several thousand deer and elk use this as summer ranges, extending into the fall.

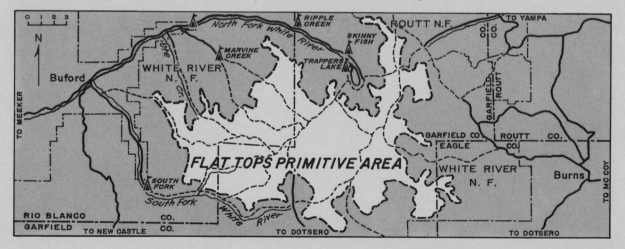

Gore Range—Eagles Nest

Season: *Peak season is June 15 to September 15; winter and spring are slower.*

Size: *61,101 acres*

Access: *From the east by roads off State Route 9 between Dillon and Green Mountain Reservoir; from the south and west off U.S. 6 by several roads east and west of Vail Village*

Camping: *Primitive camping*

Problems: *Overused; snow and very cold in winter; rain in summer; frost all year possible.*

Location: *Arapaho and White River National Forests*

Address: *Gore Range-Eagles Nest Primitive Area*
Arapaho National Forest
Golden, CO 80401

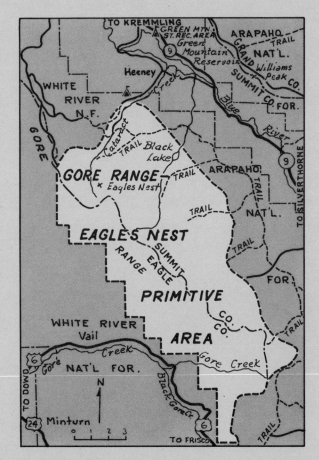

In this area there are 90 peaks which reach up over 11,000 feet—17 are over 13,000 feet and 33 over 12,000. This makes "the Gore" a favorite of climbers and backpackers alike. That fact, combined with its proximity to Denver, has created an increasingly common wilderness problem: overuse. In the case of this Primitive Area, the popularity of backpacking and ski touring has added to the problem in both summer and winter.

Baronet and sportsman Sir George Gore of Sligo, Ireland made an extended hunt here from 1855 to 1857. As if a forerunner of the groups sometimes found today, Sir George brought a party of servants, cooks and even United States soldiers with him, all guided by the famous trapper and scout, Jim Bridger.

But Gore Range is still one of the most scenic in the West. There is a vast virgin forest in which lie cascading streams and deep clear lakes. Abundant fish and wildlife are found. The mountain walls and peaks have a pronounced and spectacular vertical uplift.

A network of 11 trails, totaling about 80 miles, is maintained by the Forest Service. Most of the trails are in the northern end, but there are a few in the south. Only two, one at each end, cross the range itself.

57

La Garita

Season: *Trails clear generally from June 15 to October 15*
Size: *48,486 acres*
Access: *From State Route 114 at Upper Saguache Fireman Station; from Creede on the south by dirt road or trail*
Camping: *Primitive camping*
Problems: *Rough terrain; summer storms; low temperatures*
Location: *Gunnison and Rio Grande National Forests*
Address: *La Garita Wilderness*
Gunnison National Forest
Gunnison, CO 81230

In English, "la garita" means "the lookout," and it is an apt name for this high alpine country. Two peaks, San Luis and Stewart, are over 14,000 feet, both north of the Continental Divide as it cuts through the Wilderness. The alpine terrain and remoteness of La Garita make it a favorite for those who seek and can enjoy wilderness solitude.

Steep talus slopes, glacial rock deposits, alpine meadows and rushing streams make a natural habitat for wildlife. Bear, coyote and mountain lion live here along with ptarmigan, grouse and the cony, sometimes called the "rock rabbit." Elk, deer and mountain sheep use La Garita as a summer range and beavers have built numerous dams to form high mountain ponds along the many creeks.

Fishing is good in all the streams and in Machin Lake, a popular destination for hikers looking for rugged trails. Two lead in from the north, one from Big Meadows and one from Stone Cellar Guard Station. From Big Meadows, Trails 469 and 784 are 10 miles; Trails 783 and 784 from Stone Cellar make the trek 15 miles.

Pack animals are available for a Wilderness trip by writing to the chambers of commerce in Gunnison and Creede, Colorado.

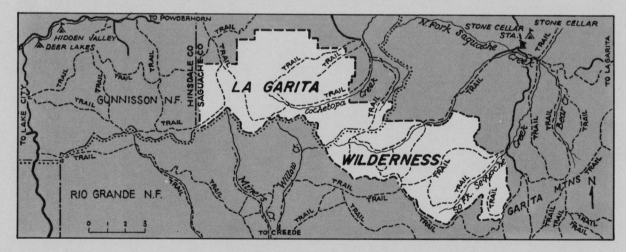

Maroon Bells-Snowmass

COLORADO

Season: *November 1 to May 15 for ski touring and snowshoeing; July and August for hiking and riding*

Size: *71,060 acres*

Access: *On the west from State Route 133; on the east from Aspen*

Camping: *Primitive camping*

Problems: *Winter snow avalanches; storms any time of year; low temperatures; lightning; overused in some areas*

Location: *White River National Forest*

Address: *Maroon Bells-Snowmass Wilderness
White River National Forest
Glenwood Springs, CO 81601*

An excellent climbing area, "the Bells" is also a family favorite for hiking and pack and saddle trips. Climbing varies from simple scramble to hard tension, difficult mountaineering. This is an extra hazardous area because of the decomposing nature of the rock on all peaks. Capitol Peak (14,130 feet) has the only good, long solid pitches, but the falling rock hazard still exists. A register is placed on each of the 14,000-foot peaks to record climbs.

One of the climbing features is the Capitol Knife Edge, which is on the northeast ridge of the climbing route to Capitol Peak. There are very few true knife edges, though many ridges are said to be. This one is: the apex of the ridge varies from less than one inch to two inches. Both sides of the ridge drop sharply down to lower ledges and cliffs. Climbing routes in the Wilderness are marked on Forest Service maps.

In the southern section, Conundrum Hot Springs await the cold and weary hiker. Near timberline on Conundrum Creek, this spring gushes hot water at just a little above body temperature. Early visitors in days gone by built a pool below the spring. The pool makes a comfortable bathing spot, but it can also be crowded.

Aspens are the most common trees in this Wilderness, joined by spruce, pine and fir. A host of small plants, wildflowers and grasses flourish in the summer. Including Colorado's state flower, the columbine, the range of wildflowers is dazzling. Bristlecone pines are found, and the mingling of aspens and evergreens make fall colors spectacular.

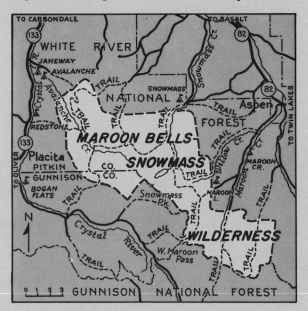

Mount Zirkel

Season: *June 15 to September 30*

Size: *72,472 acres*

Access: *From the west via Route 129 to Slavonia; from the south at Buffalo Pass on State Route 38; from the east on State Routes 6W, 16 and 22*

Camping: *Primitive camping*

Problems: *Snow anytime; heavy spring runoff; cold temperatures all year*

Location: *Routt National Forest*

Address: *Mount Zirkel Wilderness*
Routt National Forest
P.O. Box 1198
Steamboat Springs, CO 80477

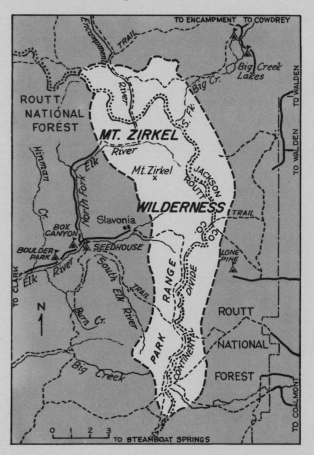

The remoteness of Mount Zirkel is probably best shown by noting that 35 of the 65 lakes in the Wilderness are unnamed. Hiking varies greatly here, with some portions generally level and easily hiked and others steep and rugged. Scenery is on a grand scale. The main north-south trail sections generally follow the Continental Divide, twisting among 14 peaks over 12,000 feet high.

The streams and lakes hold brook, rainbow and native cutthroat trout. All three are of exceptionally high quality, but are quite difficult to catch. Many of the best fishing spots can be toured in a relatively short time with pack and saddle animals. Fishermen and hikers should be aware that there are only about 30 frost-free days a year, and the average annual temperature is about 35 degrees.

Sizeable herds of elk and a few mule deer make their summer range in the Wilderness. They are kept company by black bear, fox, coyote, bobcats, marmot, cony, blue grouse and ptarmigan.

The many lakes in the area make excellent camping sites, surrounded by spruce and fir. Even along the Continental Divide trail, lakes are not far away. Several one-day hikes to lakes from access points are possible.

A number of state, federal and private areas near the Wilderness offer fine camping, fishing, skiing, snowshoeing and cross-country skiing.

Rawah

Season: *July 1 to October 1*

Size: *26,674 acres*

Access: *State Route 14 to Chambers Lake; accesses along Larmie River road north of Chambers Lake*

Camping: *Primitive camping to improved campsites*

Problems: *Summer storms; some very rough terrain; low temperatures*

Location: *Roosevelt National Forest*

Address: *Rawah Wilderness*
Roosevelt National Forest
211 Canyon
Fort Collins, CO 80521

The northern and southern portions of this Wilderness are fittingly named. "Rawah" is a Ute Indian word which translates into English as "wilderness." Lying in the rugged Medicine Bow Range, Rawah elevations average 11,000 feet, with the lowest at 9,500 feet.

In an area 14 miles long and 3 miles wide, there are over 25 lakes. Some are prominent and easy to find, while others seem well hidden. Mostly alpine lakes, they feature quality fishing, which makes the Wilderness one of the most popular in the Rocky Mountains.

Climbing in Rawah is excellent, but most is safe only for experienced mountaineers. The southern portion, reached from Tunnel Campground and Chambers Lake Campground, is especially challenging.

Two of the most popular camping spots are at McIntyre Lake and Rawah Lakes Back Area Camps, accessible, as all portions of Rawah are, from the Laramie River road. In the north and south, hikers find lakes to themselves.

It would be possible—with wide experience and proper preparation—to hike from Rocky Mountain National Park south of Rawah through the Medicine Bow Range and into Wyoming. Rawah itself, however, would be enough for the average hiker for a few weeks. The main trail north and south in Rawah itself is an exploration of alpine barrens and spruce and pine forests.

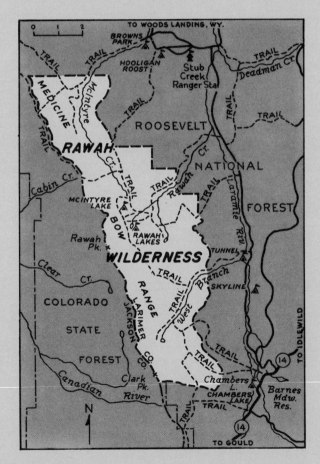

San Juan

Season: *July to September*

Size: *238,407 acres*

Access: *North from U.S. 160 at Durango, Bayfield, Pagosa Springs and Bruce Resort*

Camping: *Primitive camping*

Problems: *Extremely rugged terrain; heavy snows; low temperatures*

Location: *San Juan National Forest*

Address: *San Juan Primitive Area*
San Juan National Forest
West Building
Durango, CO 81301

Stretched along a southern slope of the Continental Divide, the San Juan is a very wild and rough country of outstanding mountain scenery. The Window, a famous landmark mentioned by early explorers, is here on the Divide. Soldiers and missionaries came first, then trappers and surveyors, and finally miners and cattlemen came before today's hikers and climbers.

Scenic beauty is the main attraction, with high mountain peaks and rich forests. Climbing is excellent in the Needle Mountains, between Animas River and Vallecito Creek. It is one of the roughest ranges in the United States. Windom Peak, Mount Aoleus and Sunlight Peak are all over 14,000 feet. Along with a score of others, they make the Needles a climber's mecca. Usually it is impossible to reach the high country before July, and by mid-September the snows have closed the peaks again. The two months between mid-July and mid-September are best for climbing. The Grenadiers are also good for mountaineering, as well as for rugged hiking.

There are many streams, lakes, waterfalls and meadows. Wildlife is abundant and there is a grizzly bear management area in the Primitive Area. Fishing is excellent here.

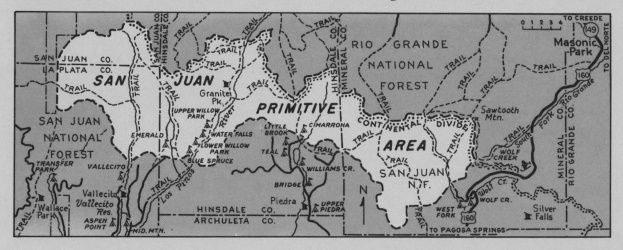

Uncompahgre

Season: *July and August*

Size: *53,252 acres*

Access: *Trails lead off of U.S. 550 and State Route 361 southwest of Ouray*

Camping: *Primitive camping*

Problems: *Boil all water; carry water on wilderness trips because of high mineral content.*

Location: *Grand Mesa-Umcompahgre National Forest*

Address: *Umcompahgre Wilderness*
Grand Mesa-Umcompahgre National Forest
P.O. Box 138
Delta, CO 81416

Few Primitive Areas are within a mile of a town the size of Ouray, Colorado, even at a thousand or so residents only. Few of these wild areas are in mining districts of current importance. But the Umcompahgre claims both places. As a matter of fact, it practically surrounds the town of Ouray and may continue to be the center of a controversy over its continued existence. The Forest Service wants it excluded from the National Wilderness Preservation System; conservationists want it expanded and included.

Mining history is evident in both parts of the Umcompahgre in the half-hidden ruins of old mines and camps. U. S. 550 cuts the area into two sections.

Rough, barren rocks, rolling and level areas and sheer cliffs hundreds of feet high characterize these mountains of superlative scenic beauty. Some peaks are over 14,000 feet, with countless lesser peaks overlooking lakes and waterfalls. Spruce and aspen, grass and wildflowers grow in the deep, colorful canyons.

Wildlife of all kinds can be seen along the trails. Living here with deer, elk, bear and bighorn sheep are wild turkey and ptarmigan. Trout fishing is excellent.

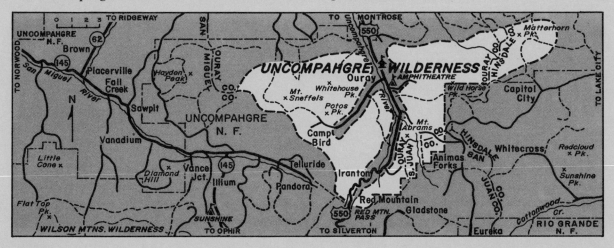

Upper Rio Grande

Season: *July and August*

Size: *56,600 acres*

Access: *West of Creede by Forest Service Road 7 to Forest Service Road 1364; several trails go south into the Primitive Area.*

Camping: *Primitive camping*

Problems: *Snow much of the year*

Location: *Rio Grande National Forest*

Address: *Upper Rio Grande Primitive Area*
Rio Grande National Forest
Rural Route 3, Box 21
Monte Vista, CO 81144

The name of this Primitive Area is derived from the fact that within its borders are the headwaters of the Nation's third longest river, the Rio Grande. Separated from the San Juan Primitive Area by the Continental Divide, the mountains offer a rich wilderness experience to expert climbers and families alike, whether backpacking or using saddle and pack animals.

This is very high country, with elevations ranging from 9,500 feet to 14,091 feet. Much of the land is alpine terrain, but about 47 percent is conifer forest cover, and the many streams and open parks give hikers a sense of solitude.

Elk, deer, black bear, bighorn sheep, coyote, bobcat, mountain lion and smaller mammals are residents of the area. Trout fishing is excellent.

While winter snows make the Upper Rio Grande unfeasible for hikers, there are fine possibilities for snowshowing and cross-country skiing. July and August are the peak season, when climbing, hiking, fishing and riding are the attractions.

Trail 818, from Rio Grande Reservoir, is a good one for reaching the Continental Divide. The trail continues across Weminuche Pass, named for the early Indians in the region.

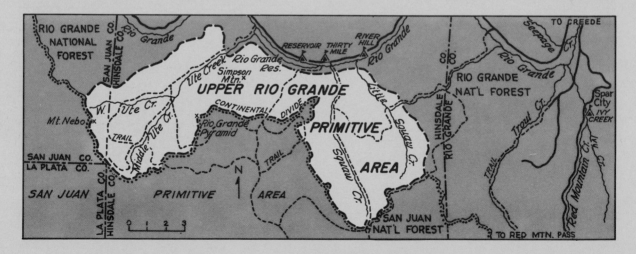

West Elk

COLORADO

Season: *All year with heavy winter snow*
Size: *61,412 acres*
Access: *From Gunnison via Forest Service Road 730: from the south via Blue Mesa Reservoir on Forest Service Road 723*
Camping: *Primitive campsites*
Problems: *Loose rock trails in some areas*
Location: *Gunnison National Forest*
Address: *West Elk Wilderness*
Gunnison National Forest
Gunnison, CO 81230

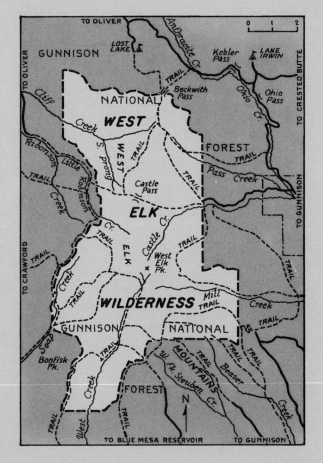

Situated on the "Western Slope" of the Rockies, West Elk is a rugged, wild, natural area in much the same condition as it was when Spaniards and mountain men first came here. Numerous streams run in the steeply carved canyons where ten major waterways have their headwaters. Most of the streams and lakes have a good supply of trout, either native or stocked rainbow and brook.

One of the main geological features of the Wilderness is The Castles, sharp walls hundreds of feet high. Erosion has formed towers, minarets and battlements which call to mind the castles of Europe.

Throughout West Elk are stands of spruce, grasses and high mountain parks of aspen. There are also barren peaks, with West Elk the highest at 12,920 feet.

In the summer, a large population of deer and elk range here. Also at home in West Elk are bear, mountain sheep and many types of local fur-bearing animals.

One good two-day trip begins at Mill Creek on Trail 450 and goes above timberline. The return is down Castle Creek on Trail 450 to the trailhead at Castle Creek, with some spectacular views of The Castles.

Pack and saddle animals are available (see address above) for several long trips in the Wilderness. One of the best trips is from Beckwith Pass to Soap Creek Campground.

Wilson Mountain

Season: *July and August*

Size: *27,347 acres*

Access: *From the north, east and south by State Route 145; from the west by Forest Service roads from Miramonte Reservoir*

Camping: *Primitive camping*

Problems: *Boil all water; pack in water for long trips because of high mineral content.*

Location: *San Juan and Uncompahgre National Forests*

Address: *Wilson Mountains Primitive Area*
Grand Mesa-Uncompahgre National Forest
P.O. Box 138
Delta, CO 81416

For a Western Primitive Area, Wilson Mountains is small. It, like Umcompahgre, is in the area of one of the greatest mining regions of Colorado. But flora and fauna abound, along with three peaks over 14,000 feet and fine lake and stream fishing, along with quite a few mines.

The area has survived despite mining and other attempts by man to conquer it, and it lives as a wildland which offers much to hikers, fishermen, climbers and backpacking families. Navajo Lake, featuring golden trout, is a good family destination. It is accessible by trail from Burro Bridge Campgrounds, which is just off State Route 145 on the south side of the Primitive Area. Mid-July is the peak season for wildflowers, when the countryside sparkles with color.

Large and small game are as abundant as wildflowers. Elk, mule deer, mountain sheep, bear and mountain lion live in the region. Of the smaller animals, there are marten, weasel, mink, fox, coyote, bobcat, snowshoe hare and beaver. Living with them are many birds—ptarmigan, bald eagle, golden eagle and many common small birds.

This is an ideal area to combine the history of mining and ghost towns with nature study in one trip.

Other Wilderness Lands

Colorado is high country, hiking and climbing wilderness. The second highest peak in the United States outside of Alaska is here at Mount Elbert, 14,431 feet. The Rockies reach massive, spectacular proportions throughout Colorado, and in many places snow can come in any month, temperatures can drop sharply.

National Forests

Most of the National Forests in Colorado have designated Wildernesses in them and practically all have fine backcountry possibilities. On Routt National Forest, in addition to Mount Zirkel Wilderness, there are two areas with excellent backpacking opportunities. The Never Summer Range, open from July 1 to October 1, features alpine tundra, conifers and subalpine meadows with awesome peaks over 12,000 feet. In the Rabbit Ears-Buffalo Pass area there is excellent hiking on 15,000 acres of gentle terrain. Winter is good for snowshoeing and ski touring. September and October are the slow months.

San Isabel National Forest is not only the location of Mount Elbert, but also of 12 peaks over 14,000 feet. It has the highest average elevation of all the national forests, with more than 40 timberline lakes. Hiking, climbing and fishing are all excellent, but hikers must come prepared for any kind of weather.

National Parks

The Black Canyon of the Gunnison National Monument covers 13,000 acres stretched along the Gunnison River near Montrose, Colorado. It is a strange and fascinating canyon, in places almost 2,500 feet deep with walls so close together that the whole day seems to be dusk. There are a number of trails into the canyon, but hiking at the bottom is difficult and dangerous—for the skilled and well conditioned only.

Rockhounds and fossil buffs will appreciate hiking in Dinosaur National Monument in the deep canyons of the Green and Yampa Rivers. The largest fossil deposits in the country are here, as well as curiously tilted, colorful rock formations and Indian caves and petroglyphs.

Rocky Mountain National Park is a vast, high-mountain area of 410 square miles. Three hundred miles of trails carry hikers up mountains, into deep valleys and past lakes and streams. Near Estes Park, Colorado, the Park is so impressive and so accessible that many areas are overused, and some are closed to camping. Other wilderness sections of the Park have a maximum set on the number of hikers allowed at one time.

For more Colorado information, write:

Forest Service
Federal Center
Building 85
Denver, CO 80225

National Park Service
1709 Jackson Street
Omaha, NB 68102

State of Colorado
Department of Game, Fish and Parks
6060 Broadway
Denver, CO 80200

CONNECTICUT

Except for the portion of the Appalachian Trail (see page 166) going through Connecticut, there are no lands which could be called wilderness for backpacking. The Connecticut Department of Environmental Protection is planning on establishing some areas where hiking and camping would be feasible.

For more Connecticut information, write:

State of Connecticut
State Office Building
Hartford, CT 06115

DELAWARE

Although there are wildlife areas, both state and federal, and state forests and campgrounds in Delaware, there are no areas suitable for wilderness trips. Camping is not even allowed in some State Parks, which are small and receive heavy use.

For more Delaware information, write:

State Park Commission of Delaware
3300 Faulkland Road
Wilmington, DE 19808

FLORIDA

In Florida, it might be more accurate to speak of wilderness "waters" rather than of "lands." So much of the wilderness is water—swamps, sloughs and rivers—that it is fine backcountry for boaters of all varieties. Florida has its own Scenic and Wild Rivers System and a Canoe Trail System. The Department of Natural Resources publishes a booklet about each one.

National Forests

On Apalachicola National Forest, the main interest for wildland enthusiasts is the canoe trail on the Ochlockonee River. It begins at State Route 20 about 23 miles southwest of Tallahassee and ends 67 miles downstream. The area around the river is sometimes impassable to foot travel, but there are stands of trees now and then. This is a fluctuating river because of water releases from Lake Talquin Dam above the trail, and is best for experienced canoeists. South of this national forest is the forbidding swamp known as Tate's Hell. It is a huge area where hiking is impossible and boating of any kind very nearly so. It is rugged and dangerous, especially because of the possibility of getting lost. Few people enter it.

Ocala National Forest is our southernmost national forest on the continent and the only one with subtropical vegetation, including, palm, pine and hardwood trees. Although there is considerable logging here under the so-called "multiple use" program, there are areas where solitude in a natural setting is available. There is much wildlife, many lakes and canoeing opportunities. Part of the Florida Trail winds 64 miles through Ocala, where it is called Ocala Trail. The Florida Trail will eventually go the length of Florida, with over 700 hiking miles. Winter and spring are the best times, and maps will be available in June, 1973. Part of the Florida Trail also passes through Osceola National Forest, which is near Lake City. (Florida Trail Association, 33 S.W. 18th Terrace, Miami, FL 33129)

Everglades National Park

The Everglades is 1,400,533 acres of subtropical wilderness administered as a natural area. Its size makes it our last real wilderness in a subtropical zone. There are some truly impenetrable areas, and foot trails are minimal compared to the unlimited possibilities for water trails. The Wilderness Waterway is a boat trail 99 miles long on an inland route from Everglades to Flamingo. Four other marked canoe trails are in the Flamingo area.

Heavy rains from June 1 to November 1 bring great numbers of insects, especially the mosquito. As everywhere in Florida, campers should be well prepared for the insect population. There is a bewildering number of animals, birds, and types of flora here, some unique to the area. The peak use season is from December 15 to April 15.

State Parks

Florida has 26 state parks, four state forests and other state lands with special designations. There are nine rivers up for inclusion in the Scenic and Wild Rivers System of the state and 16 rivers already are included in the Canoe Trail System.

Of the State Parks, three are the most appropriate for the wilderness experience. Collier

Seminole State Park is 4,760 acres of flat, swampy wildland near Marco. Its special features include the large numbers of mangroves, with creeks, rivers and lagoons. It is part of the estuarine complex of southwest Florida. Birds—including ospreys and pelicans—inhabit the Park, where canoeing and primitive camping are the best backcountry activities.

Florida prairie and flat swamp characterizes Myakka River State Park near Sarasota. It is 7,540 acres of freshwater marsh and pine flatwoods on the flood plain of the Myakka River. In the backcountry, just about every living creature native to Florida can be seen.

St. Joseph State Park, near Port St. Joe, is a small shoreline park of 1,763 acres. It is a barrier sand spit of beach, pine flatwoods and freshwater ponds. Shore birds are diverse and plentiful, and bobcats, foxes and skunks have been seen. It is also the home of the rare beach mouse.

For more Florida information, write:

Forest Service
1720 Peachtree Road N.W.
Atlanta, GA 30309

National Park Service
3401 Whipple Street
Atlanta, GA 30344

State of Florida
Department of Natural Resources
Larson Building
Tallahassee, FL 32304

GEORGIA

The famed Okefenokee Swamp sits mostly in Georgia, but restrictions on camping and the danger of going very far into the swamp without guides limit its wilderness possibilities.

There are a few state parks in Georgia, but they are relatively small and frequently used, though Jekyll Island has some good camping and ocean views.

Chattahoochee National Forest

The two main wilderness attractions on this 720,000-acre forest in northern Georgia are the last southern miles of the Appalachian Trail, going from Maine to Georgia (see page 170), and the Chattooga River.

To hikers coming in from North Carolina, the Appalachian Trail in Georgia can be surprisingly remote and rugged. The southern terminus is at Springer Mountain.

The Chattooga River is a Study River for possible inclusion in the Wild and Scenic Rivers System. Along the 50-mile stretch of the river itself, all three classifications—wild, scenic and recreational—have been proposed. The river goes through a deep gorge, with 20 to 80 percent slopes 200 to 400 feet high. Wildlife, fish and plants are abundant. The final six miles to Tugaloo Lake is the most difficult stretch, rated by canoe experts as one of the most hazardous white water runs in the United States. Parts of the river are also on Nantahala National Forest in North Carolina and Sumter National Forest in South Carolina.

For more Georgia information, write:

Forest Service
1720 Peachtree Road N.W.
Atlanta, GA 30309

Information Officer
Georgia Department of State Parks
7 Hunter Street S.W.
Atlanta, GA 30334

HAWAII

Hawaii's backcountry can come as a surprise—or even as a shock—to mainland hikers. The wildlands of the 50th state are like nothing else experienced by foot travelers in any other state. There are remote beaches, two desolate mountains over 13,000 feet and dense, wet, tropical forests. Climates range from the hot sun of the beaches to snow on the high mountains, life forms from marine species to wild pigs to some escaped wallabies reverting to a natural, if unaccustomed, state.

National Parks

On the island of Maui, Haleakala National Park is one of the most fascinating scenes in the entire system of parks. Haleakala, which means "house of the sun" in Hawaiian, is a dormant volcano over 10,000 feet high. In its crater are many colorful, symmetrical cones as much as 600 feet high.

No roads enter the crater, but there are 30 miles of trail with possibilities of long and short trips, but water and fuel must be toted along. More trails are in the Seven Pools area, situated in a long foot of the Park which reaches down to the ocean.

There are some rare flora and fauna here, for in Hawaii over 90 percent of all native species are found nowhere else. Haleakala has one of the rarest of plants, the silversword, with hundreds of flowers on a stalk in summer. All the mammals seen here except for a small brown bat were introduced by man.

Hawaii Volcanoes National Park on the island of Hawaii can be a crowded place, but backcountry camping is still possible in some areas, with a free permit. One trail leads up to the top of

Mauna Loa, at 13,680 feet. There are two cabins along the way, which may be used on advance notice. Trailless areas may be explored with permission of the Park Service.

State Parks

The state Department of Land and Natural Resources has proposed two wilderness parks, one on Hawaii and one on Kauai. They are both essentially beach wildernesses, with inland tropical cover.

The Honomolino Wilderness Park would be a thin strip along the southwestern coast of the island of Hawaii. Its 25 square miles would pass along rough terrain, by lava flows and coastal bluffs with sparse vegetation. There are no roads in the area, though one leads to each end, and all water must be brought in. The major interests besides the scenery are considerable archeological remains of early Hawaiians and excellent shore fishing.

On the fabled northern coast of Kauai, the Na Pali Coast Wilderness Park would contain five square miles with 15 miles of coast and 11 miles of trail. Steep cliffs drop into the ocean, with changes in altitude which can be as much as 4,000 feet in a half mile. There are occasional valleys and sandy beaches, and the inland tropical forest ranges from moderately wet to dry. His-

torical evidence of early Hawaiians may be seen here, too, in the larger valleys; some smaller valleys are inaccessible even to make a trail. The winter season is the wet one—and the slow one.

Other parts of Hawaii are good for backpacking, too. Trails in Mauna Kea State Park and Kalopa State Recreation Area on Hawaii go around and up the 13,796-foot Mauna Kea, highest spot in Hawaii. On Oahu, the trail on the Koolau Range ridge varies from easy to very rugged, and is usually quite wet, but can be a good, solitary retreat from Honolulu.

For more Hawaii information, write:

National Park Service
c/o Hawaii Group
677 Ala Moana Boulevard
Suite 512
Honolulu, HI 96813

State of Hawaii
Department of Land and Natural Resources
P.O. Box 621
Honolulu, HI 96809

Idaho

Season: *July and August are good and are the peak months of use; September is the slow month.*

Size: *1,224,733 acres*

Access: *From the Salmon River; from U.S. 93 on the east, State Route 21 on the south and State Route 55 on the west*

Camping: *Primitive camping*

Problems: *Early snowstorms; low temperatures*

Location: *Boise, Challis, Payette and Salmon National Forests*

Address: *Idaho Primitive Area*
Payette National Forest
McCall, ID 83638

This is the largest protected wildland in the United States. It is very rugged, scenic country, with towering peaks and deep canyons. The forest cover stretches as far as the eye can see in every direction, pratically unbroken.

Many trails, streams, lakes, abundant wildlife and plant life characterize this wildland, parts of which are little explored or not at all. Big game is plentiful along the 2,000 miles of trails, and pack animals are available.

The Middle Fork of the Salmon River, a nationally designated Wild and Scenic River (see page 203), runs through the Idaho. Float trips are possible, and are one means of access to the Primitive Area, which is under consideration as a Wilderness.

The giant Idaho Primitive Area is noted for float trips along the Middle Salmon River.

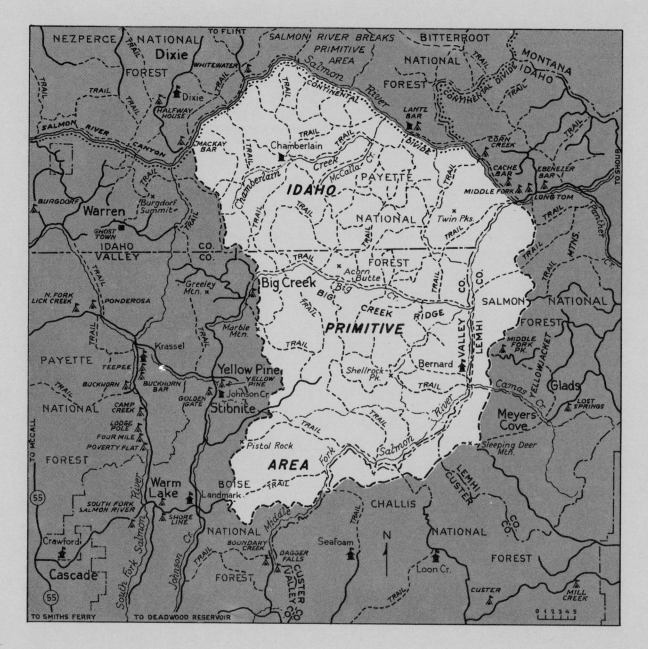

IDAHO

Salmon River Breaks

Season: *Summer*

Size: *216,870 acres*

Access: *From the east by boat from road's end below Shoup, Idaho; by dirt road and trail off State Route 14 at Elk City*

Camping: *Primitive campsites*

Problems: *Dangerous water in the Salmon; extensive use along banks and in high lakes*

Location: *Bitterroot and Nezperce National Forests*

Address: *Salmon River Breaks Primitive Area
Bitterroot National Forest
Hamilton, MT 59840*

The Salmon, the "River of No Return," runs between the Salmon River Breaks and the Idaho Primitive Areas. Together, the two areas total almost 1.5 million acres. The river here is under consideration for designation as a Wild and Scenic River (see page 73).

This Primitive Area extends for 40 miles through a roadless area along the Salmon between Riggins and Salmon, Idaho. It is a very steep, rugged, forested terrain with high mountain lakes and abundant big game such as elk and mountain sheep. The river breaks and mountain scenery are favorite subjects for photographers.

The river itself is one of the main attractions. Running its white water is strictly for the most expert boatmen, though boats and guides are available in Salmon, Idaho (write the Forest Service at the above address). Before or after the season is best because the river at this point is receiving increasing use from powerboats and float trips. But even if not on the river, hikers can enjoy it from the bank trail or others above the water. Fishing is excellent for steelhead trout and salmon.

In the Primitive Area there are still signs of Indian and white pioneer history. Miners came to the area at one time and left their marks, too.

Sawtooth

Season: *Mid-June through early September*

Size: *216,617 acres*

Access: *From the north and west via trails off State Route 21; from the east via trails off U.S. 93*

Camping: *Primitive camping to improved campsites*

Problems: *Low temperatures; rough terrain; dry periods in late summer*

Locations: *Sawtooth, Boise and Challis National Forests*

Address: *Sawtooth Wilderness*
Sawtooth National Forest
1525 Addison Avenue East
Twin Falls, ID 83301

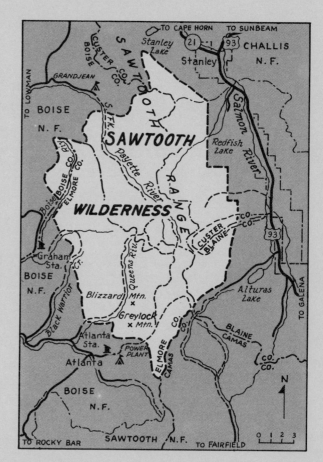

One of the new additions to the Wilderness Preservation System, the Sawtooth was slightly smaller as a Primitive Area established in 1937. It and the new Sawtooth National Recreation Area are now administered by Sawtooth National Forest.

The peaks have named the Wilderness: they are a stand of high, sharp, tooth-like mountains over deep gorges and glacial basins, giving an exceptionally scenic quality to the entire range.

The Sawtooths exhibit some classic features of alpine glaciation and block faulting. Glacial sculpturing has created highly developed cirque complexes, aretes, cols and matterhorns which together are one of the most spectacular combinations of geological features in the country.

As a result of this ice action, there are over 500 high mountain lakes set below many peaks of over 10,000 feet with perpetual snowfields. Much of the Wilderness has no trails and can only be traversed on foot. There are climbing challenges for the most experienced mountaineers.

Noted for its wildlife and good fishing, Sawtooth is the home of deer, elk, mountain goats, mountain lions and a large variety of small game. Indian artifacts in the alpine zone indicate that early cultures moved in and out of the area for hunting and fishing purposes.

Though the winter temperatures may go as low as 50 degrees below zero, Sawtooth has good possibilities for ski touring and snowshoeing.

Selway-Bitterroot

IDAHO

Season: *All year*

Size: *1,239,800 acres*

Access: *State Route 269 and various Forest Service roads surround the Wilderness.*

Camping: *Primitive camping to improved campsites*

Problems: *Low temperatures; rainstorms; very tough terrain in parts*

Location: *Bitterroot, Clearwater and Nezperce National Forests*

Address: *Selway-Bitterroot Wilderness*
Bitterroot National Forest
Hamilton, MT 59840

There are parts of this area that even Lewis and Clark found impenetrable, as do modern hikers. That might be expected on the largest designated Wilderness in the United State, but what is surprising is that access to the area is relatively easy— and there are thousands of miles of trails connecting to Forest Service and other roads at many points.

Lying in both Idaho and Montana on both sides of the Bitterroot Range, the immensity and variety of Selway-Bitterroot is hard to imagine. Elevations, for instance, range from 1,600 feet on the Selway River to over 10,000 feet in the Bitterroots. The high area is one of the toughest mountain terrains in the world, while the low spots offer peaceful meadows and streams.

Seas of fire in the past have repeatedly engulfed the forest, leaving just a few of the huge old cedars along stream beds. One of the largest fires of recent times was a 1934 blaze that destroyed about 250,000 acres of forest. There are still stands of pine and fir and larch, and the Wilderness is famous for its displays of wildflowers.

Although there are many miles of trail, some are so difficult that they should be attempted only by experienced hikers, and some require pack animals. It is said that a year of exploration in Selway-Bitterroot would still leave large areas unseen, and that, on the other hand, there are countless excellent one-day trips. Some of the one-day hikes lead to good lakes for fishing. Float trips are also available.

Other Wilderness Lands

There are more acres of designated Wilderness and Primitive Areas in Idaho than in any other state—over 2.5 million acres. And the total national forest acreage is second only to California. The State of Idaho plans on adding more protected areas. The national forests with designated areas all have other sections which are certainly backcountry in nature even though undeclared, but some with few or no lands under the Wilderness Act deserve special mention.

National Forests

Much of Clearwater National Forest has areas good for solitary hiking, and part of the huge Selway-Bitterroot Wilderness is on the Clearwater. But another area has been set aside by the Forest Service as the Mallard-Larkins Pioneer Area. "Pioneer Area" is a classification which recognizes the unique natural beauty and special wildlife qualities of this 30,500-acre sanctuary. It is on the western slopes of the Bitterroot Mountain Range 24 miles southeast of Avery. There are many lakes, trails, trout, game and furbearers, and no motorized equipment is allowed.

Kaniksu National Forest, in its 1.6 million acres, has 1,900 miles of trails. In addition to part of the Cabinet Mountains Wilderness, there is another rugged, remote mountain range backcountry along the Selkirk Crest. Its 36,000 acres are administered by the State of Idaho and the Forest Service. There are over 24 mountain lakes in this Special Management Area, maintained in its natural state. Fishing is excellent. In nearby Priest Lake in May, 1964, a 54-pound Mackinaw trout was taken. In the Selkirks, though, the catch is smaller and harder to come by because trails are few and not regularly maintained.

On St. Joe National Forest, the St. Joe and Bitterroot Mountains have some remote trails and tough backcountry, but perhaps the St. Joe River offers a greater challenge than the trails. The St. Joe is a "Study River," that is, one which was included as a potential addition to the Wild and Scenic Rivers System when it was first created. The river begins in St. Joe Lake, is a full-fledged flow by the time it reaches Red Ives Ranger Station. When it gets to Lake Coeur d'Alene it has been, in sections, a river suitable for wild, scenic and recreational classifications. The St. Joe is noted as being the highest navigable river in the world.

Twenty-six areas of Targhee National Forest, on the west slopes of the Tetons, were studied as possible additions to the Wilderness Preservation System. Of those, Forest officials recommended three for further study. The West Slope of the Tetons area is the largest, with 172,000 acres. The Webber Peaks area, near West

Yellowstone, would be 42,500 acres, and the Targhee Basin near State Route 28 would contain 13,900 acres. These two areas border on two other Wilderness proposals in Montana.

For more Idaho information, write:

Forest Service
Federal Building
Missoula, MT 59801
(For northern Idaho)

Forest Service
Federal Bldg.
324 25th Street
Ogden, UT 84401
(For southern Idaho)

Idaho State Parks and Recreation Department
2263 Warm Springs
Boise, ID 83707

ILLINOIS

Early in America's history, pioneers saw Illinois as a flat and forested place ready for the axe and plow, so most of it today is city or farm. Shawnee National Forest covers part of southern Illinois, but it has no real wilderness. Some rivers are good for boating in short stretches, though there is no backcountry around them.

For more Illinois information, write:

Forest Service
633 West Wisconsin Avenue
Milwaukee, WI 53203

State of Illinois
Division of Parks and Memorials
Department of Conservation
406 Capitol Building
Springfield, IL 62706

INDIANA

Hoosier National Forest in southern Indiana may in the next few years have some areas which will be good backpacking country with a wilderness atmosphere. Public ownership of Hoosier is scattered, but with an active acquisition program, the Forest Service hopes to bring in some wilderness areas in the future.

For more Indiana information, write:

Forest Service
633 West Wisconsin Avenue
Milwaukee, WI 53203

State of Indiana
Division of State Parks
Department of Natural Resources
616 State Office
Indianapolis, IN 46204

79

IOWA

Though Iowa is known—and rightfully so—as an agricultural state only, and there is no wilderness, one of the Study Rivers included in the Wild and Scenic Rivers Act is in Iowa. It is the Upper Iowa in the northeastern corner of the state.

For more Iowa information, write:

State of Iowa
State Conservation Commission
Public Relations
State Office Building
Des Moines, IA 50319

KANSAS

Another of the states with virtually all land devoted to agriculture, Kansas has no wilderness. Its gently rolling farmlands are more like an ocean in their open horizons, and any backcountry left is for the fortunate ones who own the land.

For more Kansas information, write:

Kansas State Park and Resources Authority
801 Harrison
Topeka, KS 66612

80

KENTUCKY

The very name of this state pulls forth images of the pioneer, like Daniel Boone, and the mountain man is a legend which still lives today. The western part of Kentucky is generally level, becoming hilly to mountainous in the east, where the best trails and streams are.

Daniel Boone National Forest

As the name suggests, this is an area of much historical interest, with the trails of Daniel Boone, Skaggs, Walker and other pioneers, as well as Civil War action and Indian history.

What is not apparent from the name is that Daniel Boone is an excellent area for slow, fast and white water and has 150 miles of trails. Almost 25 rivers provide over 600 miles of boatable waters. Most are in cliff regions, and the general forest is oak, hickory and some pine. Spring and fall are the most comfortable seasons, but also are the peak use seasons. Detailed information on the rivers and trails is available from the Forest Service.

National Parks

Though not really a wilderness area, Cumberland Gap National Historical Park does offer some interesting hiking for backpacking history enthusiasts. The Cumberland Gap was the gateway to the bluegrass lands of Kentucky from 1775 to 1810, when tens of thousands of settlers went into Kentucky. They made the land productive for their purposes under some unbelieveably hard circumstances. The Ridge Trail, 16 miles long and variable in difficulty, is the longest. Hensley Cabin, accessible only by trail, is an early mountain farm now being restored. Sand Cave is also accessible only to hikers.

Another national park in Kentucky which is not actually a wilderness land but does have some primitive areas is Mammoth Cave National Park. The northern section of the Park, over 25,000 acres, shows little sign of man's recent activity; it is an oak-hickory hardwood forest without many miles of trails. Other attractions in the Park include canoe and float trips on the Green River and the Mammoth Wild Cave Tour. Though the tour would be very tame for spelunkers, it is a good introductory, six-hour course in beginning cave exploring. It does require excellent physical condition. The surface hikes at Mammoth require preparation for ticks and chiggers from March through October and a watchful eye for abundant copperheads and numerous rattlesnakes.

State Parks

Kentucky has many state parks with streams, lakes, backcountry areas and excellent fishing with enormous variety. Most of these areas may be used freely by foot travelers. The state's Department of Fish and Wildlife Resources either manages or shares in the management of all wildlife areas, regardless of ownership. The Department of Public Information will furnish a complete compilation of backcountry lands of all sort.

For more Kentucky information, write:

Forest Service
1720 Peachtree Road, N.W.
Atlanta, GA 30309

National Park Service
3401 Whipple Street
Atlanta, GA 30344

Commonwealth of Kentucky
Capitol Annex Building
Frankfort, KY 40601

LOUISIANA

Bayou Country, as so many know it, does not have any large areas of federal land which could be called wild. Kisatchie National Forest has some very small places where solitude is possible, but none for extended backpacking. Perhaps the surprising thing about Louisiana is the extent of state-owned lands good for long trips, especially the number of Wild and Scenic Rivers established by the 1970 Louisiana Legislature.

State Lands and Waters

The total Wilderness Area state lands in Louisiana is over 1.5 million acres, most of which is stretched along the Gulf Coast and consists of coastal marshes. The inland areas are Atchafalaya Basin, Old River, Saline and Morehouse.

     The Louisiana Legislature established an astounding total of 33 rivers in the state's Wild and Scenic Rivers System in 1970. Maps are available from the state's Bureau of Outdoor Recreation.

For more Louisiana information, write:

Forest Service
1720 Peachtree Road, N.W.
Atlanta, GA 30309

State of Louisiana
State Parks and Recreation Commission
Bureau of Outdoor Recreation
P.O. Drawer 1111
Baton Rouge, LA 70821

MAINE

There is probably no other state which reminds people of the woods the way Maine does. It was the subject of Thoreau's favorite of his books, the cradle of the woodsman's lore and ethic, the land of the East where the true wilderness was, in the Maine woods. In many ways, it was this image of the great, inexhaustible woods—along with the pressures of population—that has done away with most of Maine's backcountry solitude. For over a hundred years the favorite of hikers and canoeists, Maine's woods and waters are still beautiful and can be rugged, but they are seldom places for solitary jaunts of any extent.

     The Appalachian Trail (see page 163) has its northern terminus at Mount Katahdin in Baxter State Park, and the Allagash Wilderness Waterway (see page 188), was one of the original Wild and Scenic Rivers in the national system.

For more Maine information, write:

Forest Service
633 West Wisconsin Avenue
Milwaukee, WI 53203

Maine State Park Recreation Commission
State Office Bldg.
Augusta, ME 04330

MARYLAND

Like many eastern states, Maryland is so covered with roads and so compact that there is little left today of a wilderness that was. There are some limited possibilities around the islands in Chesapeake Bay. Parts of Assateague Island National Seashore are still in a wild state, but much of the island is in private ownership, and permission may be required in many areas.

For more Maryland information, write:

National Park Service
143 South Third Street
Philadelphia, PA 19106

Maryland Park Service
State Office Building
Annapolis, MD 21401

MASSACHUSETTS

The extreme eastern and western portions of Massachusetts offer the only country which approaches wilderness, and even then solitude is a rare experience except in the off season. Late fall and early spring are the best times.

The Appalachian Trail (see page 164) runs down the western side of the state for 83 miles across several state forests. For the most part the trail is gentle as it passes through hardwood and conifer. The Berkshire Hills, through which the trail passes, are famous for their overwhelming outburst of fall colors.

In the eastern part of Massachusetts, the choices are all at the seashore. The southern reaches of Plum Island in Parker River National Wildlife Refuge present good one-day hikes on dunes, and, seasonally, many birds and waterfowl.

Like Plum Island, Cape Cod National Park has no real backcountry, but offers good dune walks for a day or more, with camping only at private campgrounds, when available.

For more Massachusetts information, write:

National Park Service
140 South Third Street
Philadelphia, PA 19106

The Commonwealth of Massachusetts
Department of Natural Resources
Division of Forests and Parks
100 Cambridge Street
Boston, MA 02202

MICHIGAN

Just about as much as Maine, Michigan conjures up the tales and true stories of the backwoodsman. Northern Michigan is still extensively covered with forest, most of it national and state forests.

National Forests

Manistee National Forest is short on real backcountry but is a canoeist's area of great diversity. A network of rivers of varying challenge spread out over the Manistee. Pere Marquette River is under study as a possible inclusion in the Wild and Scenic Rivers System. Other good canoeing can be found on the Pine and Manistee Rivers. Camping is possible just about anywhere, except on private property.

In its two sections, Hiawatha National Forest has shoreline on Lakes Huron, Michigan and Superior. There are many small lakes and excellent fishing. Like Manistee, Hiawatha is good for canoeing.

Isle Royale National Park

Made a National Park in 1940, Isle Royale was established to "conserve a prime example of Northwoods Wilderness." In its 133,000 acres there is still unspoiled backcountry on 160 miles of trails.

The Park is an island 15 miles from the mainland at its nearest point. There are no roads, and the trail that goes the length of the island is 45 miles long, recommended for five or more days, depending on side trips. The inland areas are characterized by hardwood stands, while the moister shoreline is in evergreens. Somehow crossing to the island in about 1900, a herd of moose has established itself, along with wolves, which keep the herd in a natural balance with the environment.

Some canoeing is available on Isle Royale. Short portages are frequent and such trips should be tried only by experienced canoeists.

Porcupine Mountains Wilderness State Park

The Department of Natural Resources administers this dedicated wilderness area of 58,000 acres on the Upper Peninsula. On over 80 miles of trails, hikers trek through the "Porkies" encountering steep grades and stream crossings frequently.

Of the 16 trails, the longest is Lake Superior Trail, 16 miles along the rugged shoreline of Lake Superior. Fishing for trout and salmon is good at the mouths of streams along the way.

For more Michigan information, write:

Forest Service
633 West Wisconsin Avenue
Milwaukee, WI 53203

National Park Service
143 South Third Street
Philadelphia, PA 19106

State of Michigan
Department of Natural Resources
Stevens T. Mason Building
Lansing, MI 48926

The moose came to Isle Royale, walking, some say, across the ice.

85

Boundary Waters Canoe Area

Season: *July and August have the best weather, most crowds; September is good, October for the heardy and fall color photographers.*

Size: *47,128 acres*

Access: *Main points are near Crane Lake, Ely, Grand Marais, and Tofte; also from Tower and Arrowhead Trail north of Havland.*

Camping: *Improved campsites*

Problems: *Heavily used; insects in summer*

Location: *Superior National Forest, but trips can extend into Quetico Provincial Park in Canada.*

Address: *Boundary Waters Canoe Area*
Superior National Forest
Box 338
Duluth, MN 55801

The Water Wilderness in the national system is one of a kind in many ways. There are more than a thousand lakes of 10 acres or more in size, and one acre of water for every five of land. The Wilderness Act provides that this wildland continue to be managed under special regulations of the Secretary of Agriculture which controls use of motors and the harvest of timber in portions of the area.

The network of streams and rivers which connect the lakes have portages worn deep over several centuries. First in recorded time were the Sioux, but by the time the first fur traders arrived, the Chippewas had driven the Sioux onto the plains. In 1731, with the arrival of Sieur de la Verendrye, began the legend of the Voyageurs, the fur traders who trapped and paddled the land into the 1800's.

Underlying the country here are the oldest rocks on the continent, and over it are forests of pine, spruce, fir, cedar, aspen. Wildflowers grow in profusion, including almost 30 species of orchids. Canoeists can fish for walleye, northern pike and lake trout, with others as surprises from lake to lake: bass, bluegills, rainbows.

Use of the Boundary Waters Canoe Area demands that to keep its primitive nature intact, some rules must be followed. The most important are these:

1. *All* non-burnable food and beverage containers are prohibited.
2. Mechanical portaging, motor powered watercraft and snowmobiles are subject to specific limitations.
3. No more than 15 people may form a party, and all camping at one site is limited to 14 days, unless otherwise posted.
4. There are nearly 2,000 campsites. They should be used whenever possible instead of trying to establish new sites. Fires should be made in the campsites or small stoves used instead. Otherwise, only dead wood may be used.

Meadow hiking is always a great experience.

Lakes, streams and woods cover much of the northern central wilderness lands.

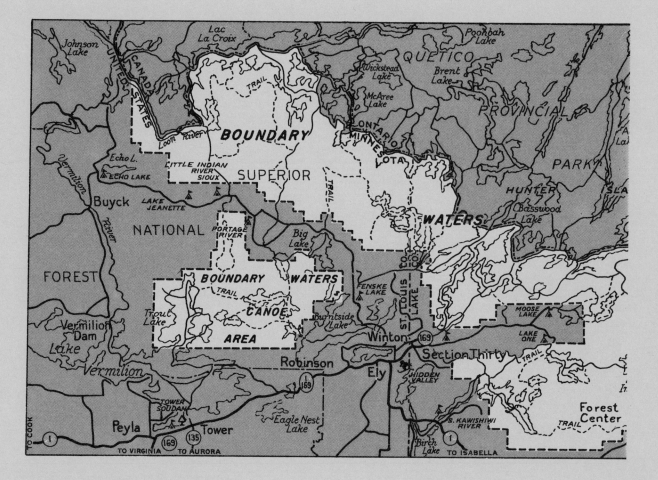

MINNESOTA

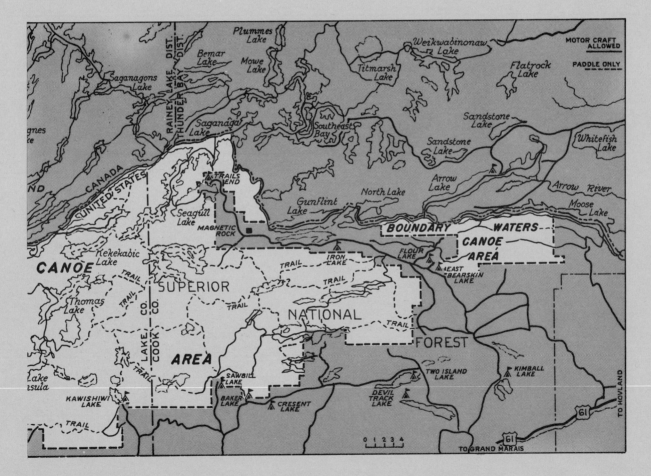

Other Wilderness Lands

As the Boundary Waters Canoe Area suggests, Minnesota is the Canoe State for wilderness enthusiasts. There are literally thousands of miles of canoeing waters on lakes and rivers, and millions of acres of forests.

National Forests

The headwaters of the Mississippi River arise in the area of Chippewa National Forest, with the source in Itasca State Park. In this home of the Chippewa Indians are large lakes and hundreds of small ones with excellent fishing among the stands of virgin red pine.

Superior National Forest is over two million acres of shorelines, islands and beaches with over a million acres of virgin forest. There are also ski areas on Superior.

Voyageurs National Park

Adjacent to the Boundary Waters Canoe Area is a recent addition to the national parks, Voyageurs National Park. It extends the great canoe area westward, adding the same remote quality for hiking, canoeing and fishing on another 220,000 acres.

Named after the early fur trappers and traders of French Canada, much of this forest and its waters is still in primitive condition and undeveloped compared to other national parks. This entire northern Minnesota region is a dramatic story of the difficulties the trappers met in their way of life, especially in transporting skins.

For more Minnesota information, write:

Forest Service
633 West Wisconsin Avenue
Milwaukee, WI 53203

National Park Service
143 South Third Street
Philadelphia, PA 19106

Minnesota Department of Conservation
Centennial Office Building
St. Paul, MN 55101

MISSISSIPPI

Of the more than a million acres of national forest in Mississippi, there are no lands which qualify as wilderness, and no other public areas which offer such an experience. Most of the forest of any kind in this state has been or is being carefully managed to produce timber.

One possible trip for river floaters is the 42 miles of Black Creek from the landing at Big Creek, near Brooklyn, to Old Alexander Bridge, near State Route 26. The current carries the floater at about one mile per hour, past six landing sites. The trip is on DeSoto National Forest.

For more Mississippi information, write:

Forest Service
1720 Peachtree Road, N.W.
Atlanta, GA 30309

Mississippi State Park System
1102 State Office Building
Jackson, MI 39201

MISSOURI

Extensive road networks and development make Missouri surprisingly lacking in wilderness opportunity for a state with mountains like the Ozarks in the south. There are national forests with backpacking areas, but few have roadless areas or the kind of solitude most hikers seek.

In south-central Missouri, the Ozark National Scenic Waterway includes the Eleven Point River, part of the Wild and Scenic River System (see page 192).

State Park officials try to keep development of parks to 20 percent, but there are no primitive camping areas.

For more Missouri information, write:

Forest Service
633 West Wisconsin Avenue
Milwaukee, WI 53203

Missouri State Park Board
P.O. Box 176
Jefferson City, MO 65101

In any wildland, good water is a treasure.

Absaroka

Season: *Very short because of snow; August is best.*
Size: *64,000 acres*
Access: *From U.S. 212 at Cooke City; from U.S. 89 at Gardiner*
Camping: *Primitive camping*
Problems: *Heavy snow; long access trails*
Location: *Gallatin National Forest*
Address: *Absaroka Primitive Area*
Gallatin National Forest
Gardiner, MT 59030

Sitting on the northern boundary of Yellowstone National Park, Absaroka is forested, high-mountain country with scattered meadows. Access trails are long from the ends of the roads that lead here. While that means a long hike before entering the Primitive Area, it also means there is solitude.

Large animals roam the area, among them deer, elk, moose, bears—including a few grizzlies—mountain goats and mountain sheep. Once in a while, along the high ridges, hikers spot a solitary old renegade bull buffalo. Fishing here is very good in the larger streams and the one lake.

This is prime country for wandering in, from the stream beds to the high peaks and ridges, where there are spectacular views of the surrounding mountains.

A leisurely, week-long trip through Absaroka can be made from Jardine to Cooke City. Jardine is off U.S. 89 on Forest Service Road 36. Out of Jardine, Forest Service Road 443 leads to an unimproved recreation site. Just before reaching the recreation site, Trail 84 heads into the Primitive Area. Then, Trail 95 skirts Hummingbird Peak and leads to Lookout Mountain, where there is a Forest Service lookout. From there, Trail 102 goes south into Yellowstone National Park, or there is an intersection with Trail 113, headed for Cooke City.

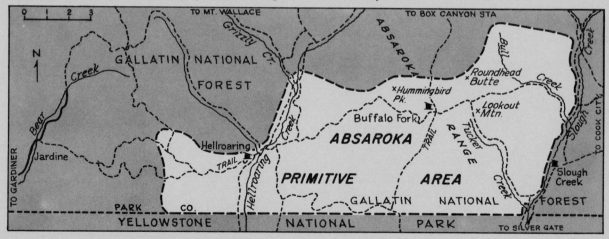

Anaconda–Pintlar

MONTANA

Season: *Mid-July to mid-September*
Size: *157,803 acres*
Access: *From the southeast via roads off State Route 43; from the north via roads off U.S. Alt. 10 and State Route 38; from the west via roads from Sula*
Camping: *Primitive camping*
Problems: *Low temperatures; heavy snow*
Location: *Beaverhead, Deerlodge and Bitterroot National Forests*
Address: *Anaconda-Pintlar Wilderness*
Wise River Range Station
Wise River, MT 59762

Charles Pintlar was a pioneer trapper and settler in the nearby Big Hole Valley. He explored and blazed trails in much of this Wilderness, as did Martin "Seven Dog" Johnson. He was famous for his strength and endurance, fabled for trapping and packing out mountain goats for zoos.

In the Anaconda Range and astride the Continental Divide for 30 airline miles, the Wilderness is thin soiled and rocky. Snow-free seasons are short, winters cold with heavy snows. A rugged land here still provides lakes, streams, forests, meadows and alpine cirques and peaks.

Many good trails cross the Wilderness, with elevations ranging from 5,100 feet to 10,793 feet. One of the best is the 45-mile trail along the Continental Divide, which covers much of the great variety. Wildlife is abundant and easy to spot and other trails and cross-country treks lead off to more alpine exploration.

A pine beetle infestation killed about 50 per cent of the lodgepole and whitebark pines in 1930-31. The dead trees are falling now, and though they can make good firewood, they also make travel more difficult.

Pack and saddle trips are possible, but forage is scarce.

Beartooth

Season: *June through September; July and August are peak months, June and September slow.*

Size: *230,000 acres*

Access: *From the south on several trails off U.S. 212; on the west from Red Lodge via Forest Service Road 71; on the north from State Route 307 and Forest Service roads*

Camping: *Primitive camping*

Problems: *Rough terrain; few trails; severe weather anytime*

Location: *Custer and Gallatin National Forests*

Address: *Beartooth Primitive Area*
Custer National Forest
2602 First Avenue North
Billings, MT 59103

All of our Wilderness and Primitive Areas are rugged and remote to some extent, but Beartooth is one of the winners in both categories. It is possible here to explore country that may never have been seen by man before, to camp near lakes where few if any have gone before. The peaks are truly majestic, the glaciers awesome, the alpine meadows peaceful.

There are only three trails in almost a quarter million acres, so much of the interior has no trails, including the area around Granite Peak, at 12,799 feet the highest in Montana. Twenty-five other peaks in this Primitive Area reach up over 12,000 feet. The difficulty of the climbs and the unstable weather make mountaineering here an activity for experienced, well conditioned climbers.

Even for hikers, the region is a true test of man's ability to endure in conditions of real primitive living. Weather can be severe any time of year and much of the terrain is challenging.

But the attractions and esthetic experiences are well worth the rough going. Wildlife takes in every size, from the moose to the dwarf shrew, the eagle to the water ouzel. Big game and fur bearers are so numerous that when Lewis and Clark made their estimates, Clark was hesitant to record them, being sure they would not be believed.

The natural features include interesting geology, occasional pink snow, and glaciers. Grasshopper Glacier is famous for the grasshoppers in it, frozen there centuries ago.

Waterfalls and cascades, alpine meadows and conifer stands, lakes and streams complete the experience in this remote and primitive land.

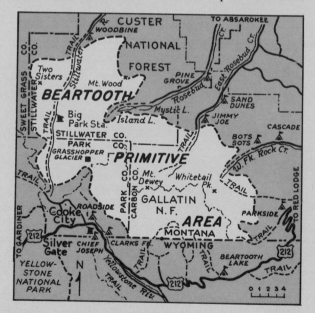

Bob Marshall

MONTANA

Season: *All year; snow in winter*
Size: *950,000 acres*
Access: *From the south and west by State Route 209; from other directions by various Forest Service roads*
Camping: *Primitive campsites*
Problems: *Snow and cold in winter; some very rugged terrain*
Location: *Flathead and Lewis and Clark National Forests*
Address: *Bob Marshall Wilderness*
Flathead National Forest
290 N. Main
Kalispell, MT 59901

The third largest of all designated wildlands, the Bob Marshall, was named after a former Forest Service Chief of the Division of Recreation and Lands. He was also one of the founders of The Wilderness Society. But one of his major achievements was as a great activist in the acquisition of wilderness lands. While many people think the Wilderness Act of 1964 was the great surge forward in protecting wildlands, the fact is that almost all lands so protected were established between 1924 and 1940. Bob Marshall died in November of 1939, and no one took his place in such an active way to create protected wilderness.

The Wilderness, larger than Rhode Island, covers an enormous range of conditions and terrains. The Continental Divide extends for 60 miles through the north-south length. Alpine meadows and lakes, forests and high-country barrens make Bob Marshall a place for hiking in solitude, fishing, excellent photography and hunting.

Hundreds of miles of trails lace the land and lead to many spectacular places, such as the Chinese Wall. For 15 miles its 1,000-foot vertical face of Cambrian limestone runs without interruption. Fossils of animals extinct a billion years lie here.

This Chinese Wall is 15 miles long.

95

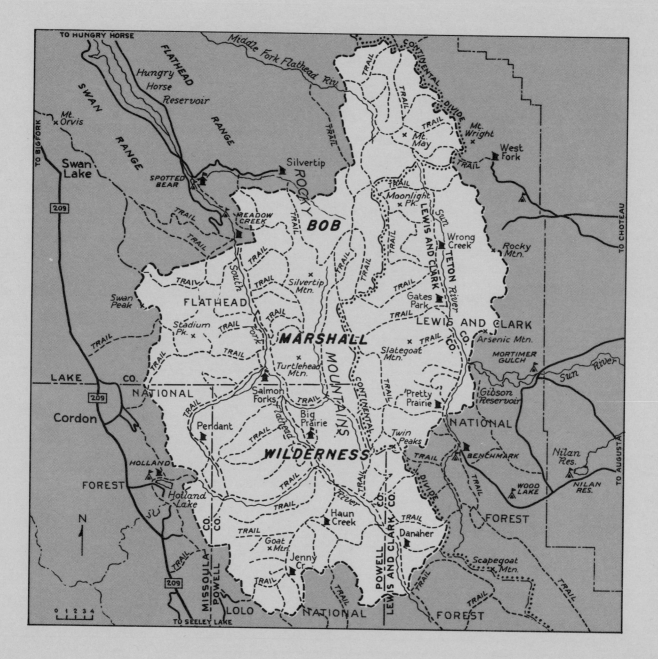

Cabinet Mountains

MONTANA

Season: *July and August are best.*
Size: *94,272 acres*
Access: *Dirt roads from Libby, Troy, Thompson Falls and Noxon*
Camping: *Primitive camping*
Problems: *Rugged terrain; low temperatures*
Location: *Kaniksu and Kootenai National Forests*
Address: *Cabinet Mountains Wilderness*
Kaniksu National Forest
Sandpoint, ID 83864

With relatively low elevations, ranging from 3,000 to 8,712 feet atop Snowshoe Peak, these peaks and valleys grow a wide variety of conifers, shrubs and flowering plants. Huckleberries are plentiful and large specimens of white pine and western red cedar grow here.

The peaks in Cabinet Mountains are a striking contrast to the surrounding timbered valleys and ridges. With snowclad slopes, glacial lakes, cold streams and cascading waterfalls, the Wilderness is a breathtaking example of subalpine scenery. Photographers have many choice subjects in the Cabinets.

Hiking is superb in the Wilderness, with fishing good along the way. Interesting geological formations are obvious and rock specimens abundant for the geology buff to study. A few peaks offer some technical climbing opportunities, though experienced mountaineers will seek higher country. Very limited forage discourages use of pack and saddle animals.

Not far from the Canadian border, Cabinet Mountains Wilderness is surrounded by remote country and small towns only. Special equipment and foods are not available in the area, and backpackers should prepare for trailless interior regions.

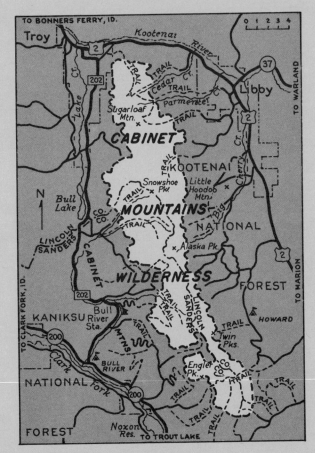

97

Gates of the Mountains

Season: *June, July and August are best, but are peak months.*

Size: *28,562 acres*

Access: *By boat from Upper Holter Lake, or on many dirt roads off U.S. 91-287 north of Helena*

Camping: *Primitive camping*

Problems: *Water scarce; some rugged terrain*

Location: *Helena National Forest*

Address: *Gates of the Mountains Wilderness
Helena National Forest
616 Helena Avenue
Helena, MT 59601*

When Lewis and Clark got to this spot on the Missouri River, the mountains seemed to bar their way, but they later thought of it as the Gates of the Rocky Mountains.

Relatively small for a Wilderness in the West, Gates of the Mountains is a favorite place for short trips, though it is also good for longer foot treks and for horseback trips.

One of the unusual things about this Wilderness is that one way—perhaps the easiest way—to reach it is by boat. Upper Holter Lake is just off U.S. 91-287. A boat goes from there to Meriwether Station, where a trail leads in.

Picturesque limestone cliffs and weathered formations are the scenic keynotes. Small streams have cut narrow gorges where trails wind past brilliant green walls. A moss-like phlox covers the rocks. One of these areas is Refrigerator Canyon, where an icy wind flows through a narrow passage.

Water is scarce here, where streams disappear into fissures. Fishing is not good anywhere in the Wilderness, but it is excellent in the Missouri River nearby.

In the canyons and along the cliffs, mountain goats are often seen. There are also deer, elk and many smaller animals and birds.

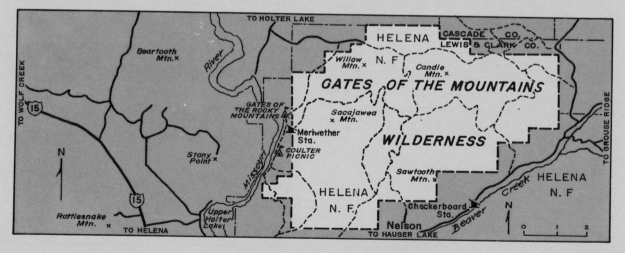

Mission Mountains

MONTANA

Season: *Summer*
Size: *73,340 acres*
Access: *From the east by roads off State Route 209; from the west off U.S. 93 through the Flathead Indian Reservation.*
Camping: *Primitive camping*
Problems: *Some very rough terrain; snow in winter*
Location: *Flathead National Forest*
Address: *Mission Mountains Primitive Area*
Flathead National Forest
290 North Main Street
Kalispell, MT 59901

Lying between Missoula on the south and Flathead Lake to the north, this eastern slope of the Mission Mountains looks east into the huge Bob Marshall Wilderness (see page 95). The few entrance trails pass through forests of spruce, fir and larch, but the trails in the area are limited. At lower elevations, underbrush such as yew and snowbrush can restrict travel.

The higher elevations have no trails and are very rugged. A combination of few trails and sparse forage limit the use of pack animals. Solitary treks are possible here not because it is a large area but because it is such challenging country.

This range got its name from the priests who did missionary work among the Salish-Flathead Tribes during the nineteenth century. The Indians developed most of the trails in use today.

The southern portion especially is a habitat for grizzly bears. Elk, deer and moose are also found, along with many fur bearers. The Rocky Mountain goat is the only big game resident all year. Birds include golden eagles, ravens, owls and hawks. There are a number of varieties of trout.

Elevations vary from 4,500 feet to 9,200 feet, with sharp peaks and broken country.

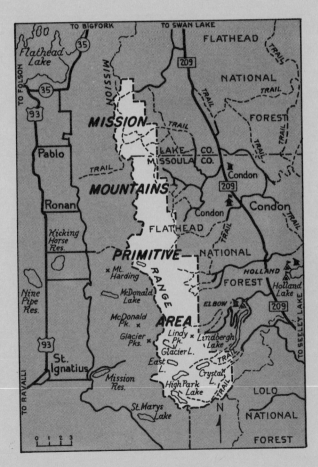

99

Spanish Peaks

Season: *August*
Size: *49,857 acres*
Access: *Several trails off U.S. 191 west of Spanish Peaks; south from Forest Service Road 166; north from Forest Service Road 982*
Camping: *Primitive camping*
Problems: *Deep snow until August; sudden summer storms*
Location: *Gallatin National Forest*
Address: *Spanish Peaks Primitive Area*
Gallatin National Forest
Bozeman, MT 59715

In about 1836, a group of Crow Indians found six Spanish trappers in this area, and the Indians from then on called it "Ol-hu-shu Ah-naht-si Ah-rah-sah-ti," or "the canyon where the Spaniards stop." The stream where the trappers worked and the peaks around it became known as Spanish Creek and Spanish Peaks.

The trappers must have been a rugged bunch, for in the high areas there is snow all year long and in the low canyons snow is possible almost all year. Gallatin Peak is the highest mountain at 11,015 feet, but there is no elevation below 6,000 feet, with timberline at about 9,000. Pine, fur and spruce stand at the lower levels, along with grassy ridges, many streams and alpine meadows surrounding lakes.

Glaciation has produced classic examples of steep, rugged peaks, sharp ridges and cirques which are now lakes. There are over 60 lakes in the region, most with fine fishing for cutthroat, rainbow and brook trout.

Ideal for solitude, Spanish Peaks is also a photographer's dream come true for mountain views and wildlife. To the west are peaceful ranches, and north of the Peaks are the golden grainfields of the Madison Valley.

Moose, elk, deer, bear, mountain sheep and goat live here along with cougar, bobcat, coyote and the fur bearers sought by the trappers.

Other Wilderness Lands

With almost two million acres of designated Wilderness and Primitive Areas alone, Montana is fourth in the country in area of such backcountry (after Idaho, Wyoming and California). Most of the national forests and Glacier National Park also have extensive undeclared wilderness acreage as spectacular as any preserved by the Wilderness Act.

National Forests

In August, 1972, the 240,000 acres of the Lincoln-Scapegoat Wilderness became part of the protected wildlands on Helena, Lolo, Flathead and Lewis and Clark National Forests. It was the end of a struggle which lasted over 20 years, led by the Montana Chapter of the Wilderness Society, to preserve the area. In the unspoiled reaches of this forest, lake and stream country, the grizzly makes his home. It is one of the last large grizzly habitats left, and its addition to the roadless areas preserves a 200-mile stretch which is the longest in the Rockies uncrossed by roads.

The Anaconda-Pintlar Wilderness is partly in Beaverhead National Forest. In addition to the Wilderness, two other areas are excellent for rugged hiking into solitude. Forest Service roads west off State Route 278 between Jackson and Wisdom lead to scores of lakes on the way to the Continental Divide, which has mountains in this area of around 10,000 feet. The Pioneer Mountains, east of State Route 278 or west of U.S. 15, also has some rough crest country with lakes and streams below it.

Flathead National Forest administers the 15,349 acres of Jewel Basin as a roadless area. It is especially abundant in mountain goats, wildflowers, lakes, streams and meadows, and is accessible on Noisy Creek Road east of Echo Lake off State Route 326. Also on Flathead, with excellent views of Glacier National Park, is a 58-mile float trip on the North Fork of the Flathead River. Mid-July and mid-August are the best times, when difficulty ratings range from I to IV, or very easy to difficult.

Glacier National Park

Northwestern Montana is the site of almost 1,600 square miles of glaciers, lakes and vast numbers of wildflowers and wildlife. Steep, sharp ridges, meadows and forests give backpackers on the 700 miles of trails many awesome sights and challenges. Summer may be crowded at some camping areas.

For more Montana information, write:

Forest Service
Federal Building
Missoula, MT 59801

National Park Service
1709 Jackson Street
Omaha, NB 68102

Montana State Highway Commission
Advertising Department
Helena, MT 59601

NEBRASKA

The flat plains, sea of grass and agricultural and ranching activities of Nebraska don't recommend, at first sight, much in the way of a wilderness experience. But a closer look shows a few interesting small areas which are unusual for a state of the plains.

Nebraska National Forest

Not exactly a sea of grass, most of this national forest was planted by man. But the Soldier Creek Management Unit is 10,000 acres of valleys and ridges of pine, cottonwood, elm and elder, with interspersed grasslands, all maintained as roadless area. It was used by the U.S. Army in 1870 as a wood supply for nearby Fort Robinson. The cool ponderosa pines are a great attraction on the tree-less plains. There are five miles of trails, with 25 more planned. The slow season is from November 15 to April 1.

State Parks

There are four State Special Use Areas in Nebraska, ranging from about 2,500 to 3,500 acres. Bazil Creek, in the northeastern part of the state, is mixed hardwood with some cedar and tall prairie grass and many birds, including a high concentration of eagles from fall to spring. The river front, on the Missouri, is nine miles long.

The other three areas, Ponderosa, Gilbert-Baker and Peterson, are in northwest Nebraska, and are in rolling to steep country with pine, grass and streams. There are no designated foot trails, and although camping is primitive, the areas are near developed sites.

For more Nebraska information, write:

Forest Service
Federal Center
Building 85
Denver, CO 80225

Nebraska Game and Parks Commission
Resource Services Division
2200 N. 33rd Street
P.O. Box 30370
Lincoln, NB 68503

Jarbidge

Season: *July to October*

Size: *64,667 acres*

Access: *North from Elko on State Route 51 to the Jarbidge turnoff and 50 miles on a dirt road; south from Rogerson, Idaho; ask directions at 76 Creek Forest Service Station, Jarbidge, Mahoney Forest Service Station or Pole Creek Ranger Station*

Camping: *Primitive camping*

Problems: *Summer thunderstorms; snow after October 1; rattlesnakes*

Location: *Humboldt National Forest*

Address: *Jarbidge Wilderness
Humboldt National Forest
976 Mountain City Highway
Elko, NV 89801*

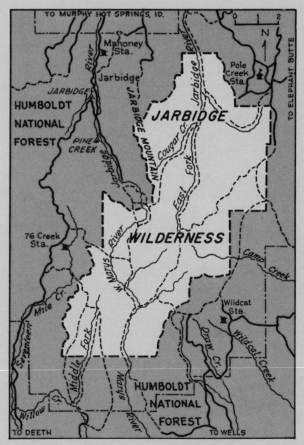

One of the most remote and scenic spots in Nevada, the Jarbidge Wilderness is difficult to get to, rugged, mountainous terrain—and unforgettable to those who reach it. From sagebrush bottoms, through pine forests and up to rocky peaks—eight are over 10,000 feet—hikers can feel the solitude and severity of high mountain environment.

Wildflowers color the area through the summer. In fall, the quaking aspen turn to yellow and orange. The streams and few lakes provide good fishing for small fish, but this is not prime fishing country.

The name "Jarbidge" is an English version of an ancient Indian name, "Tsawhawbitts," who was a huge evil spirit in human form. Little is known of the early people here, but their tribal memory of Tsawhawbitts tells of this monster who feasted on men in his crater home. Later history in the area saw trappers, cattlemen and finally a gold rush, which created the town of Jarbidge, now with a population of about 12.

One of the best trails in the Wilderness, and the trails are few, begins at Pole Creek Ranger Station and cuts southwest to Emerald Lake. It is a trip good for watching deer, the golden-mantled squirrel and a sure look at a golden eagle. It is also choice for fishing and solitary camping.

Other Wilderness Lands

It seems that there ought to be huge wild areas in Nevada good for backcountry trips, especially since 85 percent of the land in the state is under federal ownership or control. But there are not many forests and there are many arid regions and a great deal of mining evidence, both past and present. But there are some notable and rugged places for backpackers.

National Forests

Southeast of Elko in the Ruby Mountains, the Ruby Mountain Scenic Area on Humboldt National Forest offers 40,000 acres of remote mountain country. Peaks of over 10,000 feet overlook the surrounding desert, which seems to spread out forever in all directions. There are some lakes and streams, but water supplies are not dependable all year.

Wheeler Peak Scenic Area, also on the Humboldt, is in eastern central Nevada east of Ely. Trails, streams and lakes are looked over by 13,063-foot Wheeler Peak. The remains of an old U.S. army heliograph station are atop Wheeler. Some trails are easy, some quite tough, but hikers beginning at the desert base and going to the crest pass through five life zones. In the Hudsonian Zone, in two principal stands, the ancient bristlecone pine grows. It almost appears not to, and does just barely survive—but some have for close to 5,000 years.

In one section of the Toiyabe National forest near Austin, the Toiyabe Mountains present some solitary backcountry trails. The north-south trail is almost 100 miles long. Wildlife, including birds, is abundant, but water is not; local inquiry is necessary before starting out on this long trip.

For more Nevada information, write:

Forest Service
Federal Building
324 25th Street
Ogden, UT 84401

Nevada State Park System
201 S. Fall Street
Carson City, NV 89701

Great Gulf

Season: *Weather is best in summer, but hikers go in winter too.*
Size: *5,552 acres*
Access: *From the east off State Route 16; from the north off U.S. 2; from the west by cog railroad*
Camping: *Primitive camping, shelters and huts*
Problems: *Heavily used; snow and cold in winter*
Location: *White Mountain National Forest*
Address: *Great Gulf Wilderness*
White Mountain National Forest
Laconia, NH 03246

Once the smallest of all declared Wilderness, the Great Gulf is still a small, crowded area, but some wildlife refuges now in the Wilderness Preservation System are smaller by far.

Summer is the best time to backpack into this area, as far as weather goes. But at times there is a virtual stream of hikers on the trails, especially the section of the Appalachian Trail (see page 164) through the Wilderness. Spring and fall are good hiking times, too, and a little less crowded. Hardy winter campers would have more room and solitude, but it gets very cold. There are winter parties climbing Mt. Washington, at 6,288 feet the highest in New Hampshire.

The Great Gulf begins in the depths of valleys at about 1,600 feet and rises up the east slopes of the Presidential Range to 5,800 feet, just short of Washington's peak. At lower elevations, the land is covered with lush growths of hardwoods and conifers. Slowly in this glacier-gouged terrain, the spruce and fir take over then give way to a strange, barren side of the range. This is where hurricanes have torn away the trees over many a season of high winds. But every year tough alpine flowers return to cover the barren slopes.

The West Branch of the Peabody River cuts an arc through the Wilderness. There are two high lakes, Spalding and Star. Deer roam up to

about 3,500 feet, and snowshoe rabbits live up to tree line.

South of the Wilderness is Pinkham Notch Scenic Area, with skiing at Tuckerman Ravine.

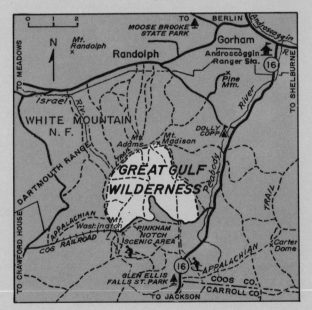

Other Wilderness Lands

Once a heavy forest with lonely trails, New Hampshire is now—like other New England states—a crowded summer and winter resort area for the heavily populated cities farther south. The Great Gulf is the only Wilderness north of North Carolina and east of Minnesota where trails lead to the far country. But even there, summers on the trail can become hiker jams, especially on the Appalachian Trail (see page 166).

About the least developed part of New Hampshire is the northern tip, up beyond State Route 110, where there are many lakes and few roads—and few public lands. Some federal officials claim there is no suitable wilderness land in the eastern U.S. for protection under the Wilderness Act. Many preservation organizations—especially in the east—are arguing the point strenuously.

For more New Hampshire information, write:

Forest Service
633 West Wisconsin Avenue
Milwaukee, WI 53203

State of New Hampshire
Department of Resources
P.O. Box 856
State House Annex
Concord, NH 03301

NEW JERSEY

The state forests of New Jersey try to offer some remote places and good trails, but it is difficult to call them wilderness by any definition. The Appalachian Trail in New Jersey is pleasant hiking on about 50 miles of trail with ten authorized campsites (see page 166).

On Lebanon State Forest and Wharton State Forest, the Batona Trail is 30 miles of forests, shrubs and streams, and much bird life. Crossing over two dozen roads, it has easy access for short hikes.

For more New Jersey information, write:

State of New Jersey
Bureau of Parks
P.O. Box 1420
Trenton, NJ 08625

Black Range

NEW MEXICO

Season: *July to October*
Size: *169,356 acres*
Access: *On the west from State Route 61*
Camping: *Primitive camping*
Problems: *Some very rough terrain; rain in July and August*
Location: *Gila National Forest*
Address: *Black Range Primitive Area*
Gila National Forest
301 W. College Avenue
Silver City, NM 88061

The Black Range Primitive Area lies just to the east of Gila Primitive Area, which in turn is east of the large Gila Wilderness. The three make up almost a quarter million acres. The Black Range was created to preserve the wild and natural characteristics of these rugged mountains.

Here, there is rough, rocky canyon, forested peak and pleasing scenery, all of which is a relief from the hot desert temperatures below.

An interesting ecological laboratory awaits backpackers in Black Range. Scars from very old fires are evident throughout the area, as well as signs of more recent fires. Though the area is still well forested, these remains of burns through time show valuable lessons in ecological succession.

Big game is not abundant, and fishing is limited. The almost extinct Gila trout lives in some streams, so fishing here would only add to the disappearance of the trout.

The famous Apache Chief Geronimo used the Black Range as a hideout. Another man from a quieter history of the West may soon be associated with the Black Range. There is a proposal before Congress to create the Aldo Leopold Wilderness here. He, more that any one man, was responsible for the first protected Wilderness, the Gila.

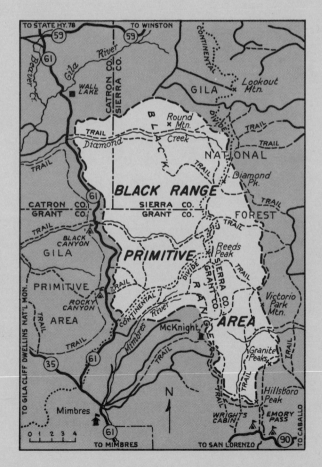

Gila

Season: *All year, with snow in winter*

Size: *130,637 acres*

Access: *There are 22 access points from State Route 25 and 527, U.S. 180 and Forest Service roads.*

Camping: *Primitive camping*

Problems: *Summer rains possible every day; lightning storms almost any season*

Location: *Gila National Forest*

Address: *Gila Primitive Area*
Gila National Forest
301 College Avenue
Silver City, NM 88061

The Gila Wilderness and the Gila Primitive Area are really inseparable. Together, and with the Black Range Primitive Area, they were the first designated Wilderness in the United States. As it was then, in 1924, the Gila Wilderness was 750,000 acres, but over the years some areas were declassified, reclassified and split up, some for mining purposes during World War II. A Forest Service wildlife management specialist, Aldo Leopold, was the one man most responsible for the first Wilderness, designated by the Forest Service.

The Gila Primitive Area as it exists now is in 11 different parcels around the edges of the Gila Wilderness. The Forest Service has proposed that the two areas become one Wilderness and that Black Range Primitive Area be created as the Aldo Leopold Wilderness.

The one large area, to be known as the Gila Wilderness, would have the Gila Cliff Dwellings National Monument at its center. Several trails begin from the cliff dwellings, and the ruins are a focal point for the historical sites around them. Once known as the *Apacheria*, or land of the Apaches, this wildland is rich in historical and prehistoric archeological evidence, all of which should be seen but, by law, not removed.

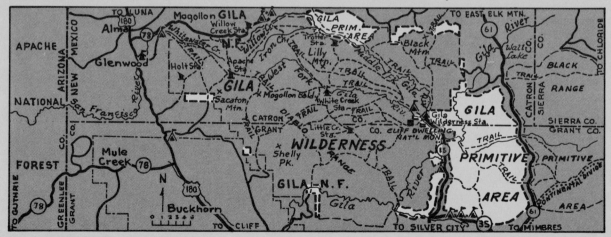

Gila

NEW MEXICO

Season: *All year, with snow in winter*

Size: *433,690 acres*

Access: *There are 22 access points from State Routes 25 and 527, U.S. 180 and Forest Service roads.*

Camping: *Primitive camping*

Problems: *Summer rains possible every day; lightning storms almost any season*

Location: *Gila National Forest*

Address: *Gila Wilderness*
Gila National Forest
301 College Avenue
Silver City, NM 88061

A part of the Mogollon Plateau, the Gila is a land of steep, rugged canyons with many streams, rivers and springs. Outstanding scenery, fishing and hunting make this a popular area, but it is large enough and rough enough that solitude is still possible on large parts of the 2,578 miles of trails. Some sections are seldom if ever visited by man.

Small animals are numerous, as are fur bearers and birds. The peregrine falcon is among several rare, endangered and peripheral species found in the Wilderness. Rattlesnakes are included in over 50 species of reptiles. In the 300 miles of streams, fishing is excellent, but the Gila trout is on the endangered species list.

Only a few areas of the Gila are crowded, but in others hikers may walk for weeks without seeing anyone. The most heavily used areas are the West Fork Trail, from Cliff Dwellings to Willow Creek; the lower part of Catwalk Trail; Gilita Creek Trail between Willow Creek Campground and Snow lake; and trails between Whitewater Baldy, Willow Creek Campground and Sandy Point.

Some trails are not well maintained and others are remote and difficult. The ones not often maintained are 175, the Clayton Creek Trail; the north-south section of 164; 156 from Bear Canyon to Prior Cabin; 260, the Manzanito Creek Trail;

and 411, Corral Canyon Trail. Trail 268 no longer exists, and Trail 164 from Prior Cabin to the Middle Fork of the Gila is almost impossible to find. From Granite Peak to Little Turkey Park, Trail 150 is very rough.

Pecos

Season: *Summer is the peak season.*

Size: *167,416 acres*

Access: *From Sante Fe via Forest Service road; from the south via State Route 63; from the northeast via roads off State Route 3*

Camping: *Primitive camping*

Problems: *Snow in winter; some very rough terrain*

Location: *Carson and Santa Fe National Forests*

Address: *Pecos Wilderness*
Santa Fe National Forest
Santa Fe, NM 87501

Lying at the south end of the impressive Sangre de Cristo Mountains at the headwaters of the Pecos River, the Pecos has been called "some of the most beautiful and scenic country in New Mexico." There is a large variety of attractions for backpackers.

Excellent fishing can be found in the lakes and many streams—more than 150 miles of them—and the scenery is magnificent for photography as well as just looking. There is a 100-foot waterfall and some rare plants and animals.

Climbers have a place here, too. Truchas Peak is the second highest in New Mexico, at 13,101 feet.

Innumerable springs and the forest cover make the Pecos home to many kinds of wildlife. Bighorn sheep live here, as do eagles and elks, beavers and martens. A small but seldom seen herd of Texas white-tailed deer makes its home in the Pecos. There is also considerable stock grazing on Santa Fe National Forest.

Even though Santa Fe is not far away, Pecos is rough enough so solitude is still possible. Basing in Santa Fe provides access to the Santa Fe Ski Basin also.

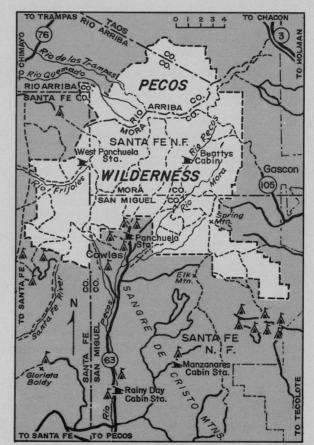

San Pedro Parks

Season: *July to October are the peak months of use.*
Size: *41,132 acres*
Access: *From the south off State Route 126; from the north off State Route 96.*
Camping: *Primitive campsites*
Problems: *Rain in summer*
Location: *Sante Fe National Forest*
Address: *San Pedro Parks Wilderness*
Santa Fe National Forest
Federal Building
Santa Fe, NM 87501

This Wilderness is named for its high, green mountain parks, some of which are at 10,000 feet. Most of the area is a high moist plateau of mountain tops overlooking canyons of pine, spruce and juniper. There are also grasslands and, at the top, alpine barrens.

Deer, bear, elk, sheep and puma draw many hunters every year. Turkey, grouse and ptarmigan also live here. Though the fishing is not the best, fishermen can usually have luck in the small, high streams.

But the main attraction is for hikers. Some access trails are steep—though short—but the going is good on the mesa and the views are superb. For a different kind of country, the winter sights are just as good, and the area is fine for snowshoeing and ski touring. Summer climbing is possible, too.

Water is generally available all year. In fact, in July, August and September rain every day is common. The first snows come in late October, and it is snow travel only from December to February, at least.

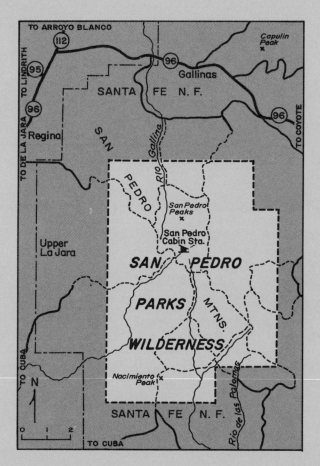

Wheeler Peak

Season: *Year round, snow in winter*

Size: *6,027 acres*

Access: *From the north by trail from Twining; from the east by dirt road from Idlewild*

Camping: *Primitive camping*

Problems: *Rugged terrain; snow in winter*

Location: *Carson National Forest*

Address: *Wheeler Peak Wilderness*
Carson National Forest
P.O. Box 587
Taos, NM 87571

Although this is the smallest Wilderness in the West, it offers some unusual and unique experiences. Wheeler Peak itself is the highest point in New Mexico, at 13,161 feet.

The alpine tundra on Wheeler Peak and other nearby peaks is very rare in the Southwest. With little that can be called true "high country," the life forms here are not found often in the Arizona-New Mexico region.

For an area of the Southwest that is such a small Wilderness, the Wheeler Peak wildlands contain a large number of small lakes and streams which provide water for downstream water users. Fishing in the lakes and streams is good, though much of the country is rough. Parts of the Wilderness provide good pack animal travel, but some areas are too rugged for any but foot travel.

Spruce and aspen mingle in this mountain country, making fall a fiery, colorful experience. It can also be a snowy one, so hikers should be prepared for winter weather.

The entire area around Wheeler Peak in Carson National Forest is laced with trails. Cabresto Creek and its Lake Fork have long trails. The north-south trail through the Wilderness continues in both directions outside it. Going south, the trail from Blue Lake follows along Rio Pueblo de Taos until it reaches Taos Pueblo.

Just a few miles from Wheeler Peak are Taos Ski Valley and Twining, with a ski lift and some accommodations. Nearby there are several campsites.

In this part of the Sangre de Cristos, there are deer, bear and wild turkey as well as mountain lion and badger.

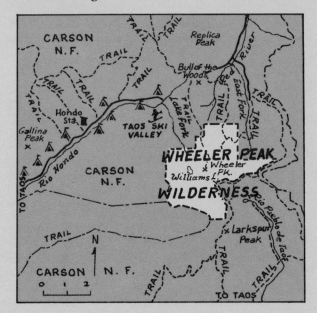

White Mountain

NEW MEXICO

Season: *Peak travel is in summer.*

Size: *31,171 acres*

Access: *From the west by roads off U.S. 54; from the east off State Route 37*

Camping: *Primitive camping*

Problems: *Extreme temperature changes; early winters without warning*

Location: *Lincoln National Forest*

Address: *White Mountain Wilderness*
Lincoln National Forest
Drawer F
Ruidoso, NM 88345

Rising with unusual abruptness from the Tularosa Basin, the White Mountains reach to over 12,000 feet just outside the Wilderness. Starting from 6,000 feet at the base of the mountains up to an altitude of 11,400 feet inside the Wilderness, five different life zones are crossed. They range from the grasslands of the desert to the subalpine. It is perhaps the most abrupt change in life zones in any Wilderness, and gives those interested in botany much to study in a relatively small area.

Hikers will encounter high mountain meadows and mixed conifers. Wildlife includes numerous and large deer, bears, occasional elk and wild pigs. Trout live in the waters of several lakes and creeks.

Evaluation and exploration of one of the few molybdenum bonanzas in the western hemisphere is going on in the Wilderness. This exploration is being done under "a carefully regulated program," but backpackers should be aware of this activity.

On the surrounding Lincoln National Forest, Mescalero Apaches operate a ski area at Sierra Blanca. T-Bars and New Mexico's only gondola lift take skiers up 12,000-foot Sierra Blanca. There are 23 miles of trails for all levels of skills. Cloudcroft, New Mexico also has a ski area, and snowshoeing and ski touring are possible in the Wilderness.

The nearby Capitan Mountains have some good trails, too. Hikers there may come across the birthplace of none other than Smokey the Bear. In 1950, after a 17,000-acre forest fire, firefighters came across an orphaned bear cub clinging to a charred tree. Nursed back to health, the bear went to the National Zoo in Washington, D.C. as "Smokey."

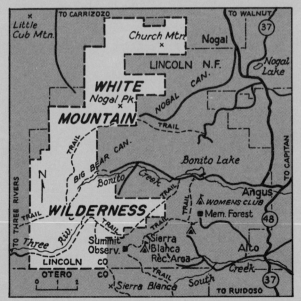

113

Other Wilderness Lands

Practically all of the good wilderness backpacking areas in New Mexico are on national forests and in the Wilderness Preservation System, though hundreds of thousands of acres in those same forests could be added.

Though much of the state is still wild and very rugged going, public lands are restricted to those of the federal government, as far as wilderness goes. The state does not have any such areas.

For more New Mexico information, write:

Forest Service
517 Gold Avenue, S. W.
Albuquerque, NM 87101

State of New Mexico
State Park and Recreation Commission
P. O. Box 1147
Santa Fe, NM 87501

NEW YORK

The recent Adirondack Master Plan has established an extensive state program to create Wilderness and Primitive Areas and Wild and Scenic Rivers. The Plan includes some 30 wild and primitive sections of over a million acres, a canoe area and 17 rivers. Intrusions by man, the "non-conforming uses," will be eliminated, prohibiting motorized vehicles and all but foot trails. The wildernesses, canoe area and wild and scenic rivers are of most interest to backpackers.

Adirondack State Park

Wilderness	Nearby Town	Acreage
Blue Ridge	Lake Pleasant	43,160
Dix Mountain	Elizabethtown	46,900
Five Ponds	Fine	62,780
Giant Mountain	Elizabethtown	22,100
Ha-de-ron-dah	Webb	26,600
High Peaks	Keene	219,570
Hoffman Notch	Schroon	35,200
McKenzie Mountain	St. Armand	35,200
Pepperbox	Webb	14,600
Pharaoh Lake	Ticonderoga	43,340
Pigeon Lake	Webb	50,800
Sentinel Range	Wilmington	23,000
Siamese Ponds	Lake Pleasant	107,740
Silver Lake	Lake Pleasant	106,650
West Canada Lake Canoe Area	Ohio	160,320
St. Regis	Santa Clara	18,100

Wild Rivers	Segment
Cold River	*The Duck Hole to*

Hudson River	*Raquette River* *Cedar River to Boreas River*	Moose River, South Branch	*North of Woodhull Mountain to Moose Middle Branch*
Indian River	*Brook Trout Lake to Moose South Branch*	Osgood River	*Osgood Pond to about Forestmere Lakes*
Opalescent River	*Flowed Lands to state lands boundary*	Oswegatchie River	*Hamilton-Herkimer County line to Wanakena*
Sacandaga, East Branch	*Botheration Pond to near Cook Brook*	Otter Brook	*Lost Pond to Moose South Branch*
Sacandaga, West Branch	*Piseco Lake to Dugway Creek*	Rock River	*Lake Durant to Cedar River*

Scenic Rivers	**Segment**
Ampersand Brook	*State land boundary to Raquette River*
Boreas River	*Cheney Pond to Hudson River*
Bouquet River	*Dial Mountain to State Route 73*
Cedar River	*Indian Lake to about five miles north*
Hudson River	*Town of Newcomb to Cedar River to Boreas River to town of North River*

For more New York information, write:

New York State Department of Environmental Conservation
Albany, NY 12201

115

Linville Gorge

Season: *All year*

Size: *7,575 acres*

Access: *From the west by trails off State Route 105; from the east by trails off Forest Service Road 210*

Camping: *Primitive camping*

Problems: *High fire hazard; copperheads and rattlesnakes*

Location: *Pisgah National Forest*

Address: *Linville Gorge Wilderness*
Pisgah National Forest
Box 2750
Asheville, NC 28802

This magnificent Wilderness is in one of the most scenic national forests in the eastern United States. The gorge of the Linville River for 12 miles is sometimes 2,000 feet below the steep cliffs above.

Hiking in the gorge is very rugged, and recommended only for experienced hikers. The southern portion has only one short trail, and there is no complete north-south trail. There are trails, though, above the gorge which are suitable for less experienced hikers and even for children. Near one trail into the gorge, but just a turnout from State Route 105, is Wiseman's View, a spectacular canyon vista point.

For climbers, popular rock climbing areas are Table Rock and the Chimneys, a scattering of spires, fissures, boulders and overhanging cliffs. Anyone who goes into the area should take extraordinary fire precautions and should always notify the District Ranger at Marion before entering.

A great variety of plants thrive here. They include laurel and myrtle, four native rhododendron species and many berries and bushes. The virgin forest is of oak, pine, maple, dogwood, ash, locust and others.

Deer, bear, squirrel, raccoon and ruffed grouse inhabit the Wilderness, and brown and native trout may be caught.

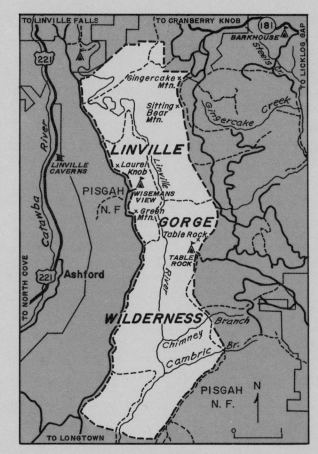

Shining Rock

NORTH CAROLINA

Season: *All year*

Size: *13,350 acres*

Access: *From the south and east off the Blue Ridge Parkway; from the north by roads and trails off U.S. 276*

Camping: *Primitive camping*

Problems: *High fire hazard; some rough terrain*

Location: *Pisgah National Forest*

Address: *Shining Rock Wilderness*
Pisgah National Forest
Box 2750
Asheville, NC 28802

Of the few declared Wildernesses east of the Rockies, North Carolina has two, and both are unusually scenic. Shining Rock is especially varied in its natural gifts.

The main topographic feature is Shining Rock Mountain, which is an outcropping of white quartz. The highest point in the Wilderness is Cold Mountain, a cone-shaped peak reaching 6,030 feet. The lower slopes of Shining Rock are steep but Shining Rock Ledge has an undulating topography with relatively gentle slopes. Hikes to Shining Rock are moderate and suitable for family hikes, but the route from Shining Rock to Cold Mountain is extremely rugged. There are many other trails in the area.

The vegetative cover here represents one of the southernmost examples of the Canadian Zone. Severe burns long ago have caused a great variety of trees, shrubs and flowers. Rhododendron, orchids, asters and mountain laurel are among them, as well as some southern fir trees in moist spots.

There are numerous springs and waterfalls at Shining Rock, and the headwaters of the Pigeon River, a tributary of the Tennessee, rise in the area. Even with such a water supply, the Forest Service urges extreme caution with fire.

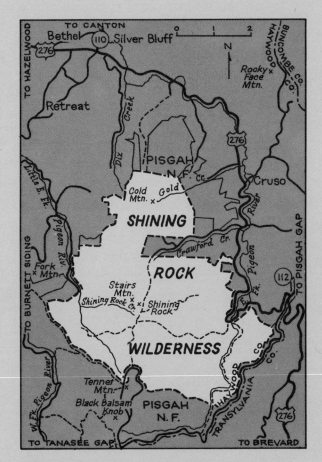

Other Wilderness Lands

The two Wildernesses in North Carolina are the only two so far in the Southeast, but there are other areas in other forests good for backpacking.

National Forests

Joyce Kilmer Memorial Forest on the Nantahala National Forest is 3,800 acres of land in a wilderness state. This is still a virgin forest, with some trees over a hundred years old, including poplar, hemlock, sycamore, oak and many others. Animal and bird life is abundant. Adjacent to Joyce Kilmer is Slickrock Watershed, which is under consideration for wilderness designation of some kind. Passing through the Nantahala is a section of the Chattooga River, which has been recommended by the Forest Service as a Wild and Scenic River. The seven areas of classification along the river cover the possibilities of wild, scenic and recreational. The Nantahala River is also a possible wilderness river, winding part of its way through a deep gorge. It is so deep that the Indians gave it its name, which means "land of the noonday sun."

The Croatan National Forest is half timber farm and half pocosin, which is a large, flat area at higher elevation than the surrounding land. It is known as a "swamp on a hill." The pocosin on the Croatan is under consideration as a Wild Area or Wilderness.

For more North Carolina information, write:

Forest Service
1720 Peachtree Road, N. W.
Atlanta, GA 30309

State of North Carolina
Department of Conservation and Development
P. O. Box 2719
Raleigh, NC 27602

NORTH DAKOTA

The Badlands of North Dakota offer some wilderness areas, but a future possibility of a national scenic trail has its western terminus in North Dakota, and is of interest to backpackers.

North Country Trail

The eastern beginning of this trail would branch off of the Appalachian Trail in Vermont. It would then pass through New York, Pennsylvania, Ohio and Michigan. Going between Lakes Michigan and Huron, it would pass south of Lake Superior into Wisconsin and Minnesota. In North Dakota, it would enter the southeast corner of the state, go between Fargo and Bismarck, then north between Bismarck and Minot. The end of the trail would join with the Lewis and Clark Trail. Unlike the Appalachian Trail and the Pacific Crest Trail, the route of the North Country Trail is neither marked nor generally established, though there are several existing trails along some parts of the route. More information on the North Country Trail is available from the Bureau of Outdoor Recreation, Office of Information, Washington, D.C. 20240.

For more North Dakota information, write:

North Dakota State Parks
State Capitol
Bismarck, ND 58501

OHIO

Ohio's wilderness is mostly long lost to the pressures of industrial and farming activities. There are some limited possibilities on Wayne National Forest, where the colors on the fall hardwood forests are worth a trip. But the State of Ohio has declared one wildland of its own.

Shawnee State Forest

The Shawnee Wilderness Area on this forest is about 5,000 acres and is so far undeveloped for public use. It will have approximately 35 miles of trails and is called "rugged (for Ohio!)." There

will be some snowshoeing in the region, as well as hiking and camping.

For more Ohio information, write:

Forest Service
633 West Wisconsin Avenue
Milwaukee, WI 53203

Ohio Department of Natural Resources
Room 207
Ohio Departments Building
Columbus, OH 43215

OKLAHOMA

Aside from a few limited river trips of short duration and rare solitude, Oklahoma has no significant wildland. Part of the Ouachita National Forest is here, with historical interest and some hiking.

For more Oklahoma information, write:

Forest Service
1720 Peachtree Road, N.W.
Atlanta, GA 30309

Oklahoma Industrial Development and Park Department
Will Rogers Memorial Building
Oklahoma City, OK 73105

Diamond Peak

Season: *Summer; winter for experienced mountaineers*

Size: *35,440 acres*

Access: *From the north by Oregon State Route 58; from the other sides by several Forest Service roads*

Camping: *Primitive camping*

Problems: *Rough terrain*

Location: *Deschutes and Willamette National Forests*

Address: *Diamond Peak Wilderness*
Deschutes National Forest
P.O. Box 751
Bend, OR 97701

In 1853, members of the Lost Wagon Train passed through what is now Diamond Peak Wilderness. They were on their way from Pennsylvania to Oregon Territory, and struggling to reach the Willamette Valley before the winter storms. John Diamond had climbed the peak named after him in 1852, searching for a route.

The settlers could not find the way, but pushed on, making their own trail, until they finally abandoned the wagons 12 miles west of Diamond Peak. Going on by foot, they eventually met a rescue party and barely missed the first snows of the season.

Under the circumstances, the pioneers would never have thought that someday people with packs on their backs would come here on purpose to experience the wilderness, which to them was a hostile thing to conquer or avoid.

But today they do come, for nature study, mountain climbing or just hiking. Geology in the area reveals intense volcanic activity and tremendous glacial movement. The Wilderness is a sometime home to deer, bear, marmot, marten, fox and other animals. And birdwatchers find the raven, Clark's nutcracker, Oregon jay and water ouzel, as well as bufflehead and golden-eyed ducks. For colors, mimulus, pentstemon and many other wildflowers coat the trails, lakeshores, streams and meadows.

Climbers follow John Diamond's footsteps up 8,744-foot Diamond Peak without much difficulty, but still with leadership, good equipment and caution. Mount Yoran, at 7,100 feet, is not high, but its steep precipices provide excellent rock climbing for experienced mountaineers. A good recreation hike follows Diamond Peak Trail to Happy and Blue Lakes, but gets rougher farther on. The Pacific Crest Trail (see page 176) goes through the Wilderness.

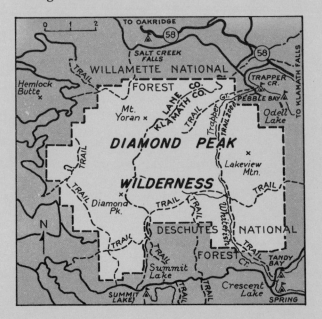

Eagle Cap

OREGON

Season: *July 1 to October 30, depending on snow; peak is July and August; September sometimes good.*

Size: *220,416 acres*

Access: *On the north from State Route 82; on the south from Selma via Forest Service roads*

Camping: *Improved and primitive campsites*

Problems: *Rough terrain*

Location: *Wallowa-Whitman National Forest*

Address: *Eagle Cap Wilderness*
Wallowa-Whitman National Forest
P.O. Box 907
Baker, OR 97814

Massive Eagle Cap, though not the highest mountain in the Wilderness, is the hub of many streams tumbling down its slopes. At the foot of the mountain and in basins on the upper slopes are over 50 lakes.

The higher mountains, nearly devoid of timber and other growth, are characterized by vast expanses of granite, sometimes capped with limestone and marble. Geology here is full of classic examples of terminal and lateral moraines and glacial cirques, with typical U-shaped and hanging valleys. Marine sediments played a large part in the formation of the mountains.

Favorites for climbing are the Matterhorn, Sacajawea and Eagle Cap. Caution is the only experience and equipment necessary.

At lower elevations, where pines, firs and Engelmann spruce grow, wildlife and flowers are varied and abundant. Hikers and horsemen see colorful buttercups, lupine, fleabane, fawnlily and many others from about mid-July to mid-August.

In this rough terrain, some of the animals are hard to find, such as the mountain goats introduced in 1950. The cougar, the marten, the mink and the fox are shy, too. Many other animals live in the area, including weasels and beavers and badgers and bobcats.

Birdwatchers fare well at Eagle Cap. The ever-present jay lives here, and the ptarmigan was introduced in 1967. They are most easily spotted in the Bonny Lakes area. But the main bird attraction here can be seen nowhere else.

The world's entire population of the rare Wallowa gray-crowned rosy finch nests only in a few spots in the Wilderness. Some of the places: Petes Point, Jewett Lake (named after the bird's first spotter) and Glacier Lake near Eagle Cap.

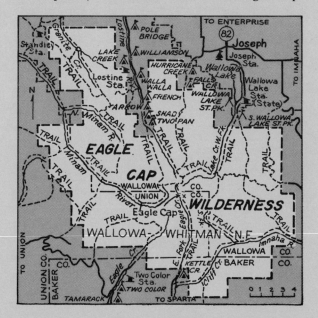

Gearhart Mountain

Season: *July to November*

Size: *18,709 acres*

Access: *From Lakeview via Forest Service Road 2913; from Bly via Forest Service Roads 3610 and 3410*

Camping: *Primitive camping*

Problems: *Some rough terrain*

Location: *Fremont National Forest*

Address: *Gearhart Mountain Wilderness*
Fremont National Forest
P. O. Box 551
Lakeview, OR 97630

In an area of many volcanic domes, Gearhart Mountain is the highest, at 8,364 feet, in this part of Oregon. It is also perhaps the oldest, beginning with thick flows and plugs of porphyritic lava. At one time, a broad and massive dome of about 10,000 feet grew up before the end of volcanic activity.

The environment cooled and moistened, bringing snow fields and glaciers, which eventually carved out the large cirque, or amphitheater, known as the Head of Dairy Creek. The glaciers are gone now, replaced by mountain parks and springs, with excellent camping spots under the impressive headwalls. The area is seven miles from the north and south entrances of Gearhart Trail 100.

Another geological feature here is The Dome and its massively eroded cliffs, stringing westward from the 7,380-foot Dome for almost a mile. The cliffs are 300 to 400 feet high. The Dome is three miles from the southeast entrance of Trail 100.

Just a half-mile from the same entrance is the Palisades. These are stark, sentinel-like formations caused by weathering. A closely spaced vertical and horizontal joint pattern, with erosion, has resulted in the "hoodoos," or columns of rock, in shapes from a fantasy. Here there are pillars, columns, pedestals and toadstools of rock.

Since the forage in the Wilderness will not support pack and saddle animals, this is a hiker's land, even though there are only 20 miles of trail. Trail 100 is 14 miles long, a leisurely two-day trip.

Blue Lake, in the north central part of the Wilderness, is always sparkling clear and cold. No stream flows in or out, indicating an underground source. Fishing is good, but sometimes crowded.

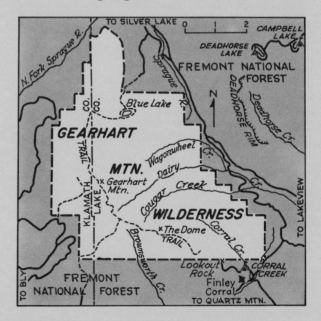

Kalmiopsis

Season: *Summer*
Size: *76,900 acres*
Access: *From State Route 101 at Brookings, up the Chetco River; road from Selma; four-wheel-drive road from near Kerby*
Camping: *Primitive camping*
Problems: *Rough terrain; rattlesnakes; yellowjackets and hornets numerous*
Location: *Siskiyou National Forest*
Address: *Kalmiopsis Wilderness*
District Ranger
U.S. Forest Service
P.O. Box 738
Brookings, OR 97415

With a character different from most other Wildernesses, Kalmiopsis has a strange fascination. There are no lofty peaks and long views. The land is one of rocky, brushy, low elevation canyons. Access is difficult. Hikers here must be self-sufficient, for it is entirely likely that no other parties will be seen.

But for the botanical hiker, this is one of the most rewarding places for a trip, possibly the most interesting in the Northwest. There are over 12 species of conifers here, including the rare Brewer or weeping spruce. Nine species of hardwood trees, 31 species of shrubs and many species of herbaceous plants join the conifers.

The major specimen is *Kalmiopsis leachiana*, a small shrub similar to a miniature rhododendron. It is a survivor of the Ice Age, the oldest member of the heath family and the only plant in its genus. Aside from one small patch on the Umpqua River, it is found only in the Chetco and Illinois River basins.

Perhaps second in importance is another relic of the Ice Age, the Brewer or weeping spruce. Here it grows in a small area of the Siskiyou Mountains.

Other rare plants include *Leucothoe davisiae*, also of the heath family, found in canyons between Pearsoll Peak and Gold Basin. The Sadler oak, a sprawling shrub with leaves like a chestnut tree, grows in parts of the Wilderness.

A few roads left on the west and east of the Wilderness are remnants of gold mining in 1851 and chromium mining after World War II. Locked gates close the roads. It is thought that miners, as well as early trappers and settlers, were responsible for most of the many charred stumps and burned-over areas.

Mountain Lakes

Season: *Summer, with frost possible anytime*

Size: *23,071 acres*

Access: *Oregon State Route 140 from the north; various Forest Service Roads from other directions*

Camping: *Primitive camping*

Problems: *Erratic weather; heavily used*

Location: *Winema National Forest*

Address: *Mountain Lakes Wilderness*
Winema National Forest
Post Office Building
Klamath Falls, OR 97601

Lakes noted for beautiful water and timbered shoreline gave this Wilderness its name, but the attraction of the lakes and the crowded area have led to heavy use. The lakes are stocked with eastern brook and rainbow trout and used in the fall by wild ducks and geese.

Around the basin containing the lakes is a natural boundary of high mountains. At 8,208 feet, Aspen Butte is the highest point. Others are Mount Harriman, 7,979 feet, Crater Mountain, 7,785 feet, Greylock Mountain, 7,747 feet and Whiteface Peak, 7,706 feet. The mountain terrain is varied enough for both novice and experienced mountain climbers.

Many of the lakes are included on a loop trail system within the basin. Most of the trees in the Wilderness are smaller-sized alpine fir, white and lodgepole pine, found above elevations of 7,000 feet. Down along the creeks and lakes, hikers walk through meadow grass and several kinds of wildflowers.

Because two-thirds of the area is over 6,000 feet in elevation, most of the precipitation comes in the form of snow, which falls in depths of from five to 20 feet, with temperatures sometimes in the minus 30 range. Summer weather brings its problems for hikers, too, with frequent thundershowers in July and August. The thermometer can go up to 95 degrees and over in summer months.

With access on all four sides of the square-shaped Wilderness, the area is used to capacity. It is not far from Klamath Falls and Medford, Oregon, and near Upper Klamath Lake. Lake of the Woods, about two miles west of Mountain Lakes is another resort area nearby.

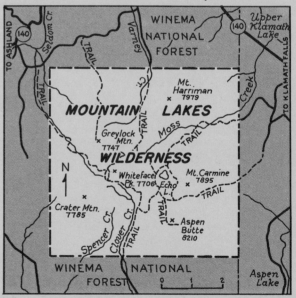

Mount Hood

Season: *August to September is the peak; slow season is November to March.*

Size: *14,160 acres*

Access: *From the south via State Route 35 and U.S. 26 at Government Camp*

Camping: *Primitive and improved campsites*

Problems: *Sudden storms; heavy use*

Location: *Mount Hood National Forest*

Address: *Mount Hood Wilderness*
Mount Hood National Forest
P.O. Box 16040
Portland, OR 97216

At an elevation of 11,245 feet, Mount Hood is said to be the most frequently climbed snowcapped mountain except for Fujiyama. Climbers and hikers register and explore the trails all year, but winter is a time for experienced mountaineers only. Even in summer, trails are not completely free of snow until mid-August, though they are open by about the middle of July.

Because there are few streams, and wildlife is not plentiful, hikers will not encounter many fishermen or hunters. The trail around the mountain is a recommended five-day trip of about 38 miles, with several stretches where water is not available and must be carried. And the purity of surface streams is not dependable, so water should be purified.

Streams around the mountain are glacier fed. That means that the melt causes high water in the streams in the afternoon and makes crossing hazardous. Either plan crossings in mornings or head upstream for more shallow water.

Wood is practically nonexistent in the high country. A fuel burning stove is a must for long trips.

In the late summer months, especially at Paradise and Eden Parks, the alpine meadows are bursting with wildflowers such as lupine, avalanche lily and anemone.

On the south side of the Wilderness is Timberline Lodge, the most popular access point to Mount Hood for hikers, climbers and skiers. There are many other trails in the Wilderness, including a short portion of the Pacific Crest Trail.

Once in a while hikers come upon Mount Hood's stone shelters. They were built in the early thirties by the Civilian Conservation Corps during the construction of Timberline Trail, and some are now just ruins.

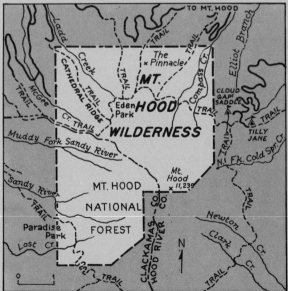

125

Mount Jefferson

Season: *July to October*

Size: *99,600 acres*

Access: *From the south by trails and roads off U.S. 20; from the west by roads off State Route 22; from the east by roads off U.S. 20*

Camping: *Primitive campsites*

Problems: *Low temperatures at higher elevations*

Location: *Deschutes, Mount Hood and Willamette National Forests*

Address: *Mount Jefferson Wilderness*
Deschutes National Forest
Bend, OR 97701

Long a favorite of lovers of wilderness, the Mount Jefferson area has seen organized hiking groups since 1900. The dominant features are Mount Jefferson, 10,497 feet, and Three Fingered Jack. Mount Jefferson, with perpetual snow, is Oregon's second highest, while Three Fingered Jack at only 7,841 feet is still a climber's favorite, but not for novices.

Good fishing can be found in half the hundred lakes of the region, where several varieties of trout are taken. Fishermen, as well as those who come to hike and look, will find a good network of trails.

Cutting from north to south the entire length of the Wilderness is the Pacific Crest Trail. It leads hikers along ridges, past alpine lakes and by perpetual glaciers. There are many spur trails, and all through the Wilderness travelers find one of the special features of the area, many mountain parks.

With relatively easy access, Mount Jefferson is especially good for one-day trips, but its size makes it also suitable for extended stays. Summer months bring lavish displays of wildflowers to go along with spectacular scenery and interesting geological formations.

Mount Washington

Season: *April to November at lower levels; summer at higher altitudes*

Size: *46,655 acres*

Access: *On the south from State Route 242; on the north via Forest Service Road 131 from U.S. 20*

Camping: *Primitive camping*

Problems: *Very rugged country*

Location: *Willamette and Deschutes National Forests*

Address: *Mount Washington Wilderness*
Willamette National Forest
P.O. Box 1272
Eugene, OR 97401

Though not a very high peak at 7,802 feet, Mount Washington has been a climbing favorite since it was first reached in 1923. A group from Bend made that first ascent and many have done it over the years, establishing various routes. The rock pinnacle on the summit has chimneys and sheer rock faces which call for experienced leaders, strict safety precautions and proper equipment.

Mount Washington is an extremely rugged Wilderness. There are not many trails. The main one, a section of the Pacific Crest Trail (see page 177), goes from north to south around the west side of Mount Washington and over lava beds.

Patjens Lakes are fished more than any of the 66 lakes in the Wilderness, but most others also have good fishing. In addition to deer, elk and bear, some cougars live in the area. Smaller mammals are common, too. Marmots, ground squirrels, pine squirrels, pine martens, conies, foxes, coyotes and snowshoe rabbits may be found.

There are few game birds—ruffed and blue grouse inhabit the area—but the summer is a peak time for non-game birds. Birdwatchers spot and study many species here.

Near the boundary of the Wilderness on State Route 242 is Dee Wright Observatory, with striking vistas of mountains and lava fields.

Strawberry Mountain

Season: *July to about November*

Size: *33,003 acres*

Access: *From the west via U.S. 395 south of John Day; from the north via U.S. 26 to Forest Service Roads 1430, 1428 and 1427; from the south via Forest Service Road 1539*

Camping: *Primitive campsites and shelters*

Problems: *Heavy use*

Location: *Malheur National Forest*

Address: *Strawberry Mountain Wilderness
Malheur National Forest
John Day, OR 97845*

In command of the scenery around Oregon's John Day country is 9,044-foot Strawberry Mountain. Spread east and west of the peak is the Wilderness, with five lakes open to fishing all year long.

Mud Lake, though it has no fish, is interesting because it is in the final ecological stage of a lake. Called an "aquatic pasture," the lake gets more and more shallow as naturally deposited materials fill it in.

Spectacular views here attract photographers and nature lovers. And to go along with the views, the Wilderness offers alpine and subalpine flora and fauna. During July and August, wild-flowers and bushes cover the meadows and hillsides, as hikers make their way on trails through pine, fir and other trees.

Birdwatchers spot Traill's flycatcher, hunters take ruffed and blue grouse. Other game found here are deer, elk and bear. The southwestern corner of the Wilderness contains a portion of Canyon Creek Archery Area, where bow-and-arrow hunting is allowed.

A good trip of two or three days begins at the junction of High Lake Trail and Road 1539. The trail goes to High Lake, Slide Lake, Strawberry Lake and out to the road again.

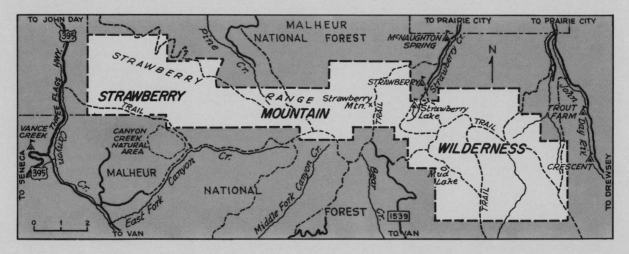

Three Sisters

Season: *April to November at lower levels; July to September on the peaks*

Size: *196,708 acres*

Access: *From the north by Oregon State Route 242; from the southwest by State Route 58*

Camping: *Primitive and improved campsites*

Problems: *Sudden storms; mosquitoes*

Location: *Deschutes and Willamette National Forests*

Address: *Three Sisters Wilderness*
Deschutes National Forest
211 East Revere Street
Bend, OR 97701

"The Sisters" is an area rich in backpackers' rewards: mountain tops, high trails and many lakes. The forest is heavy and varied, and contrasts sharply with the bare volcanic and glacial formations. The most recent volcanic activity in the Cascades was in the region of The Sisters, where hikers see lava flows and cinder cones, as well as glaciers. Collier Glacier, between North and Middle Sister, is the largest in Oregon, 1 1/2 miles wide and 3/4 of a mile long.

West and southwest of The Sisters, and near trails, many lakes fill the Wilderness with good fishing. Eastern brook and rainbow trout are the most common; there are also German browns, native cutthroats, goldens in the Chambers Lake Basin, and some Dolly Vardens. The number of lakes, pot holes and streams also means a high mosquito population, but most are gone by mid-August.

Long a favorite with climbers, the area has a great variety of challenge. From all sides the trails lead up, some to rough walks, others to difficult climbs. South Sister, at 10,354 feet, is the favorite climb; North Sister is the most difficult.

Forty miles of the Pacific Crest Trail (see page 176) lead through the Wilderness from north to south. There are 240 miles of trails.

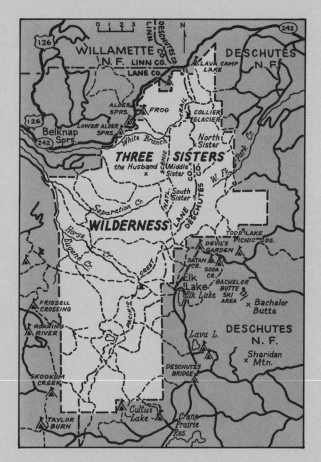

Other Wilderness Lands

When backpackers dream, Oregon is one of the places they see. In addition to the 10 declared Wildernesses, there are literally scores of other places in wilderness condition on state and federal lands, in the mountains and on the beach. And the State of Oregon is one of the most active in the country in improving and preserving its environment.

National Forests

The National Forests in Oregon and Washington have made an extensive survey of unroaded areas. They were classified, according to "public support," as areas with public support, without public support and with divided public support for further wilderness study. Whether these areas become Wildernesses or not, whether they had public support or not, they are still the prime areas for backcountry travel. Below is the list from the survey, including areas for which public support was for, against and divided.

Deschutes National Forest

1. Many Lakes
2. Metolius Breaks
3. Bend Watershed
4. North Paulina
5. South Paulina
6. Cascade Crest
7. Crescent
8. Squaw Creek
9. Bachelor Butte
10. Summit Lake-Windigo
11. Upper Little Deschutes
12. Bearwallow

Fremont National Forest

1. North Fork Twelve Mile Creek
2. Crane Mountain
3. Drake-McDowell Peak
4. Coleman Rim
5. Deadhorse Rim
6. Brattain Butte
7. Buck Creek

Malheur National Forest

1. Dixie Butte
2. Nipple Butte
3. Dry Cabin Creek
4. McClellan Mountain
5. Glacier Mountain
6. Monument Rock
7. Utley Butte
8. Myrtle-Silvies
9. Malheur River
10. North Fork Malheur River

Mount Hood National Forest

1. Lake
2. Big Bend
3. Twin Lakes
4. Bull-of-the-Woods
5. Roaring River
6. Eagle-Huckleberry
7. Zigzag Mountain
8. Badger Creek
9 Eagle
10. Gorge
11. Salmon River

OREGON

Ochoco National Forest

1. Mill Creek
2. Black Canyon
3. Silver Creek

Rogue National Forest

1. Sky Lakes
2. Butte Fork
3. Boundary Springs Extension
4. Thousand Springs
5. Rogue-Umpqua Divide
6. Brown Mountain
7. Craggy Mountain
8. Condrey Mountain
9. McDonald Peak
10. Sphagnum Bog Extension
11. Sherwood
12. Bitter Lick
13. Kinney
14. Little Grayback

Siskiyou National Forest

1. Oregon Mountain
2. Rough and Ready
3. Baldface
4. Shasta Costa
5. Collier
6. Lawson
7. Silver
8. Indigo
9. Rogue
10. Grassy Knob
11. Craggies

Siuslaw National Forest

1. Walport-Drift Creek
2. Cummins Creek
3. Rock Creek
4. Hebo 1A
5. Hebo 1B
6. Hebo 1C

Umatilla National Forest

1. South Fork Umatilla River
2. Tower
3. Jumpoff Joe
4. Greenhorn Mountain
5. Moore Flat
6. Mill Creek
7. Walla Walla River
8. Grande Ronde
9. North Fork
10. Hellhole
11. Kelly Prairie
12. Texas Butte
13. Timothy
14. North Fork John Day
15. Wenaha Backcountry

Umpqua National Forest

1. Fairview
2. Puddin Rock
3. Canton Creek/ Steelhead Creek
4. Bulldog Rock
5. Williams Creek
6. Cougar Bluff
7. Limpy Rock
8. Boulder Creek
9. Calf Creek/ Copeland Creek
10. Sawtooth
11. Windigo/Thielsen
12. Mount Bailey
13. Park/Rogue
14. Park/Winema
15. Dumont Creek
16. Lost Creek
17. Quartz Creek
18. Rogue-Umpqua Divide
19. Donegan

Wallowa-Whitman National Forest

1. Lower Minam
2. Wildhorse
3. Tope Creek
4. Joseph

5. Deadhorse
6. Lake Fork
7. Sheep Divide
8. Mount Emily
9. Twin Mountain

10. Elkhorn
11. Cook Ridge
12. Snake River
13. Imnaha Face

Willamette National Forest

1. North Breitenbush
2. Minto Mountain
3. Mosquito Creek
4. Timpanogas
5. Little North Santiam
6. Middle Santiam
7. Echo Mountain
8. McLennen Mountain

9. Packard Creek
10. Chucksney Mountain
11. Triangulation Peak
12. Big Meadows
13. French Pete Creek
14. Walker Creek
15. Rebel Creek
16. Maiden Peak

Winema National Forest

1. Cascade Crest
2. Yamsay Mountain

3. Brown Mountain
4. Sky Lakes

State Parks and Rivers

Oregon has been a pioneer state in planning for wilderness protection and establishing a Scenic Waterways System. Some interesting legislation has helped the backpacker's cause since 1967.

It was in that year that Oregon passed the Beach Law. It guarantees the public's free and uninterrupted use of ocean beaches, and controls development and traffic on the beaches. In that same year, the Willamette River Park System was begun.

The Scenic Rivers Program was started in 1970 with portions of six rivers being declared part of the system. Provisions were made for the addition of other rivers.

In 1971, the Oregon Recreation Trails System Act was passed, providing hiking and horseback trails. The Bicycle Trails Bill of the same year established the use of highway funds for bicycle trails and footpaths.

The following list shows State Parks with wilderness opportunities and the rivers in the Scenic Waterways System.

Park	Location
Humbug Mountain	*Southwest, beach*
Umpqua Lighthouse	*Southwest, beach*
Cape Lookout	*Northwest, beach*
Oswald West	*Northwest, beach*
Ecola	*Northwest, beach*
Fort Stevens	*Northwest, beach*
Silver Falls	*Northwest, mountains*
George W. Joseph	*Northwest, mountains*
John B. Yeon	*Northwest, mountains*
Wygant	*Northwest, mountains*
Guy B. Talbot	*Northwest, mountains*

Rivers	Segment
Rogue	*Applegate River to Lobster Creek Bridge*
Illinois	*Deer Creek to Rogue River*
Deschutes	*Pelton Dam to Columbia River*
Minam	*Minam Lake to Wallowa River*
Owyhee South Fork	*Oregon-Idaho Border to Three Forks*
Owyhee	*Crooked Creek to Birch Creek*
John Day	*Service Creek Bridge to Tumwater Falls*

Oregon Scenic Waterways are classified as follows: natural, scenic, recreational, natural scenic view, accessible natural, river community.

For more Oregon information, write:

Forest Service
319 S.W. Pine Street
P.O. Box 3623
Portland, OR 97208

State of Oregon
State Highway Department
Parks and Recreation Division
Highway Building
Salem, OR 97310

PENNSYLVANIA

Except for the Allegheny National Forest, which offers little of a primitive nature, there are too many roads and towns to call any area in Pennsylvania wilderness. There are several trails, including the Appalachian Trail (see page 167), which are of interest to hikers.

Baker Trail was established in 1950 by American Youth Hostels, Inc. It extends from Aspinwall to Cook Forest State Park, a distance of 133 miles. The trail is not difficult, and there are shelters 8 to 16 miles apart. For more information, write Pittsburgh Council, A.Y.H., 6300 Fifth Avenue, Pittsburgh, PA 15232.

Started in 1935, the Horse-Shoe Trail runs for 120 miles between Valley Forge and Rattling Run Gap, which is on the Appalachian Trail. The Horse-Shoe passes mountains, fields and orchards and is virtually free of any motorized traffic. Youth Hostels are located along the trail. For more information, write to the Horse-Shoe Trail Club, 51-6 Revere Rd., Drexel Hill, PA 19026.

For more Pennsylvania information, write:

Forest Service
633 West Wisconsin Avenue
Milwaukee, WI 53203

133

**Commonwealth of Pennsylvania
Bureau of State Parks**
Harrisburg, PA 17120

RHODE ISLAND

With a heading like "Wilderness Lands" for
Rhode Island, it's a little like the student who was
asked to write a travel essay. He called it "The
Mountains in Holland," and the entire essay read,
"There are no mountains in Holland." There are
no wilderness lands in Rhode Island.

For more Rhode Island information, write:

**State of Rhode Island and Providence
    Plantations
Department of Natural Resources**
*Veteran's Memorial Building
Providence, RI 02903*

SOUTH CAROLINA

There are certainly opportunities for outdoor
recreation in South Carolina, but wilderness is
hard to find unless it's by boat.

Sumter National Forest

Part of the Chattooga River, under study as a Wild
and Scenic River, passes through Sumter and
forms part of the border between Georgia and
South Carolina. Some sections are classified as
wild, others as recreation and scenic. Below U.S.
76, the river is one of the roughest stretches of
white water in the country. Part of the river is also
in North Carolina.

A 20-mile trail on Sumter leads from Long
Mountain to Walhalla Fish Hatchery. Campsites and streams line the way, part of which is
along the Chattooga River.

For more South Carolina information, write:

Forest Service
*1720 Peachtree Road, N.W.
Atlanta, GA 30309*

**South Carolina Department of Parks,
    Recreation and Tourism**
*Box 1358
Columbia, SC 29202*

SOUTH DAKOTA

About the only wilderness experience left in South
Dakota is on Badlands National Monument, which

134

takes not only a special interest in erosion and rock formations, but willingness to carry water.

Classic signs of erosion have made the Badlands a place of strange forms and colors, with cracks and crags and an interesting variety of wildlife.

For more South Dakota information, write:

National Park Service
1709 Jackson Street
Omaha, NB 68102

State of South Dakota
Department of Game, Fish and Parks
Pierre, SD 57501

TENNESSEE

New programs being implemented in Tennessee are of interest to backpackers. The state is establishing new wild areas, trails and rivers to be maintained in natural condition. There are also a few existing state parks in addition to federal lands, with limited wilderness possibilities.

Great Smoky Mountains National Park

Backcountry in this year-round park is one long lesson in biology. The plant and animal life is staggering in number: 1,400 species of flowering plants, 2,000 species of fungi, and there are 72 species of fish, 200 of birds.

The Great Smokies form one of the oldest uplands on earth. It is mountainous country, with some roads closed in winter snows. Some buildings from the mountain pioneer days are in the Great Smokies, too.

State Areas and Rivers

Of the Tennessee State Parks, five offer some rugged country. They are Roan Mountain, Chickasaw, Meeman-Shelby, Pickett and Standing Stone. Other specified sections of the state with wilderness possibilities include Catoosa and Cheatham Wildlife Management Areas and five State Natural Areas. They are Savage Gulf, Falling Waters Falls, Ozone Falls, Big Cypress Tree and Piney Falls. They are preserved for their scenic and natural values and will offer only primitive hiking trails.

The State Scenic Rivers are being preserved as natural, free-flowing waterways with controlled recreational use. At present, there are seven: the Harpeth, Hatchie, Hiwassee, Conasauga, French Broad, Collins, Roaring River-Blackburn Fork-Clear Creek and Tuckahoe. Two possible additions to the national system are the Buffalo and Obed.

Another new program in the process is the State Scenic Trails, which will have over 1,000

135

miles of trails. Part of the Appalachian Trail will be included, along with six others, the John Muir, Trail of Tears, Trail of the Lonesome Pine, Cumberland, Natchez Trace and Chickasaw Bluffs.

For more Tennessee information, write:

National Park Service
3401 Whipple Street
Atlanta, GA 30344

State of Tennessee Department of Conservation
2611 West End Avenue
Nashville, TN 37203

TEXAS

There is little true wilderness in Texas, but what there is of it is unusual enough to draw hikers into new experiences. And Texas does have a State Scenic Waterways Program with 23 rivers of wild and scenic varieties.

Sam Houston National Forest

The Lone Star Chapter of the Sierra Club sponsors the Lone Star 100-Mile Hiking Trail on Sam Houston and some private land, in Walker, Montgomery and San Jacinto Counties. It is a backpacking trail with primitive campsites.

National Parks

The backcountry of Big Bend National Park is a rugged and waterless place, where all drinking water must be carried. It is a treasure for anyone interested in geology, birdwatching and incredible varieties of plant life. The South Rim hike is one of the best, with desert terrain giving way to stands of pine, fir and aspen. It is a strenuous trail, but only 14 miles long. Color photography is good here on most of the 172 miles of trails. Heavy rains and floods occur in July and August, and hikers must watch for four species of rattlesnakes and the copperhead.

Guadalupe Mountains National Park includes "the most extensive fossil organic reef complex on record," the Capitan Barrier Reef. It was formed in the shallow water of a vast inland sea. Hiking here is a very rugged experience. On the 55 miles of trail in 77,500 acres, it is easy to become lost and very little trail maintenance is done at the present time. Backpackers find great views as well as odd mixtures of plants and trees, from desert types to pine and madrone and maple. The "rotten" rock cliffs are unsuitable for even technical climbing, but the four highest peaks in Texas—all over 8,000 feet—are here. All water must be carried.

Padre Island National Park is another unusual place to visit, though backcountry is limited.

There are astounding numbers of birds, fish and animals, including the rare whooping crane on Aransas National Wildlife Refuge to the north. Beachcombing is excellent.

State Scenic Waterways

The following list covers the wild and scenic rivers of Texas, with the warning that many portions of the banks are in private ownership and the Parks and Wildlife Department stresses getting permission to even set foot on a privately owned bank.

Wild Rivers	Section
1. Concho River	*San Angelo to Colorado River (65 miles)*
2. Guadalupe River	*Above Canyon Reservoir (62.5 miles); below (14)*
3. Lampasas River	*Kempner to Youngsport (40 miles)*
4. Little River	*Lampasas River to Brazos River (75 miles)*
5. Llano River	*Junction City Lake to Lyndon B. Johnson Lake (100 miles)*
6. Medina River	*Headwaters to the San Antonio River (116 miles)*
7. Pecos River	*U.S. 290 to the Rio Grande (100 miles)*
8. Pedernales River	*Pedernales Falls State Park to Lake Travis*
9. Rio Grande River	*Lajitas to Langtry (about 350 miles)*
10. San Gabriel River	*Headwaters to Little River (140 miles)*
11. San Marcos River	*Headwaters to Guadalupe River (59 miles)*
12. San Saba River	*Fort McKavett State Park to the Colorado River (100 miles)*

Scenic Rivers	Section
1. Angelina River	*Headwaters to Neches River (120 miles)*
2. Big Cypress Creek	*Lake O' the Pines to Caddo Lake (45 miles)*
3. Big Sandy-Village Creek	*Alabama-Coushatta Indian Reservation to Neches River*

137

River	Section
4. Brazos River	Possum Kingdom Dam to Gulf of Mexico (about 450 miles)
5. Colorado River	San Saba County to Gulf of Mexico (milage unavailable)
6. Neches River	Headwaters to Sabine Reservoir (416 miles)
7. Nueces River	Headwaters to Uvalde (35 miles)
8. Pine Island Bayou	Headwaters to Neches River (25 miles)
9. Red River	Denison Dam to Texas-Arkansas boundary (mileage unavailable)
10. Sabine River	Lake Tawakoni to Sabine Lake (340 miles)
11. Trinity River	Dallas to Gulf of Mexico (mileage unavailable)

For more Texas information, write:

Forest Service
1720 Peachtree Road, N.W.
Atlanta, GA 30309

National Park Service
P.O. Box 728
Santa Fe, NM 87501

Texas Parks and Wildlife Department
John J. Reagan Building
Austin, TX 78701

Wasatch National Forest has rugged trails.

UTAH

High Uintas

Season: *June 15 to September 30, peak from July 1 to September 10, slow in winter*

Size: *237,177 acres*

Access: *From the south by roads off U.S. 40; from the west off State Route 150*

Camping: *Primitive campsites*

Problems: *Afternoon rainshowers; can freeze any night.*

Location: *Ashley and Washatch National Forests*

Address: *High Uintas Primitive Area*
Ashley National Forest
437 East Main Street
Vernal, UT 84078

The Uinta Mountain Range is the only major one in the United States which runs east and west; all others bear north and south. The range is also the site of Utah's highest mountain, Kings Peak, 13,449 feet, along with four others over 13,000 feet and many other lower peaks for hikers.

Streams and lakes—over 250 lakes—cover the Uintas and make the western section especially popular with fishermen, who come for trout and grayling. Glacial action scooped out the many lakes and created an alpine scenery both wild and picturesque. The western boundary is a 2 to 3 hour drive from Salt Lake City.

Three-quarters of the Primitive Area is covered with conifer forest interspersed with meadows. During the fur trading period, the mountain men found a favorable beaver trapping locale under the alpine heights. There are now many trails in the entire area, with the north-south hiking perhaps the best. The trails off State Route 150 are most heavily used. Ashley and Wasatch National Forests east of High Uintas also have excellent hiking opportunities.

Winter brings snow here, but the mountains are still accessible for cross-country skiing and snowshoeing.

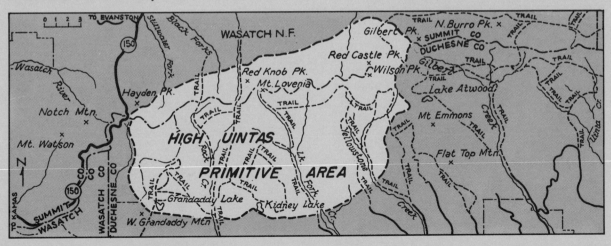

139

Other Wilderness Lands

For a state which is rich in wilderness, there are few places here kept in that condition, but still some left by chance. Many areas are under consideration for addition to the Wilderness System. But there are also dams, roads and mining activities in process or planned.

National Forests

There are many wild areas in the National Forests in Utah, such as the Aquarius Plateau and the Escalante Mountains on Dixie National Forest in the southeast and the Bear River Range on Cache National Forest in the north. Some of these areas are used heavily at varying times. There are still some wild places on Ashley and Wasatch National Forests.

One area on Manti-Lasal National Forest is of interest to desert mountain hikers. The Dark Canyon-Woodenshoe Canyon area is essentially roadless, but accessible from Blanding. April 1 to October 1 is the best time to visit this rugged cliff and canyon country. Flash flooding can be a problem and potable water sources are scarce.

Forest Service maps and brochures for Utah put an unusual stress on the commercial uses of forest lands. The primitive nature of the country administered by the Park Service is more

certain but very rugged.

National Parks

The southeast corner of Utah, in fact most of the Four Corners area, is practically one large wilderness, though of course there are roads. Canyonlands and Capitol Reef National Parks and Glen Canyon National Recreation Area, with the Escalante Canyon wilds, make up over two million acres of wildland opportunities. The chaotic geological forces, the deep canyons and eons of erosion have given the area a stark and grand quality found nowhere else. It is wild indeed, and hikes to the backcountry require experience, conditioning and planning—and in some places guides are essential. All supplies, including water and gas, must be brought in.

In Bryce Canyon National Park, 16,303 acres of the 36,010-acre park have been proposed as a Wilderness. Much photographed for its color and fantastic erosion patterns, Bryce is more of Utah's challenging wildland along the eastern side of the Paunsaugunt Plateau. Pine, oak and sagebrush grow in the lower elevations, with fir, manzanita and grasses in the middle altitudes. The high elevations have spruce and aspen, and the bristlecone pine grows in all zones. Winter brings the snowshoeing and ski touring weather. At present there are 65 miles of trails.

Zion National Park is another area of colorful desert hues and deep, eroded canyons. There are some rough trails, but even a combination of them does not produce a long trip.

Not to be forgotten in Utah are the boating possibilities. River trips are available on the Green and Colorado Rivers and others.

For more Utah information, write:

Forest Service
324 25th Street
Ogden, UT 84401

National Park Service
1709 Jackson Street
Omaha, NB 68102

State of Utah
Department of Natural Resources
132 South Second West
Salt Lake City, UT 84101

VERMONT

This is part of the New England-wilderness-that-was area, and while there is still much open space in Vermont, there is little open public land.

The Appalachian Trail is good hiking, especially in spring and fall, before and after the summer crowds, but even spring and fall can be crowded. The trail twists through 134 miles of Vermont, where 94 miles of it is known as the Long Trail.

For more Vermont information, write:

Forest Service
633 West Wisconsin Avenue
Milwaukee, WI 53203

State of Vermont
Department of Forests and Parks
Montpelier, VT 05601

VIRGINIA

The best bet in Virginia for wilderness enthusiasts is on the 29 rivers which have been proposed for the state's Scenic Rivers System. The Appalachian Trail (see page 168) passes through Virginia, including Shenandoah National Park, George Washington and Jefferson National Forests.

Scenic River System

The following list gives the section of each river proposed for the system. Most of them have public land access.

141

VIRGINIA

River	Section	River	Section
1. Appomattox River	*Appomattox Dam to Petersburg (6 miles)*		
2. Back Creek	*Mountain Grove to Gathright Reservoir (9 miles)*	11. Cripple Creek	*Entire stream (22 miles)*
3. Big Reed Island Creek	*Entire stream (34 miles)*	12. Dragon Run River	*Route 604 to Turk's Ferry (15 miles)*
4. Blackwater River	*Route 603 to Franklin (39 miles)*	13. Goose Creek	*Interstate 66 to Potomac River (15 miles)*
5. Bullpasture River	*Headwaters to Williamsville (20 miles)*	14. Jackson River	*U.S. 220 to Gathright Reservoir (21 miles)*
6. Cedar Creek	*Entire stream (45 miles)*	15. James River	*Under study*
7. Chickahominy River	*Providence Forge to James River (31 miles)*	16. Mattaponi	*Route 628 to Frazier Ferry (34 miles)*
8. Clinch River	*Blackford to Cleveland (21 miles); St. Paul to Dungannon (16 miles)*	17. Maury River	*Calfpasture headwaters to Beuna Vista (65 miles)*
9. Cowpasture River	*Headwaters to Jackson River (73 miles)*	18. New River	*U.S. 58 to Fries (6 miles); Austinville to Route 100 (11 miles)*
10. Craig Creek	*Newcastle to Strom (37 miles)*	19. Northwest River	*Entire stream to North Carolina line (16 miles)*
		20. Nottoway River	*Route 609 to Route 645 (19 miles)*

River	Section	River	Section
21. Powell River	*Dryden Southwest to Tennessee line (45 miles)*	29. Thornton River	*Sperryville to Monument Mills (20 miles)*
22. Rapidan River	*Headwaters to Rapidan (42 miles); Rapidan to Rappahannock River (35 miles)*		
23. Rappahannock River	*Remington to Fredericksburg (29 miles); Fredericksburg to Port Royal (31 miles)*		
24. Rivanna River	*Albemarle County line to James River (25 miles)*		
25. Roanoke River	*Alta Vista to Kerr Reservoir (72 miles)*		
26. Russell Fork	*Bartlick to Kentucky line (6 miles)*		
27. Shenandoah, South Fork	*Port Republic to Front Royal (93 miles)*		
28. St. Mary's River	*Headwaters to Route 608 (7 miles)*		

The Virginia Commission of Outdoor Recreation publishes a booklet, *Virginia's Scenic Rivers*, with further descriptions.

For more Virginia information, write:

Forest Service
1720 Peachtree Road, N.W.
Atlanta, GA 30309

National Park Service
143 South Third Street
Philadelphia, PA 19106

Commonwealth of Virginia Commission of Outdoor Recreation
803 East Broad Street
Richmond, VA 23219

Glacier Peak

Season: *Trails open late July to October*

Size: *464,219 acres*

Access: *From the south at Telma via Forest Service roads; from the west at Darrington via Forest Service roads; from the east at Holden near Lake Chelan; from the north via gravel road at Marblemount*

Camping: *Improved campsites; shelters; primitive camping*

Problems: *Sudden snow flurries and thunderstorms; lightning*

Location: *Mount Baker National Forest*

Address: *Glacier Peak Wilderness*
Mount Baker National Forest
Bellingham, WA 98225

Another of the Northwest's large wildland areas, Glacier Peak provides the full range of wilderness experience. Hikers can take the Pacific Crest Trail through the 35-mile long Wilderness or tread one of the many other trails.

In the southeastern section a well maintained footway leads to the Napeequa Valley, properly called the Shangri-La of the Cascades. Image Lake, in the central portion, is a popular spot to camp in the company of its image of Glacier Peak, the highest in the Wilderness at 10,528 feet. Visitors are always welcome at Miners Ridge Lookout.

The natural bounty at Glacier Peak goes from the flora and fauna of lush valley floors to barren alpine peaks which cradle over 90 glaciers. Lyman Lake is the scene of brilliant fall foliage, but the gray-green glacial silt in the lake makes it beautiful all year. Flower Dome is named for its display of wildflowers, and mountain azalea as well as the rare Lyall larch, grow in the Wilderness.

Animal life is abundant here, from the small cony and the hoary marmot to black bear and mountain goat. The State of Washington maintains open season in the Wilderness on deer, black bear, mountain goat and grouse, but no open season on ptarmigan or marmot. Most of the area is open to early-season deer hunting for those who seek high-mountain hunting. Pack and saddle animals are available (see address above).

144

Goat Rocks

WASHINGTON

Season: *All year, with seasonal snow conditions*

Size: *82,680 acres*

Access: *On the north from U.S. 12; on the northeast from Forest Service Road 134; on the east from several Forest Service Roads, principally at Packwood Lake and Walupt Lake.*

Camping: *Primitive and improved campsites*

Problems: *Sudden, violent storms, even in summer*

Location: *Gifford Pinchot and Snoqualmie National Forests*

Address: *Goat Rocks Wilderness*
Gifford Pinchot National Forest
P.O. Box 449
Vancouver, WA 98660

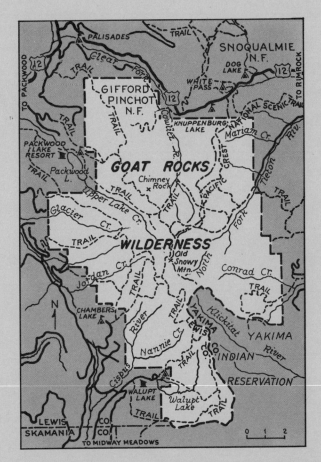

For alpine enthusiasts, Goat Rocks has just about every range of experience. Winter brings perfect snow for cross-country skiing and snowshoeing from White Pass to Hogback Mountain. Summer climbing includes glacier traverses and a number of peaks which are not too difficult for whole families. Pleasant access trails are easy to reach by good roads, and the Pacific Crest Trail (see page 173) winds the whole length of the Wilderness.

The views are as varied as the environment. Along the trails, hikers see meadows full of wildflowers, strange rock formations, forested valleys and distant snow-capped peaks. Photographers have all the choices of animal life and three vegetative life zones, the Canadian, Hudsonian and Arctic-Alpine.

Bands of mountain goats forage the crags, elk feed in the basins and the whistling marmot calls his warning. The unusual pika, or cony, which looks like a small guinea pig, lives in slide rock and gives a short, bleating call. A telephoto lens is invaluable here.

Many of the streams and lakes are good for native cutthroat, rainbow and eastern brook trout. Access to some streams is difficult.

Snowgrass Flat, located in the southern part of the Wilderness, was so popular with hikers and riders, and so accessible, that it has been closed to campers and livestock.

145

Mount Adams

Season: *Summer*

Size: *42,411 acres*

Access: *From the north on Forest Service Road 101; from the west on Forest Service Road N84; from the south on Forest Service Road N80*

Camping: *Primitive camping*

Problems: *Rugged terrain and sudden, violent storms at higher elevation*

Location: *Gifford Pinchot National Forest*

Address: *Mount Adams Wilderness*
Gifford Pinchot National Forest
P.O. Box 449
Vancouver, WA 98660

Named for the second highest mountain in the Northwest, this Wilderness has several main features, including 12,326-foot Mount Adams. Part of the Pacific Crest Trail (see page 175) goes through a large portion of the area. It connects with Round-the-Mountain Trail and others.

Well known for its rich variety of trees, shrubs, wildflowers and ground cover, this part of Gifford Pinchot National Forest has many back-packing opportunities. Families may take leisurely hikes and experienced walkers have a chance at the high country.

One of the most rugged parts of the Wilderness is in the eastern section, adjacent to the Yakima Indian Reservation, where Hellroaring Creek heads into the glaciers. In this area is also Little Mount Adams, a secondary cone thrown up after the last eruption of Mount Adams. The slope around Bird Creek Meadows, just outside the Wilderness, is noted for its August floral display.

The Ridge of Wonders is in the eastern Wilderness, too. It is the remnant of a wild lava flow between Mt. Adams and Little Mount Adams.

One of the most interesting wildlife aspects of the Wilderness is its population of coyotes. They range over the entire area, and their songs—from aria to chorus—may be heard on summer evenings. Living with the coyotes here are black bears, which may sometimes be seen in the numerous berry patches. Black tail deer roam here,

too, and an occasional elk can be caught browsing in the meadows. During a short season when berries and plant shoots are at the right stage, blue and ruffed grouse are in abundance.

Most of the lakes in the area are either too shallow or lack the food for fish, except for the eastern brook trout in Lookingglass Lake.

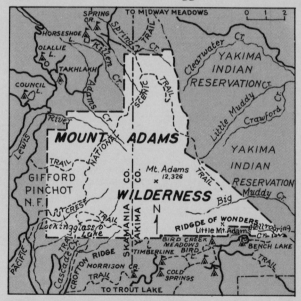

Pasayten

Season: *July to October or November*

Size: *518,000 acres*

Access: *On the east, Forest Service Road 392 north from Winthrop; on the south from Mazama on Forest Service Road 374*

Camping: *Primitive campsites and shelters*

Problems: *Variable weather*

Location: *Mount Baker and Okanogan National Forests*

Address: *Pasayten Wilderness*
Okanogan National Forest
Okanogan, WA 98840

In range of experience and in size, Pasayten is one of the giants of the National Wilderness Preservation System. Its 518,000 acres make it sixth in size nationally and first among the Pacific coast states. Pasayten's wilderness extends almost unbroken for 40 miles from west to east and 20 miles from north to south.

The experiences of the North Cascade Range are all here, with prime examples of each. For the mountaineer, there is alpine topography and challenging climbing. Or, for just about anyone, there are foot and horseback trails which cover several hundred miles. The Pacific Crest Trail (see page 173) stretches 27 miles through the Wilderness from Windy Pass to Monument 78 on the Canadian border. The terrain goes from barren alpine country to wooded stream beds and grassy meadows.

Rainbow trout are the most common in the 94 lakes, but other species are cutthroat, eastern brook, Montana blackspot, German brown and Dolly Varden. The streams of the Wilderness also carry fish, as do the Pasayten River and its tributaries.

Usually accessible for four to five months, from about July to October or November, the Wilderness is subject to snows any time of year at higher elevations.

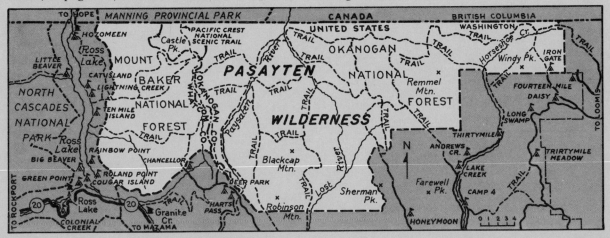

Other Wilderness Lands

Like Oregon, Washington has a vast treasure of wilderness. The total designated areas alone are over a million acres, with several national parks adding unusually beautiful places.

National Forests

The following list is a Forest Service survey of possible areas for Wilderness study. The survey was compiled with Oregon's national forests (see pages 130-132).

Gifford Pinchot National Forest

1. Green River
2. Strawberry
3. Mount Margaret
4. Upper Green
5. St. Helens
6. Siouxon
7. Trapper
8. Clear Creek
9. Shark Rock
10. Upper Lewis
11. Juniper Peak
12. Pompey Creek
13. Davis Mountain
14. Park Addition
15. Tatoosh
16. Cartright
17. Cougar Lakes
18. Limited
19. Indian Heaven
20. Big Lava Bed ·
21. Bear Creek
22. Cussed Hollow

Mount Baker National Forest

1. Twin Sisters
2. Diobsud
3. Alma Cooper
4. Higgins Mountain
5. Pressentin Creek
6. Tomyhoi-Silesia
7. Mount Baker
8. Monte Cristo
9. Diskerson
10. Boulder River

Olympic National Forest

1. Quilcene
2. The Brothers
3. Mildred Lake
4. Colonel Bob
5. Mount Zion
6. Green Mountain
7. Moonlight Dome
8. Matheny Ridge
9. Elk Reade
10. Wonder Mountain
11. South Quinault
12. Rugged Ridge
13. Mount Baldy

Snoqualmie National Forest

1. Alpine Lakes
2. Dougar Lakes
3. Mount Index
4. Miller River
5. Lake Dorothy
6. Mount Thompson-Rampart
7. Norse Peak
8. Monte Cristo
9. Grizzly Peak
10. Quartz Mountain
11. Blue Slide
12. Ragged Ridge
13. Eagle Rock
13. Clearwater

Umatilla National Forest

1. Wenaha Backcountry
2. Spangler
3. Upper Tucannon
4. Asotin Creek
6. Wenatchee Creek
7. Moore Flat
8. Mill Creek Watershed

5. Hogback   9. Saddle Creek

Wenatchee National Forest

1. Alpine Lakes   7. Slide Ridge
2. Enchantment   8. Nason Ridge
3. Kitan   9. Mission Creek
4. Grade Creek   10. Entiat
5. Lake Chelan   11. Lake Wenatchee
6. Stormy

National Parks

One of the most spectacular and most popular of Washington's national parks is Mount Rainier, with the largest mountain glacier system in the United States. Climbing the 14,410-foot mountain is the favorite attraction here for backcountry hikers. The steepness, heavily crevassed glaciers and sudden storms demand that climbers be in top condition and experienced. One of the main features at Rainier is the animal, bird and plant life—over 700 species of plants alone. The wildflower fields and mountain scenery are the most spectacular sights in the park. The peak season is July 1 to Labor Day, when the park is often heavily overused; the slow season is from November 1 to June 1, when snowshoeing and ski touring are possible.

North Cascades National Park has been proposed as an addition to the Wilderness Preservation System. It would be one of the largest such areas at 514,000 acres, and would include parts of Ross Lake and Lake Chelan National Recreation Areas. About 345 miles of trails take hikers into the heavily forested valleys and onto open ridges. There are over 300 glaciers, peaks for climbing range from easy to challenging and plant and animal life are varied and abundant.

One of the most unusual of all our national parks is the 1,400 square miles of Olympic. The Olympic Mountains are fortunately almost impenetrable for road building. They are an array of peaks with little of anything that could be called a crest. The heavily vegetated rain forests receive 145 inches of rain a year, mostly in late fall to early spring. Some 600 miles of hiking trails go into the rugged heart of the mountains. The 50 miles of Pacific coastline are among the most primitive left in the United States.

For more Washington information, write:

Forest Service
319 S.W. Pine Street
P.O. Box 3623
Portland, OR 97208

National Park Service
1424 4th Avenue
Seattle, WA 98101

**Washington State Parks and
Recreation Commission**
*522 South Franklin
Olympia, WA 98502*

WEST VIRGINIA

About the only West Virginia backcountry left
is on the Monongahela National Forest. Of interest
to hikers in the forest is the Seneca Indian Trail,
the curious Cranberry Glades, unexplored limestone caves and bear colonies. There is some
rugged scenery in the mountains, and almost
2,000 miles of fishing streams.

For more West Virginia information, write:

Forest Service
*633 West Wisconsin Avenue
Milwaukee, WI 53203*

**State of West Virginia
Department of Natural Resources**
*1709 Washington Street, E.
Charleston, WV 25311*

WISCONSIN

Like Minnesota, Wisconsin is prime canoe country. On the Chequamegon National Forest there
are hundreds of lakes of all sizes and good canoeing on the Flambeau and Chippewa Rivers. Nicolet
National Forest also has canoeing on many scenic
rivers.

Part of the St. Croix River (see page 201)
is in Wisconsin, and the Wolf (see page 205) is
here, too.

There are three state administered areas
with limited wilderness trips. The Elroy-Sparta
Trail goes 30 miles over an old railroad grade,
where tunnels and depots still remain. The
Northern Unit Kettle Moraine State Forest is a
rolling to hilly oak, grassland and marsh area of
26,162 acres. And Northern Highland State Forest
is lake and northern forest country with 144,007
acres.

For more Wisconsin information, write:

Forest Service
*633 Wisconsin Avenue
Milwaukee, WI 53203*

**State of Wisconsin
Department of Natural Resources**
*Box 450
Madison, WI 53701*

Bridger

Season: *July 1 to October 1; limited winter showshoeing and ski touring*

Size: *83,300 acres*

Access: *From the west via many Forest Service Roads off U.S. 187*

Camping: *Primitive and improved campsites*

Problems: *Snow in any month; permits required for pack stock and groups over 20.*

Location: *Bridger National Forest*

Address: *Bridger Wilderness*
P.O. Box 31
Forest Service Building
Kemmerer, WY 83101

The Continental Divide in the Wind River Range forms the eastern boundary of this Wilderness. Running from north to south on the Atlantic drainage slopes are Glacier Primitive Area, the Wind River Indian Reservation and Popo Agie Primitive Area.

As the name suggests, this was the land of early trappers and explorers such as Jim Bridger, Kit Carson, William Sublette, Captain B. L. Bonneville, Lieutenant John Fremont and many others.

Gannett Peak, 13,804 feet, is the highest in Wyoming; it and other peaks are becoming more and more popular for climbing. In the Wilderness, there are over 600 miles of trails and large expanses of trailless areas (outlined, incidentally, on Bridger National Forest maps). Some of the trails have portions which are not passable for pack and saddle animals. Short trail distances from entrances to scenic lakes make Bridger truly a family Wilderness.

There are literally hundreds of lakes and streams up and down the Wilderness. They produce fine catches of golden, rainbow, brook, mackinaw and cutthroat trout and whitefish. Spinning gear and fly fishing tackle both work well.

While large animals are not abundant, the variety is great, from the moose down to the cony, which Fremont called "Siberian squirrel."

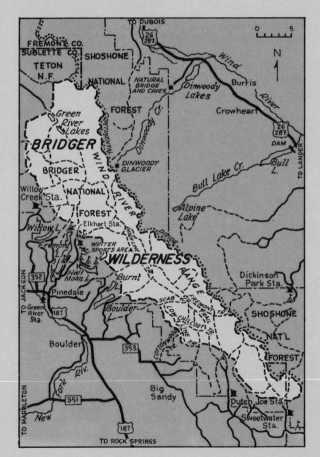

151

Cloud Peak

Season: *June 15 to September 15*

Size: *137,000 acres*

Access: *From the north on Forest Service roads off U. S. 14; from the south off U. S. 16*

Camping: *Primitive camping to improved campsites*

Problems: *Snow anytime; severe winters*

Location: *Bighorn National Forest*

Address: *Cloud Peak Primitive Area*
Bighorn National Forest
P.O. Box 2046
Sheridan, WY 82801

The lowest point in Cloud Peak is the Main Fork of Paintrock Creek—at 8,500 feet. Cloud Peak, 13,165 feet, is the highest spot, and the Primitive Area has a mean elevation of 10,000 feet. This makes for low temperatures, plenty of snow and a short season. But the air is so invigorating and the views so striking, that Cloud Peak is worth some cool weather. Just the sight of the Bighorn Mountains rising abruptly off the plains is unforgettable. Some of the vertical walls are 5,000 feet high.

Within the region, not only views but bodies of water abound. There are 256 lakes and 49 miles of streams—all good for fish. Solitude Lake is the largest, with Crater, Cliff and Geneva Lakes also exceptional for fish. The lower lakes and streams are set in stands of fir, pine, spruce, cottonwood and aspen.

Several large species of animals inhabit Cloud Peak: the elk, moose, deer, mountain sheep, bear. Smaller ones include the fox, coyote and the little rock cony.

All of the Bighorn National Forest is good for hiking, and one of the best sections is the northern area. As well as hiking here, there is the curious Medicine Wheel. It is a wheel, laid out on the ground, stone by stone, with a diameter of 70 feet. From the wheel's hub run 28 spokes. There is no certainty about who built it or why, but it predates the Crow Indians.

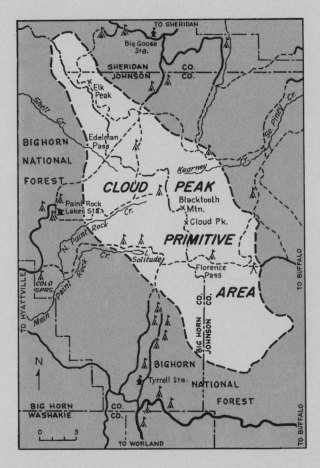

152

Glacier

WYOMING

Season: *July and August*
Size: *177,000 acres*
Access: *Various roads off U.S. 26-287 between Burris and Dubois*
Camping: *Primitive camping*
Problems: *Rough terrain; snow anytime*
Location: *Shoshone National Forest*
Address: *Glacier Primitive Area*
Shoshone National Forest
P.O. Box 961
Cody, WY 82414

Here in this high and very rugged country, the name "Glacier" applies to present geological activity, not just to a dim past. Some of the largest "living" glaciers in the continental United States are still scouring the rock in this Primitive Area.

Hiking here is for the experienced and those in good condition. Much of the area is bare granite, planed and sometimes broken by past and present glacial movement. The main north-south trail, which begins in the north near Torrey Lake, leads to Gannett Peak. It is the highest peak in Wyoming (13,804 feet) and is on the border of Glacier and the Bridger Wilderness. The trail is about 25 miles long and passes many lakes. The area, in fact, is peppered with hundreds of lakes, named and unnamed. The fishing is good.

The southern part of this Primitive Area has very few trails and is rough, remote country. It is bordered on the west and south by the Bridger Wilderness and on the east by the Wind River Roadless Area, which is part of the Wind River Indian Reservation.

Animals found in Glacier include elk, deer, mountain sheep and goats, antelope, moose and black and grizzly bears. In addition to waterfowl and songbirds, it is possible to spot bald eagles and golden eagles.

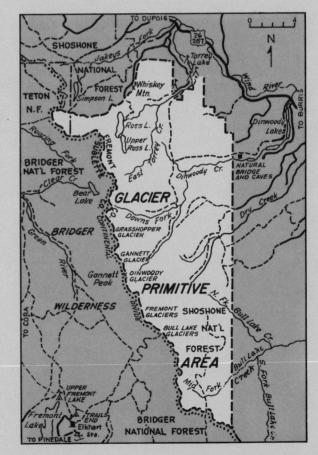

153

North Absaroka

Season: *August and September*

Size: *351,104 acres*

Access: *From the west off U. S. 212 and Forest Service roads; short access from the south off U. S. 16*

Camping: *Primitive camping*

Problems: *Snow anytime at higher elevations*

Location: *Shoshone National Forest*

Address: *North Absaroka Wilderness*
Shoshone National Forest
P.O. Box 961
Cody, WY 82414

Shoshone National Forest contains almost a million acres of Wilderness, with North and South Absaroka cut only by a narrow corridor. The land here is rough, marked by steep canyons; it easily overwhelms those who roam in it with one majestic view after another.

The rushing streams and remote canyons were the home of the Shoshone Indians and once served as a haven for Chief Joseph and his Nez Perce in their effort for freedom in Canada. The first white man to see the Yellowstone country, John Colter, was one of the early mountain men to travel here. Even now, many parts of the Wilderness seem to remain untouched by the footsteps of man. To keep the area in a wilderness condition, the Forest Service limits the length of stay at one campsite to ten days and the number in one party to 25. Further restrictions may be imposed when necessary.

The peaks here reach over 12,000 feet. Geologically young, North Absaroka contains alpine rocks, glaciers, a natural bridge and petrified trees still standing.

Firewood is scarce, so small campstoves are a must. In addition to hiking, climbing and riding, the area is popular for fishing and big game hunting. Winter snows close the Wilderness to all but the most experienced and conditioned wilderness travelers.

Many miles of trails cover the area, and it would be possible to spend an entire summer on them, with proper preparation for sudden snow. The eastern boundary joins Yellowstone National Park, with connecting trails. Pack trips are available (see address above).

PopoAgie

WYOMING

Season: *August and September*
Size: *70,000 acres*
Access: *From the west through Bridger Wilderness; from the east by Forest Service road from Lander*
Camping: *Primitive camping*
Problems: *Snow anytime; rough terrain*
Location: *Shoshone National Forest*
Address: *Popo Agie Primitive Area*
Shoshone National Forest
P.O. Box 961
Cody, WY 82414

On the east slope of the Continental Divide, Popo Agie is a treasure of mountain environment. Glacial action in this rough, remote terrain has made it a photographer's paradise of dramatic jagged peaks and deep narrow canyons. Seven major trails take backpackers up and down through geological history.

One of the trails, as well as a pass and a mountain, is named after Washakie, a Shoshone Indian chief. After listening for hours while his men and white officials argued about Indians doing small truck farming, Washakie made a grandly simple speech: "God damn a potato!" He lived to be almost 100 years old, and his grave (and Sacajawea's) are on the Wind River Indian Reservation next to Popo Agie on the north.

In a relatively small area, there are over 200 lakes, almost half of them with fish. But all visitors here should beware of weather. Snow storms and cold temperatures can be expected any time of year above timberline. The high country is rarely open before mid-July.

There are no very close access roads to Popo Agie. The road through the Wind River Indian Reservation must be checked to make sure it is open for travel.

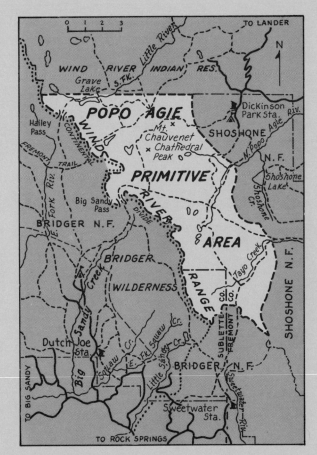

South Absaroka

Season: *Mid-July to mid-September*

Size: *483,130 acres*

Access: *From the north off U.S. 16; from the east via State Route 291 and Forest Service Road 479*

Camping: *Primitive camping*

Problems: *Rough terrain; snow at any time*

Location: *Shoshone National Forest*

Address: *South Absaroka Wilderness*
Shoshone National Forest
P.O. Box 961
Cody, WY 82414

The northwest corner of Wyoming has, in addition to Yellowstone and Grand Teton National Parks, almost 2.5 million acres of Wilderness and Primitive Area. South Absaroka is second only to Teton in size among the eight areas here.

Long a favorite of the big game trophy hunter, South Absaroka is home to mountain sheep, elk, deer, moose and black and grizzly bears. Wolves, coyotes, eagles, wildfowl and songbirds also live here.

This vast wildland has many excellent trails, some of which connect on the west with trails in Teton Wilderness and Yellowstone, on the south with Stratified Primitive Area. The abundance of lakes and streams make fishing, hiking and trail riding a pleasant experience with striking scenery.

Many of the trails in South Absaroka were first made by Shoshone Indians. They prized the mountains for its herds of big game and fur-bearing animals. Hundreds of miles of trails connect with each other in this part of Wyoming, making it possible to hike from the Lander area up into Montana while crossing only two highways.

Climbers will find many peaks in the 12,000-foot range. Glacier Basin holds several glaciers on the slopes of Overlook Mountain.

Stratified

WYOMING

Season: *June 1 to September 30; slow in May and September*
Size: *203,930 acres*
Access: *From the south via dirt road off U.S. 26-287 at Dubois*
Camping: *Primitive campsites*
Problems: *Snow and storms nine months a year*
Location: *Shoshone National Forest*
Address: *Stratified Primitive Area*
District Ranger
Wind River District
Dubois, WY 82513

Like the other wild country in the Absaroka Range, Stratified is noted for its big game. It is the home of deer, elk, bear, mountain sheep, antelope, moose and small fur bearers, too. It is hunter's domain in the fall.

But unlike the rest of the Range, this area has become nationally famous as a discoverer's treasure for geology buffs. The main attraction is the agatized and petrified wood. Petrified remains of forests, ferns and animal life are relics on a trip backward in time. Gravel bars of almost all the streams contain pieces of petrified trees, and some trunks are still standing at the head of Frontier Creek.

Although there are numerous lakes and streams here, fishing is poor because of unstable channels. So though hikers will have available water, fish as a food source is more unreliable than usual.

The trail system is only fair to poor, but there are many trails, some connecting with South Absaroka Wilderness to the north.

Pack animals are available (see address above), but a special permit is required for commercial and large groups. The peak season is from June 1 to August 31 every year.

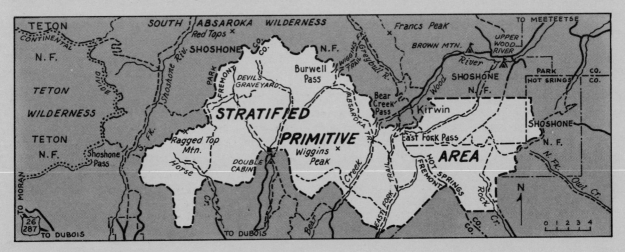

Teton

Season: *May to October; trails open July 1.*

Size: *563,500 acres*

Access: *Best on the south from U.S. 26-287; on the west from U.S. 89-287.*

Camping: *Primitive camping*

Problems: *Electrical storms; high water and runoff May to mid-July*

Location: *Teton National Forest*

Address: *Teton Wilderness*
Buffalo Ranger District
Blackrock Ranger Station
Box 78
Moran, WY 83013

A country of high plateaus, large valleys and open mountain meadows, Teton is only part of a chain of Wilderness and Primitive Areas totaling over 1.5 million acres. Just east of Teton and stretching north to the Montana border are Stratified Primitive Area, South Absaroka and North Absaroka Wilderness. And much of Teton and Shoshone National Forests outside of these designated areas is in a primitive condition.

Teton is especially popular with pack and saddle animal fans and with fishermen. The Outfitter Trail virtually circles the inner edge of the Wilderness. It leads past waterfalls, lakes, through mountain valleys and meadows and to the "Parting of the Waters." On the Continental Divide, Two-Ocean Creek parts to become Atlantic Creek and Pacific Creek, one emptying into the Atlantic 3,488 miles away and the other into the Pacific 1,353 miles away. This is the only spot where such a phenomenon is known to occur.

With over 400 miles of trail in Teton, the Outfitter route is far from the only great hiking experience. Another trail, along Thorofare River, was once a principal route of the Shoshone and Blackfoot Indians.

Part of the Jackson Hole elk herd summers in the mountain ranges and the animals are easily spotted by approaching their feeding ridges and meadows cautiously. There is also habitat for moose, bighorn sheep and a few deer. Trumpeter swans are often sighted on Enos and Bridger Lakes. Black and grizzly bears are found, as are numerous fur-bearing animals.

For determined winter sports enthusiasts, this entire area is good for rugged, exciting cross-country skiing and snowshoeing. Winter solitude is easy.

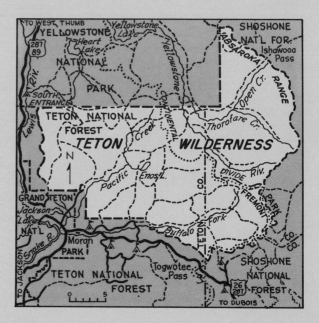

Other Wilderness Lands

Just about anywhere in Wyoming is where the wilderness is. The southwestern portion of the state has the Red Desert, a barren, windy place, while the northwestern corner is a giant, forested wildland with almost 2.5 million acres of designated Wilderness.

National Parks

As a Grand Teton National Park hiking information sheet points out, the Tetons have very likely had too much praise as a hiking area of unsurpassed beauty. The trails are overused in summer, and solitude is hard to find on them. Some hikers prefer to leave the trails, which Rangers discourage because of increasing numbers of people. Though it is incredibly beautiful country, it needs a rest.

The same can be said of much of Yellowstone, except its outer fringes. The four corners and the north-south boundary lines touch several Wildernesses in adjoining national forests, where backcountry still exists.

For more Wyoming information, write:

Forest Service
Federal Center
Building 85
Denver, CO 80225

(For Bighorn, Black Hills, Medicine Bow and Shoshone National Forests)

Forest Service
Federal Building
324 25th Street
Ogden, UT 84401
(For Bridger, Targhee and Teton National Forests)

National Park Service
1709 Jackson Street
Omaha, NB 68102

Wyoming Travel Commission
2330 Capitol Avenue
Cheyenne, WY 82001

A trail rider smiles on a Teton pack trip.

159

Basin Ponds lie far below Mt. Katahdin, where the Appalachian Trail begins in Maine.

III Scenic Trails

Appalachian

A 2,000-mile footpath anchored in the north at Mount Katahdin, Maine and in the south at Springer Mountain, Georgia winds its way along the Appalachian Mountains through 14 states near some of the most densely populated centers of the country. On October 2, 1968, the Appalachian Trail and the Pacific Crest Trail were designated as the first two in a series of trails to make up the National Scenic Trails System.

The idea of the Appalachian Trail was Benton MacKaye's. He wrote of his plan in 1921 and helped unite a group of people similarly interested in joining some existing trail systems and extending the whole project some 1,200 miles. As the trail grew, so did the pioneering interests of others, both individuals and clubs, who volunteered their efforts. The sheer magnitude of the task inspired some, though mere length was never the real goal. Rather the opportunity to explore some of the more remote tracts of Maine and the Southern Appalachians helped to stimulate the most interest.

In 1935, after the project almost collapsed for a time, the Appalachian Trail Conference (ATC) was born, joining existing clubs under this common federation. It provided further impetus. The 2,000-mile trail was completed on August 15, 1937, through such efforts as well as those of the Forest Service and other public agencies.

Since that time, use of the trail has constantly multiplied. The trail passes through 8 National Forests and 2 National Parks. More than half is in publicly owned lands, but the 866 miles of privately owned lands through which the Trail winds have often been subject to development requiring trail relocation and finally threatening the continued existence of the Trail. The National Trails System Act now gives permanence to the entire route.

Because of their long and fruitful association with everything connected with the Trail, anyone intending an extended trip on it would do well to contact The Appalachian Trail Conference, P. O. Box 236, Harpers Ferry, West Virginia 25425. The ATC also published a series of booklets that detail a great deal of information for the traveler.

The Trail is a 4-foot wide footpath open neither to motor traffic nor horses. It is a wilderness trail with extensive systems of side trails feeding from it. A chain of lean-to's has been built over most of the route to serve hikers. Water, toilet facilities and fireplaces are usually located there as well. More of these are planned, but in most areas they already occur every 8 to 10 miles, handy for family excursions.

The Trail is well marked with blue on white markers approximately every 100 yards. White on blue is used on side trails. What follows

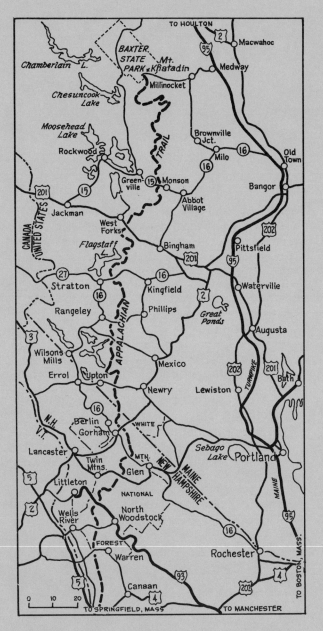

is a state by state verbal trip along the route of this longest completed recreational trail in the world.

Maine

Mount Katahdin (5,267 feet) in Baxter State Park is both the highest peak in Maine and the northern tip of the Appalachian Trail. This "Greatest Mountain" as the word translates from the Indian, overlooks a forested wilderness remote from towns and rich in scenery, lakes, rivers and ponds. The trail immediately works its way across rivers (Nesowadnehunk and Penobscot West Branch), past lakes (Rainbow, Nahamakanta, Joe Mary) and up White Cap Mountain. It crosses an old road with side trails to "Gulf Hagas." From Long Pond it passes along the range over Chairback, Columbus, Third, Fourth and Barren Mountains, and then drops into the valley following Little Wilson Stream to a lovely 50-foot waterfall.

The Trail pushes through Savage's Mills, abandoned to the forest in 1858 and on to Monson with its slate quarries. Monson is one of the two towns one passes through in Maine. The route to Lake Hebron follows old wooded roads. Ahead are Moxie Bald and Pleasant Pond Mountains. Then come Wyman Lake and the Kennebeck River crossing at Caratunk. Here again pleasant side trips are possible.

163

From "The Great Bend of Dead River" the Trail pushes on to Bigelow mountain (4,150 feet) and to the town of Bigelow. Sugarloaf and Spalding Mountains are fine ski areas. After crossing Orbeton Stream, the Trail follows the long range of the Saddleback from which one has a marvelous view of the Rangeley Lakes below. The Trail now lifts itself over a series of disconnected peaks: Bemis, Elephant, C Pond Bluff, Spruce and Baldpate.

At Old Speck above Grafton Notch begins the trail system of the Appalachian Mountain Club. Between Goose Eye Mountain and Mount Success one crosses into New Hampshire. The portion of the Appalachian Trail in Maine accounts for 277 miles.

Swimming and canoeing are popular throughout Maine. Public accommodations are available along some streams and lakes, open generally from April through November, and the network of lean-to's in Maine is uninterrupted.

New Hampshire

Much of the Trail in New Hampshire is above the timberline where temperatures are subject to sudden changes.

The Mahoosuc and the Peabody Brook Trails join the Appalachian Trail and leave it at the Androscoggin River. As it crosses U.S. 2, the Trail enters the White Mountain National Forest, following the Rattle River, Kenduskeag, Wildcat, and Lost Pond Trails to Pinkham Notch. It climbs Mount Madison in the Presidential Range and passes by the Gulfside Trail past Mounts Jefferson and Clay and over Washington, the highest peak in New Hampshire at 6,288 feet. The route follows the Webster Cliff Trail to drop to Crawford Notch near Mount Jackson. After crossing the Saco River, it climbs Mounts Zeacliff, Buyot, South Twin, Garfield and Lafayette, and heads for the Whitehouse Bridge at Franconia Notch. Beyond U.S. 3 the Trail passes through excellent ski country and on to Lost River at the junction of State Route 12. The Appalachian Mountain Club has 9 furnished huts at Lost River providing meals and lodging for travelers during the summer months.

At Kinsman Notch the Dartmouth Outing Club trail system begins. From Mount Moosilauke with its panoramic view, the Trail goes on to Glencliff and then on Cube, Smarts and Moose Mountains to Hanover where it crosses the Connecticut River into Vermont. The Trail in New Hampshire runs 154 miles.

Vermont

In Vermont, public accommodations can be found along the route. There are as well the familiar

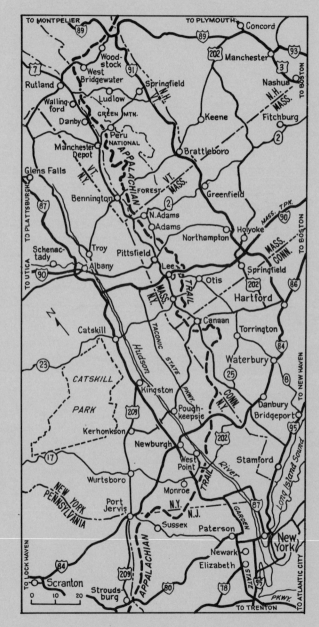

lean-to's regularly spaced for hikers.

The Trail through the Green Mountains is through high country, abandoned farmlands and woodlands. There are 134 miles of the Appalachian Trail in Vermont; the last 95 miles follows the famous Long Trail of the Green Mountain Club.

The first 21 miles follows the White River to State Route 12. This is ski country and the high point is Griggs Mountain. From there the Trail leads west to Sherburne Pass where it turns south into the Green Mountain National Forest, over White Rock, Green Mountain, Mount Tabor, Bromley, Stratton, Glastenbury and Bald Mountains to The Dome near the Vermont-Massachusetts border.

Massachusetts

The 83 Massachusetts Trail miles begin in the Clarksburg State Forest and then pass through the Mount Greylock State Reserve. Mount Greylock at 3,491 feet is the highest point in this state. It too is a strong ski area. The Trail continues through Chesire and from there on old wood roads into Dalton in the October Mountain State Forest of the Berkshire Hills. It crosses Interstate 90 and forges on to Goose Pond, and from there across the Tyringham Valley where the Trail joins Beartown State Forest, another popular ski area. The route is now across the Housantonic River and south along the Taconic Range over Mount Everett to Sages Ravine on the Connecticut border. The Massachusetts portion of the Appalachian Trail provides pleasant walks through hills and valleys and forests. Accommodations of all sorts are available, as they are in the next two states.

Connecticut

Pleasant walks and scenic variety are the features of the 55-mile Connecticut Trail. The Trail begins at the highest point in the state (2,380 feet), over Bear Mountain, Lions Head, and Prospect Mountains and then returns to the Housatonic River at Falls Village, formerly an iron and charcoal center, and recrosses the Housantonic to enter the Mohawk State Forest. There the side trails provide a series of scenic hikes. From Cornwall Bridge the trail leads up through St. Johns Ledges and into the Macedonia State Park through to the foot of Mount Algo near Kent. Cobble Mountain and Pine Hill afford the best views. The Trail parallels the Housantonic and ascends to the New York line at Schaghticoke Mountain, named for the Indian Reservation at its base.

New York

The New York terrain is even tamer than the hill walks of Connecticut. East of the Hudson the Trail follows old roads. The Palisades Interstate Park section is the oldest portion of the Trail and the most heavily used.

From Schaghticoke Mountain, the Appalachian Trail descends to Webatuck and climbs again to Lake Hammersley and down into the Harlem Valley at Pawling. Across that valley to Mount Tom and beyond to Hortontown and Shenandoah Mountain the Trail crosses Fahnestock State Park and slides down Anthonys Nose to Bear Mountain Bridge where it crosses the Hudson into Bear Mountain State Park and Harriman State Park. It skirts Greenwood and Wawayanda Lakes in New Jersey and crosses the Pochuck Mountains, arriving at the foot of the Kittatinny Range. On the crest, just below High Point State Park, the Trail passes into New Jersey once and for all, having flirted for a time with the New York border.

New Jersey

Here the Trail follows a topographic route along mountain crests, and here Benton MacKaye formulated the idea of the Appalachian foot trail. The passage through the Kittatinny Mountains to the Delaware Water Gap is more rugged and remote than any since leaving Vermont, but it is also heavily used. Only three of the six lean-to's in New Jersey are within a day's hike so that a tent on this

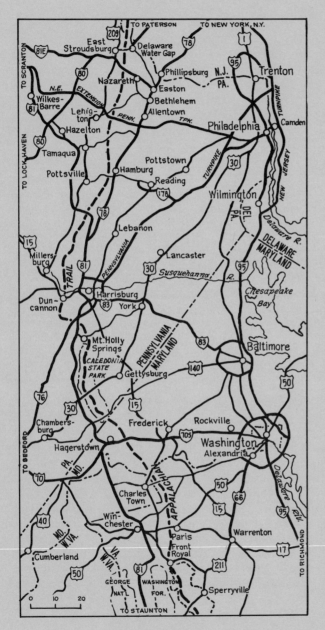

portion of trail can be very useful. The New York-New Jersey segment of the Trail runs 157 miles.

Pennsylvania

One enters Pennsylvania by crossing the Delaware River. The Trail follows the Blue Mountain Range to the Susquehanna River. It crosses the Cumberland Valley and winds into the northern Blue Ridge Mountains. For the eastern portion of this route it would again be prudent to carry a tent because camps are irregularly spaced. But in the last half of the Pennsylvania segment and through Maryland, lean-to's and public accommodations are easy to come by. In this state the trail mileage is 225 miles.

The Blue Mountain Range is an uninterrupted range except for gaps where the Lehigh, Schuylkill and Swatara Rivers cut through. Along the way are a line of old forts that protected the borders during the French and Indian wars. At Swatara Gap the Trail veers northwest to avoid the Indiantown Military Reservation. It crosses St. Anthony's Wilderness and climbs Peters Mountain. Shortly thereafter the Trail crosses the Susquehanna at Clarks Ferry Bridge.

After climbing Cove Mountain and North Mountain, the Trail turns south again away from the Alleghenies on the west. Using secondary routes, it crosses the Cumberland Valley over beautiful farmlands, finally reaching the northern extension of the Blue Ridge.

From South Mountain to Pine Grove Furnace is a broken range. At this historic resort the Trail joins the Michaux State Forest along a terrain of flat ridges. It crosses U.S. 30 at Caledonia State Park and heads for the Maryland border.

Maryland

The 38 miles of the Trail in Maryland provide a marvelous 3 to 4 day trip with towns and highway access nearby. It is one of the most historic regions for the Civil War battlefields it traverses. Most of the trail route is through wooded hills along a narrow ridge that ends at Weverton on the Virginia border.

Virginia—West Virginia

The Virginia portion of the Trail is 463 miles, better than a fourth of its entire length. For the southern portion of any hiking excursion a tent should be carried since accommodations for camping are widely spaced.

At Weverton the Trail picks up the old Chesapeake and Ohio Canal towpath, and follows that west across the Potomac. Ahead is Harpers Ferry, the national headquarters of the Appalachian Trail Conference. The Trail takes the narrow crest of Blue Ridge across Snickers, Ashby and Manassas Gaps. It reaches the Shenandoah National Park near Chester Gap. A wide variety of side trails developed by the Potomac Appalachian Trail Club can be explored here. The chief landmarks of the main Trail are Skyland and Big Meadows. At the southern end of the Park one arrives at Jarmans Gap.

There begins a series of high summits to Rickfish Gap, and from there the Trail parallels the Blue Ridge Parkway at varying distances. At Reeds Gap the Trail swings east and climbs a series of 4,000-foot peaks that include Three Ridges, The Priest, Rocky Knob, Tarjacket, Bald Knob, and Bluff Mountain. In the Jefferson National Forest one crosses the James River. At Apple Orchard Mountain the Forest Service has relocated the trail, taking it west and finally south to Bearwallow Gap. Seven miles later the Trail finally leaves the Parkway area and continues through the National Forest and some private lands to the junction of Interstate 81 north of Roanoke, at the same time crossing the western fork of the Blue Ridge.

Once the Trail crosses the valley, it follows the Tinker Mountain crest southwest where the Roanoke Appalachian Trail Club had to relocate the trail to a remoter area in the 1950's. It winds through the Jefferson National Forest where the scenery is awesome for some 150 miles. Big

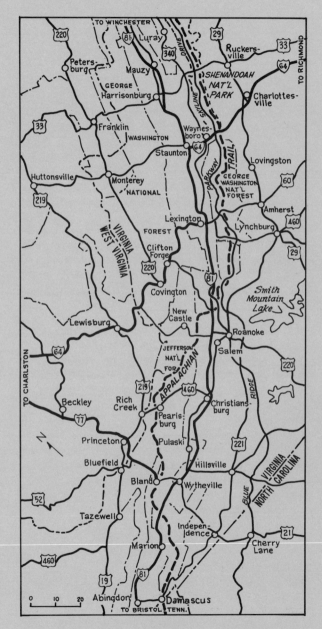

Tinker, Cove Mountain, Dragons Tooth, and Sinking Creek Mountains provide vantage points for the most exhilarating views.

The Trail crosses New River, skirting Pearisburg and heads for Angels Rest; this is followed by Dismal Peak and Dismal Creek and a long hike to Walker Mountain. Beyond the Galde-Brushy Range the Trail bridges the upper Holston River. Relocation will shift the Iron Mountain Range section to the Pine Mountain and Wilburn Ridge area. High meadows and the two highest peaks in Virginia, Mount Rogers (5,719 feet) and Whitetop Mountain (5,520 feet) are outstanding features of the area. The Trail enters Tennessee just south of Damascus.

Tennessee—North Carolina

The Great Smoky Mountains National Park, flowering shrubs in profusion, and an assortment of spectacular views from 4,000- and 5,000-foot peaks make a walk through the Southern Appalachians unforgettable. Camping sites are irregularly located in the last 90 miles of the Cherokee National Forest where tents should be carried. For most of the route to Georgia, the natural border between Tennessee and North Carolina is followed.

Holston Mountain leads through the Cherokee National Forest. In 1954 the Tennessee

Eastman Hiking Club relocated the trail to the top of Iron Mountain and past the T.V.A.'s Watauga Dam. From there it reaches into the rugged Laurel Fork Gorge and follows the crest of White Rocks Mountain.

At the Tennessee-North Carolina line the Trail heads for Hump Mountain (5,587 feet), and follows the border along the Unaka Mountains over Yellow Mountain, Grassy Ridge and Roan High Knob (6,285 feet). The rhododendron display along this route is spectacular. After Little Rock Knob, Little Bald Knob and Big Unaka, the Trail descends to the Nolichucky River and its sheer canyon walls. The crossing is at Unaka Falls.

From here the Trail follows the Bald Mountains to Big Pigeon River, the high point being Big Bald (5,530 feet). It leads on to the Pisgah National Forest with trails diverging to the lookout stations providing splendid vistas. The French Broad River is crossed at Hot Springs, North Carolina. From there the route is over the slopes of Max Patch and Snowbird Mountains to the gorge of the Big Pigeon River West at Waterville.

There the Trail enters The Great Smoky Mountains National Park following the crest of the range to the Little Tennessee River at Fontana. It passes through spruce and fir forests and after climbing Clingmans Dome, the highest point on the entire 2,000-mile trail at 6,643 feet, it passes through the magnificent hardwood forests of this region. The Trail climbs all the major peaks in the Smokies: Old Black, Buyot, Chapman, Laurel Top, Kephart, Clingmans Dome, Silers Bald, and Thunderhead. Much of the trail was relocated to this area in 1947 and 1948 by the Smoky Mountain Hiking Club. After passing over the Fontana Dam, the Trail again climbs to the Yellow Creek Mountains and Yellow Creek Gap.

The Trail has now left the natural border line it has been following, and it enters Nantahala National Forest along the Cheoah Mountains with a series of impressive views of these Southern Appalachians. It crosses the Nantahala River at Wesser and climbs into the 5,000-foot mountain range of the same name, including Copper, Burningtown and Wayah Balds. The Trail then follows a ridge crest to Standing Indian (5,500 feet), drops down into the Tallulah Gorge and on into Georgia. This Tennessee-North Carolina segment of the Trail has covered 342 miles.

Georgia

The remainder of the Trail is entirely in the Chattahoochee National Forest. The ruggedness of this portion of the Trail comes quite unexpectedly, but the familiar lean-to's are comfortably spaced over these last 76 miles.

The first focal point is Tray Mountain,

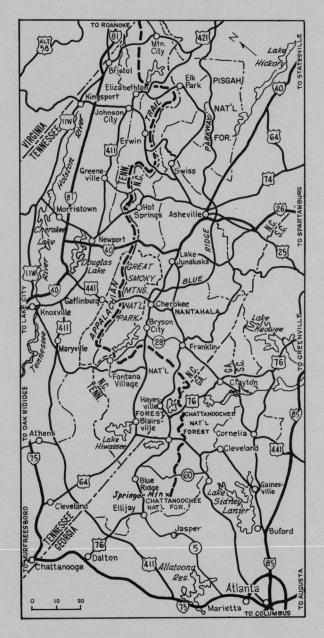

dominating the northern Georgia Blue Ridge. The Trail winds around the headwaters of the Chattahoochee River and heads southwest across Tesnatee to Little Hightower Gaps. Blood Mountain near Neel Gap is the outstanding peak of this area. The southern anchor of the Appalachian Trail is Springer Mountain, at 3,920 feet. There the Trail ends, but as is true so often along the way, a system of side trails leads to scenic points. Once, the southern terminal point was located at Mount Oglethorpe, but commercial developments and road building made this final relocation necessary. The protection of the federal government should fortunately see little further relocation for such reasons.

Few people have hiked the entire length of the Appalachian Trail. Rather it has been the path taken on afternoon walks, weekend hikes or longer vacation trips.

171

Pacific Crest

Adopted in October, 1968, as one of the two National Scenic Trails, the Pacific Crest Trail stretches 2,313 miles from the Canadian border to the Mexican border, following the mountain tops of Washington, Oregon and California. Statistics rarely bring life to a subject, but a few bearing on the route of this Trail suggest something of the accomplishment, as well as the magnitude of the task remaining, since nearly one third of the Trail has yet to be completed.

The Pacific Crest Trail crosses 24 National Forests, 23 Wildernesses, 7 National Parks, 6 State Parks and 2 Primitive Areas. From its low point near sea level at the Columbia River crossing, it climbs to a 13,200-foot height at Forester Pass in California. It climbs 109 mountains, 47 of which are glacier peaks and reaches some 1,000 lakes, ponds, pools or tarns.

The idea for such a trail was Clinton C. Clarke's. In 1932 he organized the Pacific Crest Trail Conference to further his idea. Today the Pacific Crest Club, founded 1972, carries on that work in much the same way as the Appalachian Trail Conference has done in the East. Their primary objective is to coordinate knowledge and service under the supervision of the U.S. Forest Service and National Park Service in preserving this wilderness trail. The Quarterly published by the Club will provide detailed information on all matters related to the Trail. Their first issue contained a listing of Post Offices in the more remote regions where provisions could be sent for later pick-up by backpackers, and it listed the bus routes that serve dozens of areas where the Trail intersects major roads and highways.

The entire route, most of it so well known and loved by the famous naturalist John Muir, requires the frequent use of superlatives in description. A generous share of the most verdant forests, the tallest and oldest trees, the highest mountains, the most breathtaking waterfalls, lie along the route of the Trail. The unique golden trout, and the nearly extinct giant condor and California grizzly live in these regions with hundreds of other more common wildlife species.

Portions of the Trail had their own names by which many will still know them, names such as the Cascade Crest Trail in Washington, the Oregon Skyline Trail, and in California the Lava Crest Trail, the Tahoe-Yosemite Trail, the John Muir Trail and the Desert Crest Trail. The proper designation for the entire route is now the Pacific Crest Trail, and it is this designation on the trail markers.

Only horse and foot traffic are allowed, but highway and road access to most areas puts the Trail within reach of almost anyone willing to make use of it. The main trail is only the main

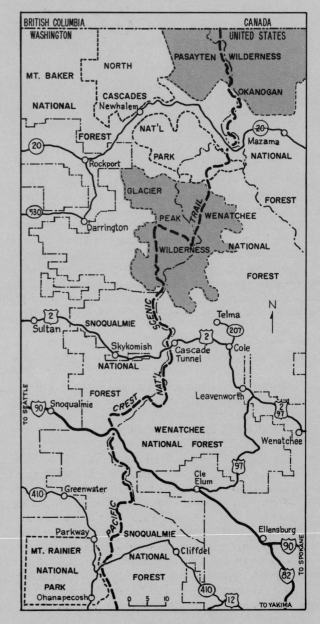

artery of miles of scenic side trails that lace the national parks and forests.

In many areas campsites are easy to come by, but overuse in recent years has made it necessary to reserve sites ahead of time in the most frequented locations. Some stretches of the route require camping without established sites.

Careful planning for trips is imperative, since supply points are infrequent, and one can rely on several days' distance from supply and communications points.

Washington

The 457 miles of Pacific Crest Trail in Washington pass through the Pasayten Wilderness, Okanogan National Forest, North Cascades National Park, Mount Baker National Forest, Glacier Peak Wilderness, Wenatchee National Forest, Snoqualmie National Forest, Mount Rainier National Park, Goat Rocks Wilderness, Gifford Pinchot National Forest and Mount Adams Wilderness.

At or near each of the Trail locations throughout Washington and Oregon, primitive campsites exist unless otherwise indicated. From these points a system of feeder trails diverge to areas famous for their interest and beauty.

In Canada the Trail starts in the E. C. Manning Provincial Park at Monument 78 on the Canada-U.S. border. There the elevation is 4,250 feet. The Trail heads for Castle, Hopkins, Woody, Holman, Windy and Harts Passes. Only the first two locations do not have camp locations developed. At Harts Pass a narrow gauge wagon road was built in the 1890's to reach Slate Creek mines. This 38-mile section of trail winds through high subalpine timber growth and open meadows with patches of scattered timber.

From Harts Pass the Trail follows the mountain crests to Glacier, Methow, Cutthroat and Rainy Passes. There State Route 20 intersects. The route continues to the North Cascades National Park boundary and the Glacier Peak Wilderness-Lake Chelan National Recreation Area. Recent construction along this 52-mile trail section has improved the condition of the Trail. Horse feed should be carried since it is scarce along the way. The National Park area is especially rich in scenic side trails to places of great beauty.

Following Agnes Creek, the Trail passes Suiattle Pass (5,983 feet) and Glacier Peak Mines, where an alternate route is in use until the Middle Ridge section is completed. Until one has passed Sky Bridge, few campsites exist in this section. The route heads for Fire Creek Pass, Sitkum Creek, White and Cady Passes, with high, open meadow views. At Wenatchee Pass, water is scarce, and at Union Gap the intersecting Smith Brook Trail leads to U.S. 2. This section of trail accounts for 80 miles.

At Stevens Pass, where the Great Northern completed its Cascade Railroad crossing in 1893, U.S. 2 intersects. The area is very popular among skiers, and the camper would do well to resupply here. Skykomish, 16 miles west is a good supply base. For many miles the Trail now overlooks the Cascade lake country with a trail network hunting out many of the most beautiful among them. The Trail route leads to Trap Lake, Deception Pass and Dutch Miller Gap. Beyond Hardscrabble Creek Crossing, and Goldmeyer Hot Springs, the Trail reaches Snoqualmie Pass Summit, the junction of Interstate 90 and U.S. 10. This again is an excellent supply point with the town of Snoqualmie only 24 miles to the west. This again is ski country. Those using horses must use the Snow Lake Trail to reach Snoqualmie Pass since the last portion of trail is impassable to them and other sections are very risky except on foot. The Stevens to Snoqualmie route covers 78 trail miles.

The Trail now pushes past Yakima, Stampede and Tacoma Passes on its way to Blowout Mountain. The view is panoramic, and huckleberries can be picked in season. Windy Gap, the junction for the Pyramid Peak Trail, Arch Rock Camp, Norse Peak and Bear Gap lead to Chinook Pass (5,447 feet), where State Route 410 crosses the Trail. Skiing is popular here too, and supplies

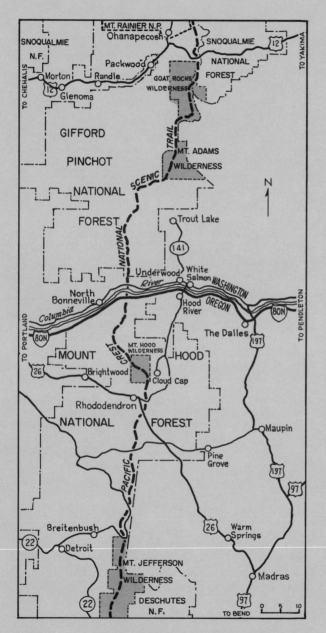

can be purchased at Enumclaw 42 miles west. This 60-mile stretch of the Trail is characterized by numerous high mountain passes and highly scenic vistas. Well marked detours are occasionally met.

At Chinook Pass the Trail enters Mount Rainier National Park for eleven miles, providing a series of magnificent views of this giant. Fires are never permitted in the Park, so campers might prefer to use Dewey Lake nearby. Laughingwater Junction is ahead, followed by the White Pass Campgrounds. At White Pass, U.S. 12 intersects, bringing skiers during their season. From there the route is through Tieton Pass and Snowgrass Flats, an area noted for its wildflowers, and then to the junction with the Nannie Ridge Trail. Feed for horses must be carried over this 55-mile segment of the Trail. In the Goat Rocks Wilderness, picture postcard scenery is common.

Next on the route comes the junction of the Walupt Lake Trail, the Forest Service Station at Midway near Lava Spring and Green Timber Camp. Few campsites exist until this last point is reached. The Trail then joins the Round-the-Mountain Trail in the Mount Adams Wilderness, and goes on to Steamboat Lake, Bear Lake and Blue Lake. Along this 57-mile passage one can enjoy the huckleberry fields around Midway (berries are ripe in September and October), the splendid wilderness region around Mount Adams and the

175

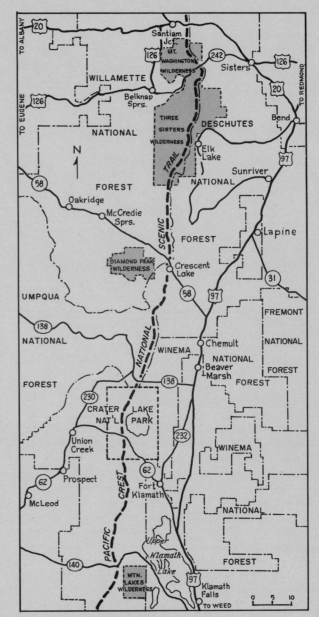

lakes in the Indian Heaven country of Cultus Creek.

The last 33 miles of Washington Trail intersects Carson-Guler Road 8 miles south of Blue Lake, then follows the western edge of lava beds to Grassy Knoll, and drops down Dog Mountain to State Route 14 where the Columbia River serves as the natural boundary between Washington and Oregon. The river is best crossed on the Bridge of the Gods.

Snow covers much of the Trail even into early summer on occasion, and cold weather clothing is generally welcome at the higher elevations.

Oregon

In Oregon the Pacific Crest Trail route leads through the Mount Hood National Forest, Mount Hood Wilderness, Willamette National Forest, Mount Jefferson Wilderness, Mount Washington Wilderness, Deschutes National Forest, Three Sisters Wilderness, Umpqua National Forest, Crater Lake National Park, Winema National Forest, Mountain Lakes Wilderness and Rogue River National Forest.

The general route climbs out of the Columbia River Gorge, along the skyline of the Cascades for 400 miles, high on the flanks of Mount Hood, past Mount Jefferson, Three-Fingered Jack, and

Mount Washington, through the Belknap lava fields, past the Three Sisters, and into the beautiful lake country; then on the Crater Lake, along Mount McLoughlin, past Lake of the Woods and down to the California border.

At the Columbia River Gorge work center, the Trail wends its way to Wahtum Lake and Lost Lake, both with improved campgrounds, past Lolo Pass where there is no campsite and to the junction of the Timberline Trail. It climbs on to Paradise Park and Timberline Lodge with the U.S. 35 junction only a few miles away at Barlow Pass. There the first wagon route through the Cascades was built in 1845, enabling immigrants to avoid the dangerous rafting of the Columbia. The first 56-mile segment ends at Wapinitia Pass. Water is scarce in the Bald Mountain area; Herman Creek and the Sandy River can be dangerous at high water time. Much good camping is available in this area with fine improved campgrounds dotting the entire region. Both Government Camp and Lost Lake are used as supply points. Timberline Lodge, sitting on the shoulder of Mount Hood, provides the luxury of a resort for those who want a change as well as fine campgrounds. This is Oregon's most popular ski area.

From Wapinitia Pass the Trail heads to the Skyline road junction with U.S. 26 just 10 miles north, and then on to Olallie Meadows with its improved campgrounds. In winter this too is a ski area; in fall it is a huckleberry area where Indians still do some picking. (The Indian word Olallie means "huckleberry.") Some supplies can be purchased here. This segment of the Trail measures 48 miles.

The Trail winds through rough mountain country to Breitenbush Lake Camp. (Another improved campground is located here.) At Pamelia Lake, side trails lead to a number of other fine lakes, but the Trail heads for Minto and then Santiam Passes. Here U.S. 20 and 126 intersect. Parts of this 47-mile portion of trail are in poor repair when wet weather causes frequent slides. Horse feed should be carried. The snow field near Mount Jefferson should only be crossed in daylight since the trail marking there is difficult and often obscure.

Over the next 48 miles the Trail is first rough and abrasive as it cuts through lava flow. But from the McKenzie Pass on, it is in excellent repair. Snowstorms can be expected as early as mid-September. The Trail at McKenzie Pass intersects State Route 242 with Sisters, 15 miles east, serving as a good supply area. The lava flow over which the Trail passes came from Belknap Crater. At the Pass is located the Dee Wright Observatory overlooking eleven peaks. It was named for a famous mountaineer, guide and trail builder. Farther

177

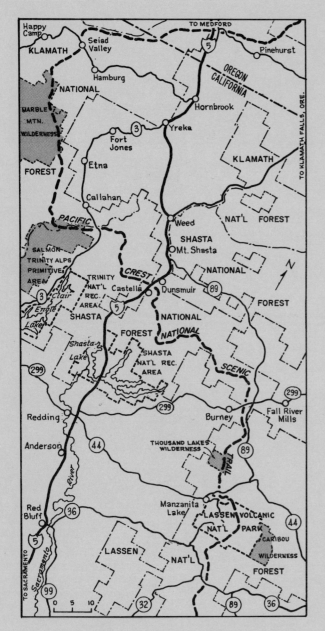

along, the Trail reaches Sunshine Campsite with inviting trails spreading on either side, and Horse Lake Forest Service Station with an even broader network of side trails.

Over the next 43 miles one passes through some of the most impressive and beautiful lake country. The direct route passes Stormy Lake and Charlton Lake, but these points diverge on a system of excellent trails to Irish, Taylor, Waldo, Cultus, Lily, Betty, Davis, Maiden and Rosemary Lakes. Ahead lies the Willamette Highway Junction leading to Eugene 66 miles distant. Odell and Crescent Lakes can be reached from this point by anyone with the time for this excellent trip. Both areas are also good supply points.

The section from Windigo Pass to Crater Lake National Park requires carrying a water supply. Access to Chemult 13 miles east of the Pass is possible. In this 46-mile stretch, established campsites are often quite distant from each other, but intersecting side trips are often possible. One can reach Diamond Lake from the Mount Thielsen Trail junction. With State Route 138 only a half mile away, this junction is a good supply point. At the northern boundary of Crater Lake National Park, the Trail is 6,050 feet high. Throughout the Park a wide variety of trails lead to points of interest, with none more spectacular than the lake itself. It lies at the bottom of the extinct Mount

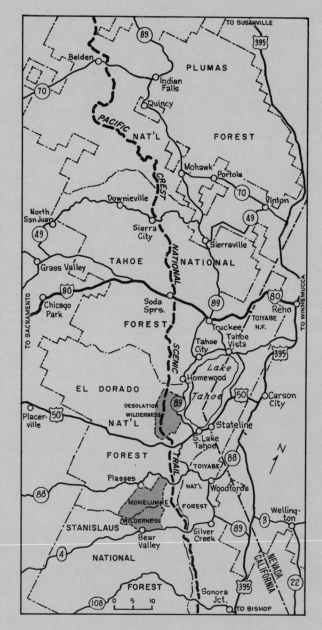

Mazama volcano and is 2,000 feet deep, deeper than any fresh water body in the country. Most of all it is a uniquely beautiful sight.

The next 42 miles of Trail within the Park and as far as Four Mile Lake is in good repair. At Devils Peak Lookout, one can encounter snowdrifts even in summer, while the 10-mile passage through the Oregon Desert requires that one carry water and horse feed. Side trails from the junction of Fire Road, the southern Park boundary, Marguerette Lake Camp and Four Mile Lake provide an array of trips in all directions to isolated streams, lakes, mountain peaks, vista points, fishing sites and campgrounds.

To this point the Oregon route of the Pacific Crest Trail has been located at elevations ranging between 4,000 and 7,000 feet. Deep snows until mid-July and after mid-October make it impassable during those months. But the last 44 miles are usually open between May and November. South of the National Forest boundary the Trail crosses private lands and is not as well maintained or marked as on public lands. The scenic highpoint is Lake of the Woods with its resort, improved campsite and excellent fishing. This is also a good supply point. From there the Trail heads for the boundary of the Rogue River and Winema National Forests. When it has passed through this area it crosses State Route 66 leading to Klamath

Falls 37 miles east, and Ashland 25 miles west. The last leg of the Trail heads for Copco Lake 2 miles south of the Oregon-California line.

For both Washington and Oregon, fine detailed Trail maps are available through the Forest Service.

Northern California

In California the Pacific Crest Trail passes through Marble Mountain Wilderness, Salmon-Trinity Alps Primitive Area, Klamath National Forest, Shasta-Trinity National Forest, Castle Crags State Park, McArthur-Burney Falls Memorial State Park, Thousand Lakes Wilderness, Lassen Volcanic National Park, Caribou Wilderness, Middle Fork of the Feather River (Wild River), Plumas National Forest, Tahoe National Forest, Desolation Wilderness, Eldorado National Forest, Mokelumne Wilderness, Toiyabe National Forest, Emigrant Basin Primitive Area, Hoover Wilderness, Yosemite National Park, Devils Postpile National Monument, Sierra National Forest, Minarets Wilderness, John Muir Wilderness, Kings Canyon National Park, Sequoia National Park, Inyo National Forest, Domeland Wilderness, Sequoia National Forest, Mojave Desert, Angeles National Forest, San Gabriel Wilderness, Cucamonga Wilderness, San Bernadino National Forest, Hart Bar State Park, San Gorgonio Wilderness, Mount San Jacinto State Park, San Jacinto Wilderness, Cleveland National Forest, Anza-Borrego Desert State Park and Cuyamaca Rancho State Park. This accounts for 1,048 Trail miles on public lands; an additional 402 miles of private lands are crossed by the Trail.

In Washington and Oregon the Trail is virtually complete; in California the total length of uncompleted trail measures almost 600 miles. Temporary travel routes are being identified around these sections, using other trails or lightly traveled roads. Local inquiry is the best way to determine the exact route until all of the Trail has been constructed.

The first highly detailed map of the California route will be published in 1973. In isolated areas a compass is an essential tool, as are the topographical maps published by the U.S. Geological Service. It is a good rule to inform someone where you expect to be at various points of your route, and to call in when these points have been reached. Most of the first two-thirds of the California Trail route are at such high elevation that passage is not possible before late July or after the beginning of October. The best supply points along the route are at road and highway junctions with towns nearby.

In California the Trail begins in the Rouge River National Forest near Condry Mountain. Its

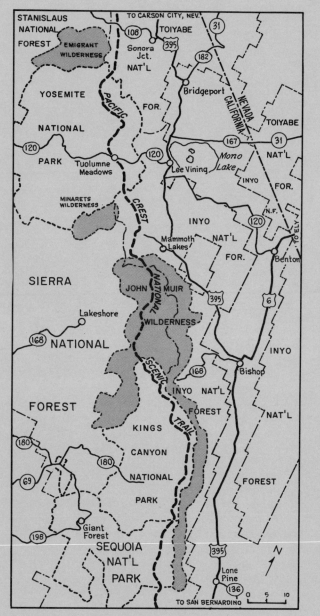

direction is southwest until it reaches Seiad Valley where State Route 96 intersects. After crossing the Klamath River, the Trail heads for the northwestern tip of Marble Mountain Wilderness. It cuts diagonally west to east across this area emerging at the road leading to Sawyers Bar and Etna. Next it crosses the road between Cecilville and Callahan and turns east to pass through a corner of the Salmon-Trinity Alps Primitive Area. Side trails explore this fine wilderness region. The Trail then follows the beautiful Scott Mountains through the Shasta Recreation Area heading for Lake Britton. At Castle Crags near Dunsmuir, the Trail crosses Interstate 5 following a route that passes McCloud River and Lake, Grizzly Peak and the town of Cayton near Rock Creek. At Cayton, State Route 89 intersects. The Dunsmuir area is a popular ski area lorded over by Mount Shasta (14,162 feet).

Shortly after leaving the Lake Britton area, the Trail heads south crossing State Route 299 near Burney. As the route enters Thousand Lakes Wilderness, Eiler Lake and Crater Peak are of particular interest on side trails. State Route 89 is again crossed just before the Trail enters Lassen Volcanic National Park. Recent volcanic activity has left the area with a fascinating series of hot springs, lava beds, caves and cinder cones, all amid green forest growths to hike through. The Trail

181

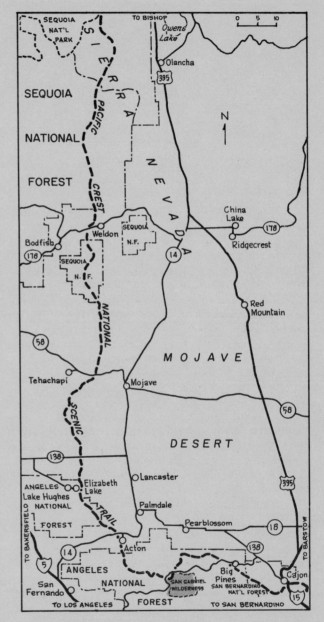

bed is abrasive here. Of particular interest are Cinder Cone, Juniper Snag and Lassen Peak itself. In winter this is a popular ski area.

The Trail continues south through the beautiful recreation lands of Lassen and Plumas National Forests. It crosses the North Fork of the Feather River near Belden where State Route 70 intersects. Lake Almanor lies to the east. After passing Bucks Lake, the Trail crosses the Middle Fork of the Feather River, one of the nine original Wild and Scenic Rivers in the country. From there the Trail veers southeast climbing through ski country, the Lake Basin Recreation Area to Sierra City where State Route 49 crosses. A marvelous lake region lies ahead. Milton and Jackson Meadow Reservoirs, Bowman, Spaulding, Webber and Summit Lakes are only the largest lakes tied together by scenic side trails. At Soda Springs near Emigrants Gap, the Trail has a junction with Interstate 80. For the next 150 miles popular ski areas are near the Trail.

The Trail enters the Lake Tahoe region. It can be reached by side routes but lies hidden by the high mountains that protect it on the east. The route is through French Meadows Reservoir, Squaw Valley, Alpine Meadows, Wentworth Springs and Loon Lake. Through Desolation Wilderness, near Lake Aloha, Pyramid Peak, Echo Lake and Echo Summit, the Trail makes its way to

182

the U.S. 50 junction.

Still following mountain crests, the Trail cuts State Route 88 at Carson Pass. Before crossing State Route 4, it passes through another lake region including Blue and Meadow Lakes and Grover Hot Springs, all near the Mokelumne Wilderness. Then through Ebbetts Pass, past Highland Peak and Sonora Peak (11,429 feet) and on to the junction of State Route 108 at Sonora Pass. Skirting Emigrant Wilderness, the Trail enters Yosemite National Park near Tower Peak (11,704 feet). In this high country even summer nights can be quite cold. Proper clothing is important.

The long stretch of 150 trail miles from Yosemite to the headwaters of the Kern River follows a continuous strip of mountain lakes, all competing in their charm and beauty. Fortunately the network of side trails to many of these lakes makes the choice even more difficult, but if a choice must be made, a random one will not disappoint. Access to the region is possible from U.S. 395 paralleling the Trail on the east. State Routes 120 into Yosemite, 168 into the Sierra National Forest and 180 into the Kings River Canyon are the chief east-west arteries. This is the heart of John Muir country, an area one can spend a lifetime exploring.

The Trail winds past Buckeye Pass, Burro Pass, through Matterhorn Canyon to Tuolumne Meadows. For a time it follows Lyell Fork, then takes the Donohue Pass by Thousand Island Lake and Garnet Lake to Devils Postpile National Monument. In the Mammoth Lakes district it heads for Duck and Purple Lakes and Lake Virginia, then through Silver Pass and between Rose and Marie Lakes to Selden Pass.

Side trails lead to some of the most loved recreation areas in California: Mono Lake, Hetch Hetchy Reservoir, Tuolumne Canyon, Yosemite Falls, Badger Pass, groves of giant sequoias, small and large mountain lakes and streams, and such 10,000-foot mountains as Eagle Peak, Mount Dana, Parsons Peak, Triple Divide Peak, Red Slate Mountains, Mount Morgan and Three Sisters. More lies ahead.

Southern California

As the Trail winds through the John Muir Wilderness into Kings Canyon National Park and through Sequoia National Park, the temptation to follow each side trail increases. South of Florence Lake the Trail follows the South Fork of the San Joaquin River, enters Evolution Valley and Evolution Basin, and follows Le Conte Canyon. Along the way the traveler has passed Desolation, Davis, Wanda and Helen Lakes as well as Mounts Humphreys, Darwin, Goddard and Pinchot, all more than 13,000 feet tall.

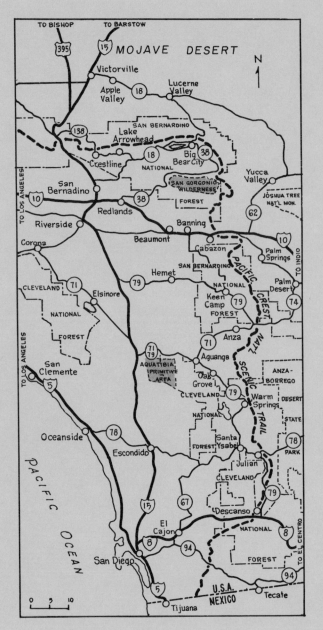

South of Kearsage Pass the Trail reaches its highest elevation of 13,200 feet at Forester Pass, from which a side trail leads to Mount Whitney, the highest peak in the continental United States at 14,495 feet. From its summit one can look down into Death Valley where Bad Water marks the lowest point in the United States at 282 feet below sea level. Whitney is flanked by two other 14,000-foot giants, Mounts Williamson and Langley.

The Trail now descends to the Mojave Desert, passing through the southern Sierra Nevada. It follows the Kern River past Kern Peak, the Needles, Sherman Peak and near Salmon Falls. It reaches Weldon on State Route 178 after having passed through the Dome Land Wilderness. One should carry water during the desert passage leading over the junction of State Route 58 between Tehachapi and Mojave. The Trail now leads on through the San Gabriel Mountains.

At Lake Hughes it veers off to Bouquet Reservoir and its junction with State Route 14. From there it winds southeast past Pacifico Mountain, Devils Punchbowl, Mount San Antonio (better known as Old Baldy, 10,064 feet). This is popular ski country for southern Californians. The route goes to the intersection with Interstate 15 leading to San Bernardino, and on to Silverwood Lake, Lake Arrowhead, Big Bear Lake and Baldwin Lake in the San Bernardino National

Glacier Peak rises above Buck Creek Pass.

Forest. Summer and winter resorts are common in the area. The highest peak in this range is San Gorgonio Mountain at 11,845 feet.

The last portion of the Trail now leads south across Interstate 10 through the San Jacinto Mountains and past the Agua Caliente Indian Reservation near Lake Hemet. It crosses the Cahuilla and Santa Rosa Indian Reservations, the Cleveland National Forest, the Santa Ysabel Indian Reservation and U.S. 80 near Descanso. Both State Routes 79 and 94 are crossed before it finally reaches International Boundary Marker 251 near Tecate, the southern terminus of the Pacific Crest Trail.

Because the southern end of the Trail passes through mountains less imposing and difficult than those encountered in the north, some prefer this approach as a start on a border to border crossing since it conditions the traveler for the difficult climbs ahead. The southern portion of the Trail also contrasts with the northern in vegetation, terrain and wildlife. Naturally many parts of the Trail throughout its length are suitable for shorter trips of a weekend or a few weeks.

The scale of this Wild and Scenic River dwarfs the half-hidden figure on the rocks.

IV Wild and Scenic Rivers

Allagash

Season: *Year round; best between May 15 and October 15*

Size: *200,000 acres, 30,000 of which are water.*

Access: *Telos Lake is 50 miles west of Patten on Grand Lake Road, across the northern Baxter Wilderness Park. Umsaskis Lake is 55 miles west of Ashland on American Realty Road and Churchill Lake about 23 miles from Umsaskis. Permits for this private toll road can be obtained in advance from Paper Industry Information Office, 133 State Street, Augusta, Maine 04330.*

Camping: *Primitive camping*

Guides and rentals: *Not generally available*

Difficulty rating: *Waters range from smooth to sections of long rapids with intricate maneuvering.*

Address: *Department of Parks and Recreation
Augusta, ME 04330*

The longest trip through the Waterway begins at Telos Lake and ends at West Twin Brook, a distance of 92 miles. Many prefer to continue for another five miles to Allagash Village, where the Allagash joins the St. John River. This longest trip takes from 7 to 10 days. Those with less time might prefer a shorter trip from Umsaskis north to West Twin Brook, a section which is mostly river, or from Telos north to Churchill Dam, which is mostly lake.

Contrary to normal expectations, the Allagash flows north so that downstream always seems headed the wrong way. Across Telos Lake and through Round Pond takes the canoeist into Chamberlain Lake, and ten more miles brings him to Lock Dam, built in 1841 to divert the Allagash waters into the East Branch of the Penobscot River. A side trip of six miles just west of Lock Dam up the mouth of Allagash Stream takes him to the memorable solitude of Allagash Lake where no mechanized equipment is permitted. But the water level of the side streams, such as Allagash Stream, is extremely variable, especially late in the season, and considerable portage may be necessary.

A 12-mile paddle across Eagle Lake follows a short portage from Lock Dam. A two-mile run through the thoroughfare precedes five more miles of lake water to Churchill Dam.

The most spectacular portion of the trip is directly ahead, the nine-mile Chase Rapids to Umsaskis Lake. This is the most taxing stretch of water. It takes an experienced stern man to guide a canoe through the rocks when the water is high.

Those who do not wish to run Chase Rapids will find private portage service at Churchill Dam, but that service is not always available after October 1.

The trip across Umsaskis Lake is five miles to the thoroughfare at Long Lake. Another five miles through this lake is followed by the 10-mile run down river to Round Pond. At the end of the next 18-mile paddle, one arrives at the scenic climax of the trip, Allagash Falls, some 40 feet high. The Falls require a portage of one-third of a mile. The final eight-mile run ends at West Twin Brook.

All provisions must be carried in. There are no supply stops until the end of the trip at Allagash Village, or farther down the St. John River at St. Francis or Fort Kent.

In winter these waters are used for fishing and trapping on snowshoes. With the arrival of snowmobiles, winter traffic has increased, though there are few snowmobile trails.

Warm clothing is necessary for nights and rainy days. Before the middle of May, ice is a serious problem. Trips should not be planned before that time. In the month of June the black fly season is at its worst. Most of the common insect repellents afford enough protection. Both the river and the lakes provide drinking water, but normal purification procedures should be followed. The only hiking trails lead to fire towers from which spectacular views can be seen.

Regular state licenses govern hunting and fishing. Brook trout, togue and lake whitefish are plentiful. Moose, whitetail deer, black bear, hunting cats, eagles, loons, ruffed grouse, the Canadian jay and pipit, mink, weasel and snowshoe hare are all found in this area.

Primitive man has left his mark here at grave sights and through stone age tools. The Indians followed and left a legacy of myths and place names. French trappers and lumbermen were followed by the English. Today the forests, already in their fourth and fifth growths, are impressive in their size. Spruce, fir and pine are the most common species, but birch, maple and beech are also common. There are various grasses, rushes, mosses and lichens.

This is a land explored and recorded by Thoreau. He was working on his favorite book, *The Maine Woods*, when he died. We can still enjoy much that Thoreau described because of the 1966 legislative act that sets this area apart to "preserve, protect and develop the natural beauty, character and habitat of a unique area."

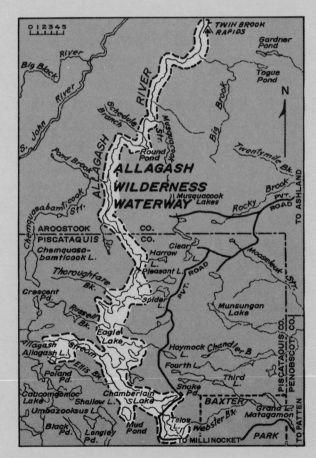

Clearwater Middle Fork

Season: *Year round*

Size: *56,000 acres, 185 miles*

Access: *U.S. 12 and State Route 13 both lead through Kooskia; U.S. 12 follows the Middle Fork of the Clearwater and Lochsa.*

Camping: *Primitive and improved camping; some commercial services available*

Guides and rentals: *Commercial outfitters and guides are available in the Lowell and the Smith Creek-Syringa areas.*

Difficulty rating: *These are not waters for canoeing. Boat floating and river rafting range in difficulty from moderate to hazardous even for the expert.*

Address: *Office of the Forest Supervisor*
Clearwater National Forest
Orofino, ID 83544

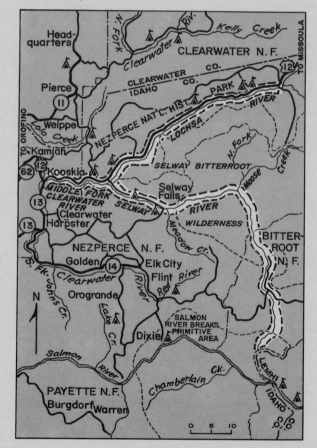

The Recreational River classification includes the Middle Fork of the Clearwater from Kooskia to Lowell, the Lochsa from Lowell to the Powell Ranger Station, and the Selway from Lowell to Race Creek and from Paradise to the Magruder Ranger Station. This accounts for 131 river miles.

The Wild River classification includes the Selway from Race Creek to the Paradise Guard Station, and from the Magruder Ranger Station to the headwaters of the Selway. These areas have no access roads. Trails reach into the area and five low-standard airstrips requiring experienced mountain pilots provide access. The Wild River sections account for 54 miles of the river system.

The Selway to Paradise Recreational section is so classified only because of the road beside it. In all other respects, this area should be treated as a Wild River area.

Simple float and trail camps are spaced along the river banks. Trails lace the entire area along some of the scores of creeks that feed the rivers, and through the mountainous country.

Trout fishing yields rainbow, cutthroat, brook, German brown and Dolly Varden. Salmon and steelhead spawn in these waters and whitefish are also caught. In-season hunting offers elk, deer, moose, mountain goat, black bear and bighorn sheep. The hiker and camper might see coyote, wolverine, mountain lion, mink, marten, otter,

Selway-Bitterroot is near the Clearwater.

marmot and badger among the more unusual species. In the subalpine areas one can see the glacier lily, alpine poppy, columbine, white dryad, globeflower, Indian paintbrush, violets and asters. At the higher elevations grow Rocky Mountain laurel, white and purple heather and Labrador tea.

Bird hunters take blue, Franklin and ruffed grouse and Merriam turkey. Besides the many songbirds the raven, Canada jay and osprey are common, and both the bald and golden eagles do their hunting here.

Ponderosa pine, Douglas fir, lodgepole pine, Engelman spruce and western larch cover the mountains and foothills.

The river traveler can expect pleasant and moderately difficult challenges on the Recreational sections of the river system. The most hazardous challenges occur in the Wild River sections containing for the rafter a variety of vicious and long rapid stretches, falls, boulders, rough currents and the dangers of steeply walled canyons.

Side trips to some of the many hot springs that dot the area are possible.

Eleven Point

Season: *Year round*

Size: *14,191 acres, 45 miles*

Access: *On State Route 99 near Thomasville for the northern access; on State Route 142 near Gateswood for the southern approach*

Camping: *Primitive and improved campsites*

Guides and rentals: *Some recreation services such as canoe rentals are available.*

Difficulty rating: *Easy to medium for canoeing and floating; some rapids*

Address: *Mark Twain National Forest*
3001 E. Trafficway
Springfield, MO 65802

Some say the Eleven Point River has been used by man since 10,000 B.C. when hunters roamed the banks. Village life developed here by 1000 A.D. The Pigman Mount archeological site is of considerable significance in tracing this history. Arrowheads and tools of the Osage Indians testify to their presence until 1830, when they were driven away. This was just 21 years after the arrival of the first white settler. The Spanish and French, who also explored the area, have not left their marks.

By 1930 the population of the area reached its peak. The decline since that time has been accounted for by the increased land holdings of some farmers and timbermen.

The classification given to the entire 45-mile section of this river is Scenic. Forested hills account for 85 percent of the terrain through which the river runs. The remainder is private farmlands in pasture and hay meadows.

At Thomasville the river is small, slowly gaining in volume from the many springs that feed it in its course. Shallow riffles and long deep holes characterize its run here as well as its clear blue-green color and the purity of the water.

The tempo changes at the junction of the Greer Springs Branch where that underground river boils out of a rock bottom, changing the Eleven Point into a long, swift, cold river. The boater can expect fast tumbling shoals and long

deep pools from this point on.

The feeder springs that continue their input deserve a comment. Posy Spring emerges at the base of a bluff, tumbling over moss covered sandstone boulders. Roaring Springs bursts out of a horizontal crack on the face of a bluff. Graveyard Spring bubbles out of sand in a nearby field. Geer, Blue and Morgan Springs emerge like underground rivers.

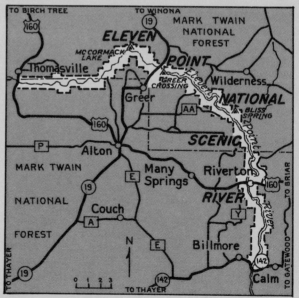

ELEVEN POINT

As the river carved its channel it left the large bluffs and caves of dolomite sandstone for which the area is justly famed. It is a river inviting family use. Float camps are available for that purpose. Infrequently the river is subject to fast rises, a precaution the boater should be aware of.

The most unique botanical values are concentrated at Greer Springs and at the Narrows. The 20 miles of trails serve to make such areas of this Ozark wilderness available to campers and hikers, but during the peak summer season the area is sometimes overused.

Gnarled junipers twist out of the cracks along the bluffs. Hardwood forests alternate and mix with pine along the hills. Common to the area are the sycamore, willow, river birch, ash, box-elder, Ozark oak, elm, sugar maple and basswood. Mixed in one finds dogwood, wild rose, sweet william, blue bell, redbud, azalea, serviceberry and a wide range of wildflowers.

The river banks and forests are home to squirrel, woodchucks, quail, white-tailed deer, beaver, muskrat, blue heron, wild turkey and fox. Sometimes the coyote and bobcats are seen, and occasionally an eagle can be sighted.

The Eleven Point is not famous as a fishing river although it provides recreational enjoyment. There are trout and largemouth, smallmouth and rock bass to be caught.

The Ozarks have long been famous for their special beauty. This Scenic River area is graced with some of the most memorable, gentle wilderness scenery to be encountered.

Scouting is always required on Wild Rivers.

193

Feather Middle Fork

Season: *Year round; best between May 1 and October 31*

Size: *25,000 acres, 108 miles*

Access: *The Recreation portion of the river is reached by driving State Routes 49, 70 or 89 to the mountain communities of Portola, Clio, Graeagle, Blairsden, Mohawk or Sloat. The Oroville Lake end of the river area can be reached on paved roads as far as Berry Creek or Feather Falls, and on dirt roads thereafter.*

Camping: *Accommodations range from resorts and motels to improved and primitive campsites.*

Difficulty rating: *Portions of the river are so treacherous and rescue operations so difficult to come by and dangerous to execute that they are considered impassable.*

Address: *Plumas National Forest
Quincy, CA 95971*

The Rio de las Plumas, translated into the Feather River, was named by Captain Luis A. Arguello in 1820. Apparently the cottonwood trees were shedding their blooms into the river, giving the appearance of drifting feathers.

Until 1850, the mountainous segment of the Feather River was little known to the white man. The Gold Rush changed that completely so that today, old machinery, abandoned water ditches and faint trails still slightly suggest the fevered activity of that time. Although mining has almost disappeared, campers are allowed to do simple recreational gold prospecting along the river.

The emigration resulted in the use of Beckwourth Pass, the lowest crossing in the Sierra Nevada Mountains at 5,212 feet. This is four miles from the origin of the Middle Fork. Logging, lumbering and farming sprang up along the Middle Fork and continue today.

Between Little Last Chance Creek and Lake Oroville, the river drops from 4,900 feet to 900 feet. From that northeast corner of the Sierra Valley, the river flows generally southwest across the Plumas National Forest. Rivers usually flow first through rugged terrain, and gradually into more gentle valleys. But the Middle Feather River is unusual in that it begins in a gentle valley, switches into moderate mountain terrain, and finally plunges into the canyons above Lake Oroville.

The Recreational zone stretches from Little Last Chance Creek, past mountain towns for some 65 miles to a railroad tunnel. The scenery is sagebrush that becomes rangeland, small rocky canyons, timbered flats and meadowland. Swimming, boating, fishing, riding, camping and even golf can be enjoyed on day trips using motel or resort accommodations as well as both improved and primitive campsites. Visits to Frenchman Reservoir, Lake Davis, Lakes Basin, and Gold Lake can be managed.

English Bar Scenic River zone is an almost tame wilderness. Timber stands are close to the river and less rock and steep terrain is visible than in the lower portions. The Quincy road to La Porte crosses at Nelson Point and access on unimproved roads is possible. Trout fishing here and on all parts of the river is excellent. This stretch of river is six miles long.

The Upper Canyon Wild River zone extends 27 miles from Nelson Creek. The river is rugged and rocky. Slopes are well vegetated but steep. Access is available on three roads and also on trails. At Hartman Bar the trail bridge and camp are on the crossing for the Pacific Crest Trail (Canada to Mexico, see page 172). Travel along the river here is often difficult. It is usually easier to get above the river using old mining trails and deer trails which skirt the break made by the river channel. These trails are not maintained.

Travel from end to end of this zone has rarely been accomplished because of the cliffs and swift flowing water.

The Milsap Bar Scenic River zone is 3½ miles long. Again the area is rugged, but fishing in three streams, the Middle Fork, the Little North Fork and the South Branch, is inviting. A mile upstream from Milsap Bar Campground on the South Branch one comes upon Seven Falls.

The final 5½ miles of river before it pours into Lake Oroville is the Bald Rock Canyon Wild zone. The scenery is dominated by massive boulders, rock cliffs, waterfalls and canyon walls of sheer rock. Feather Falls, the third highest waterfall in the 48 contiguous states is a memorable side trip. Again, travel from end to end of this zone has rarely been accomplished because the natural barriers are so great.

The upper river is in the snow belt, but paved roads are usually open. Unimproved roads can be too soft for vehicles in wet weather. In general, the weather is dry in summer and wet in winter, with summer daytime temperatures often being uncomfortable. Nights are cool or cold. In late spring, high water can be a problem.

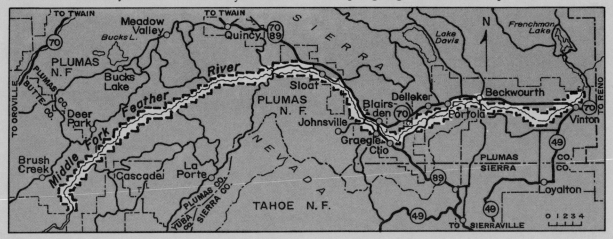

195

Rio Grande

Season: *Year round*

Size: *16,880 acres, 52.75 miles*

Access: *East-west access on State Route 96 to the Taos Junction bridge connects with U.S. 285 21 miles south of Tres Piedras. State Route 111 to the Rio Grande high bridge connects with U.S. 285 and State Route 3 ten miles north of Taos.*

Camping: *Primitive and improved campsites*

Guides and rentals: *Available in the Taos-Santa Fe areas*

Difficulty rating: *Expert boaters can negotiate the entire Wild River section when conditions are ideal. The fluctuating water level makes this an unpredictable event.*

Address: *Bureau of Land Management*
1304 Fourth Street
Albuquerque, NM 87107

Early in its journey through a sagebrush valley in New Mexico, the Rio Grande slips into a basalt-rimmed trench 50 miles long and 300 to 800 feet deep. There the river withdraws from man, renewing itself in rapids and pools. It descends 1,500 feet in the 50 miles, polishing basalt to glass-like smoothness, sheltering and feeding giant trout. Eagles nest in and hunt the canyon's rims. The Spanish named it El Rio Grande del Norte, "the great river of the north." Only in this 50-mile trench does the river today resemble the one of yesterday. The river feeds on generous springs and four small tributaries—Red River, San Cristobal Creek, the Arroyo Hondo and Taos Creek, where the Wild River designation ends. The lower four miles of the Red River match the Rio Grande gorge in depth and primitive character and have therefore been included with the section of the Rio Grande.

Indian tribes first lived here and some still do so today. Spanish explorers, fur trappers and settlers have also left their marks.

A series of springs, misnamed Arsenic Springs, are located above Red River. They produce water in such volume and of such quality and temperature that they have created a superb natural trout fishery. It can be reached from Questa on State Route 3.

The Rio Grande trough was formed by complex geologic processes involving uplift, faulting and a series of overlapping andesite-basalt lava flows. Ute Mountain (10,120 feet) and Cerro la Olla (9,450 feet) are striking examples of extinct volcanoes.

The widest and deepest portion of the canyon occurs at the confluence of the Rio Grande and Red Rivers where it is 800 feet deep and 4,000 feet wide.

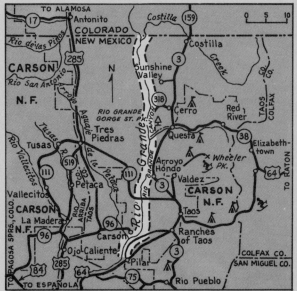

A broad selection of hiking trails wind through this area, but passages along the riverbank are few.

Land ownership consists of Federal lands, Indian lands and parts of three Spanish land grants that have never been surveyed.

The entire Wild River section is certainly scenic without the official scenic designation, since 98 percent of the river is designated Wild. The remaining 2 percent is designated Recreational because of the accessibility by automobile.

Mallard, teal and merganser are the most common waterfowl; a few quail and a goodly number of mourning doves are the major game birds. Brown and rainbow trout ranging from 2 to 16 pounds have been caught and are the chief wildlife value. Smallmouth bass are of less importance. Nongame species are varieties of sucker, carp, dace and chub. Deer and antelope are the chief big game; nongame species include varieties of songbirds, raptors, mammalian predators and rodents.

Fluctuating water depths, canyon walls, boulders, rough water rapids and treacherous currents are problems that await boaters, but the spectacular scenery makes the hardship worth enduring.

Steep-walled rivers are among the roughest for navigation, camping, hiking and rescue.

Rogue

Season: *Year round*

Length: *84 miles*

Access: *From Gold Beach east along the gravel road that follows the river to Lobster Creek. Both U.S. Highway 199 and Interstate 5 meet in Grants Pass where it is a short drive west on a paved road to the mouth of the Applegate River.*

Camping: *One improved campsite, otherwise primitive*

Guides and rentals: *Both are available in the Grants Pass area and the Gold Beach area.*

Difficulty rating: *Designated portions of the river range in difficulty from easy to so treacherous that canoes and kayaks are banned.*

Address: *Bureau of Land Management, USDI*
310 West Sixth Street
Medford, OR 97501

The Rogue is born in the high Cascades near Crater Lake and carves its way west through Oregon's coastal mountains to the sea. The 84-mile stretch designated as Wild and Scenic between the mouth of the Applegate River and Lobster Creek provides quiet waters beside timber covered slopes, and the rushing torrent of swirling waters crashing over boulders or churning through narrow defiles.

Below Grave Creek the Rogue can only be explored in boat or on foot, since horses, pack animals and all motorized transportation is banned. At Grave Creek begins a 40-mile trail that follows the north bank of the river to Illahe. There the hiker can continue on to Gold Beach by following the road. The trail is well constructed and of moderate grade. Although few other trails provide the hiker with an opportunity to explore, this trail should satisfy the most demanding. There are a series of shorter trails and roads in various stages of passability that link the area.

Hikers usually take five days for the trip to Illahe. This allows time to enjoy the scenery, study the geology, plants and wildlife and to note some of the vestiges of gold mining. Water purification tablets and full provisions must be packed since many campsites don't provide pure water, and no supply stations are to be found enroute.

Above Hellgate, willows line the banks. Oregon ash and big leaf maple occupy most areas.

Pacific madrone and Oregon white oak can be seen on the dry ridges. On lower stretches of the river, western red cedar, Port Orford cedar, Pacific yew, canyon live oak, golden chinkapin, tanoak and Oregon myrtle occur among stands of Douglas fir, western hemlock, grand fir and sugar pine. Botanical rarities such as weeping spruce, knob-cone pine and pitcher plants are found in a few remote areas. Rhododendrons, azaleas, Pacific dogwood, Oregon grape, salal, salmonberry and varieties of fern can be found on the banks of side streams. Only along the lower Rogue does the golden iris grow.

The Rogue cuts through dissected plateaus exposing rocks of the Mesozoic Era, including serpentine, greenstone, granite, sandstone, slate and shale.

Species of fish found in the Rogue include Chinook Salmon, coho Salmon and steelhead trout, all of which migrate up the river to gravel beds suitable for spawning. Additionally, cutthroat and rainbow trout, shad, sturgeon, bullhead catfish, black crappie, bluegill, largemouth bass, carp, sucker, lamprey, red-sided shiner, sculpin, stickleback and dace use these waters.

The great blue heron does his fishing beside the shore. These large birds stand four feet tall and have a six-foot wingspan. Common mergansers, belted kingfishers, water ouzels, cliff swallows, ospreys, bald eagles, pileated woodpeckers, bandtailed pigeons, blue and ruffed grouse, quail, hummingbirds, thrushes, juncos, ducks and shore birds can be spotted by the alert bird watcher.

Black-tailed deer, Roosevelt elk, black bear, otter, racoon, mink and the Douglas squirrel are rather common, while the ringtailed cat or cacomistle is a rare find. Lizards, skinks, newts and salamanders abound, while the ring-necked snake, king snake, rattlesnake and Pacific pond turtle are rather frequent. (Antivenin snake serum should be part of every first aid kit.)

The McKenzie-type high-bowed drift boats or six-man rubber rafts are generally used for floating the Rogue. Boaters are urged to go in boat groups of two or three to provide greater safety and emergency aid. Power boats of any type are allowed only above or below the Wild and Scenic stretch of river. Commercially guided float trips begin at several boating spots between Grants Pass and Grave Creek. They offer trips of three to eight days duration stopping at commercial lodges or at public recreation sites.

The 19 miles of river between Grants Pass and Hellgate Canyon is a mild, easy stretch, but the next 13 miles to Grave Creek provide a

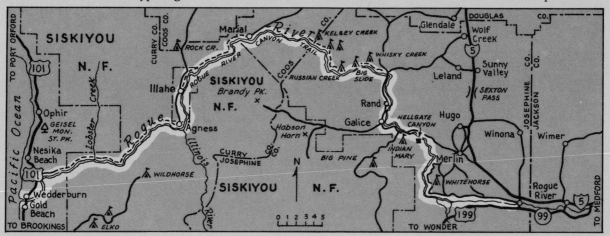

medium stretch of water. Rapids have irregular waves but passages are clear though narrow with expert maneuvering needed. Inspection trips on land before running rapids is strongly recommended. The next 20-plus miles of long rapids, powerful and irregular waves, dangerous rocks and boiling eddies makes maneuvering difficult. Inspection is mandatory before going through. Below Grave Creek 1.7 miles waits Rainie Falls, a 10-foot drop that one must portage or where the boat must be lined around the falls. Mule Creek to Blossom Bar Rapids (2.2 miles) is an extremely dangerous run, with violent rapids following without interruption. Vertical walls of rock on either side make scouting difficult but no less important. The river bed has big drops and violent currents. From there to Brushy Bar is another hazardous stretch (3.7 miles), followed by seven miles of moderate river and a final 24 miles of comfortable navigation, despite rapids.

A driftboat passes through Mule Creek Canyon.

ST. CROIX

Season: *Year round, but ice and snow limit river use in winter.*

Length: *200 miles*

Access: *East-west traffic reaches Taylors Falls and St. Croix Falls on U.S. 8; State Routes 87 and 95 serve north-south traffic. Riverside is reached on State Route 35. Trego on the Namekagon is served by U.S. 53 and 63.*

Camping: *Primitive and improved campsites; picnic areas*

Guides and rentals: *Guides are not available or considered necessary, but canoe rentals are available in the Trego and the St. Croix Falls areas.*

Difficulty rating: *Both rivers provide the canoeist with a variety of water ranging in difficulty from easy to moderate.*

Address: *National Park Service*
St. Croix Falls, WI 54024

The combined length of the St. Croix and Namekagon Rivers is the longest among the original nine Wild and Scenic Rivers. Of the 200 miles, only 19 are classified as Recreational, the remaining 181 miles being classified as Scenic. The St. Croix River serves as the boundary between Minnesota and Wisconsin for most of its length. It empties into the Mississippi.

The southern terminus of the St. Croix is located at Taylors Falls in Interstate Park. Picnic and camping grounds can be found here. A number of trails serve hikers, but few trails presently exist throughout the area, with many more presently planned.

The St. Croix originates, as does the Scenic portion of the river, at Gordon Dam on Lake Gordon and develops over 35 rapids in the first 12.5 miles. These rapids are of low to medium risk. Until one reaches the last 12.5 miles before Taylors Falls, the river flows south providing waters with some moderately difficult rapids, currents that range from slow to fast, one high hazard rapid at Big Fist Trap and magnificent forest scenery. The Recreational portion or last 12.5 miles is busier.

One of the principal tributaries of the St. Croix is the Namekagon river. It flows generally

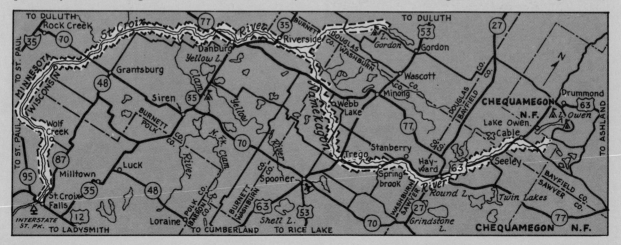

west from its origin in Lake Namekagon. The first 63.5 miles are classified as Scenic until the river reaches Trego. There a 6.5 miles stretch is classified as Recreational. The last 28 miles until the Namekagon joins the St. Croix at Riverside are again designated as Scenic. The scenery here as on the St. Croix is marked by rolling hills and almost endless tracts of pine and hardwood forests.

For the avid fisherman or for the neophyte, a better choice of rivers could hardly be imagined. Good catches of smallmouth bass, trout, northern pike, walleye, musky, catfish and panfish are the rule rather than the exception.

Deer and black bear are the most common large game. A wide variety of ducks are also hunted as are several species of grouse. The snowshoe hare, beaver, otter, procupine and muskrat are often spotted.

Several types of maple, yellow birch, hemlock, aspen, ash and red oak make up the hardwood forests. White, red and jack pine forests cover the hills.

Both rivers have their source in lakes, a fitting origin since the entire region is dotted with hundreds of lakes, one more beautiful than the next, most of them remote from access roads. Hikers and campers can discover peace and solitude and the thrill of stumbling upon a remote lake surrounded by dense forests.

River areas often offer good side trips, too.

Salmon Middle Fork

Season: *June to October*

Size: *32,000 acres, 106 miles*

Access: *From Boise north on State Highway 21; from Sun Valley north on U.S. Highway 93 to Stanley and from there 20 miles on the Dagger Falls Road.*

Camping: *Primitive camping*

Guides and rentals: *Idaho Outfitters and Guide Association Inc., P.O. Box 95, Boise, Idaho 83701*

Difficulty rating: *From placid water and quiet pools to long continuous rapids without let-up; very tortuous, irregular, powerful cross currents. No canoes allowed. Rubber rafts and kayaks only.*

Address: *Boise National Forest*
413 Idaho Street
Boise, ID 83702

The Middle Fork of the Salmon is a mighty river flowing through one of the deepest gorges in North America. Born at the confluence of Marsh and Bear Valley Creeks, the Middle Fork plunges 106 miles northeast to join the main Salmon.

Some of the descriptive place names along its route suggest the ruggedness of the river: Dagger Falls, Powerhouse Rapids, Artillery Rapids, Cannon Creek Rapids, Pistol Creek Rapids, Broken Oar, Haystack Rapids, Porcupine Rapids, Cliffside Rapids and Rubber Rapids.

In order to preserve the wilderness aspect of this Idaho Primitive Area (see page 73), no motorized transportation is permitted except for the use of airplanes to established landing fields. The river cuts through parts of the Boise, Challis, Payette and Salmon National Forests.

Archeologists have found bone chips, tools and mussel shells in rock shelters along the canyon walls dating to a culture over 8,000 years old. Indian paintings and writings in caves and on cliff walls are still in evidence. In 1879 a party of Shoshone Indians sought hiding here from being hunted for an alleged ambush and massacre that has been attributed since to refugees of the Bannock War. Troops at Fort Boise under Captain Reuben V. Bernard set out to capture the Shoshones in what is known today as the Sheepeater Campaign. Fifty-one Indians surrendered.

Literally hundreds of creeks empty into the Middle Fork in its rush to meet the Salmon. The many pools and deep holes provide outstanding fishing spring through fall. Salmon, steelhead, cutthroat, rainbow and Dolly Varden offer excellent angling.

Nearly a third of the Chinook Salmon spawning nests are found in the Middle Fork or its tributaries. The Chinook leaves the ocean between March and July, migrates up the Columbia, and spawns in the Middle Fork during August and September. The young spend a year or two in fresh water, descend to the ocean for one to four years and return to their ancestral waters in turn to spawn and die.

The steelhead, an ocean going rainbow trout, migrates up the Salmon during fall and winter and spawns in the Middle Fork each spring.

This area is also rich in game that again suggests the ruggedness of the terrain. Deer, elk, bighorn sheep, mountain goat and bear may be hunted in season. And there are cougar, lynx, bobcat, coyote, fox, porcupine, badger, beaver, marten, mink, otter, muskrat and skunk. Hunting is open most seasons to chuckar partridge, and Franklin, blue and ruffed grouse. Because this is rattlesnake country it is important to carry snakebite kits with antivenin serum. For information on seasons and bag limits contact

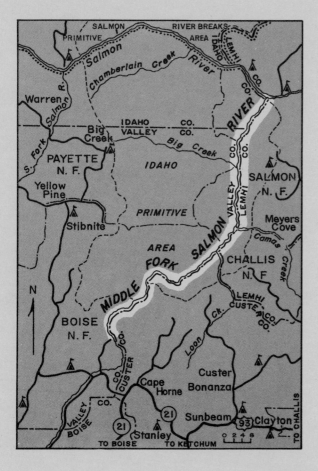

Idaho Fish and Game Department, 600 S. Walnut Street, Boise, Idaho 83706.

Some hunters boat down the river because much of the canyon is virtually impassable on foot or horseback.

Float boating down the Middle Fork is unforgettable. Placid green pools alternate with swift currents and the boiling waters of the rapids. These rapids are not a place for the novice boater. Chances of rescue from a boating mishap are very poor. A licensed guide should be hired for any such trip. Before July and after October, float boating is too hazardous. Most trips begin at Dagger Falls, but in late summer when the water is low it is best to begin float trips from one of the downstream landing fields.

There are many trails weaving through the area. Some link a network of lookout stations, some climb along the Yellowjacket Mountains or through the spectacular Bighorn Crags studded with their 9,000- to 10,000-foot peaks. Still others search out the mountain lakes or follow some of the creeks to their sources. One trail takes the route of the Middle Fork as far as Big Creek, offering a wide variety of side trips on the way.

Wolf

Season: *April to October is the best time. Ice and snow are problems at other times.*

Length: *24 miles*

Access: *North on State Routes 47 and 55 from Shawano to Keshena, or south on State Route 55 from Langlade, Hollister and Lily*

Camping: *Primitive and improved camping facilities, picnic areas and motel accomodations at Keshena Falls*

Guides and rentals: *Canoe rentals are available. Guides are not considered necessary.*

Difficulty rating: *This is not a river for canoe beginners. There are many falls and rapids that are dangerous for experts.*

Address: *National Park Service*
St. Croix Falls, WI 54024

The Scenic River portion of the Wolf River runs 23.5 of the 24 miles. The remaining half mile at Keshena Falls is designated as Recreational because of the heavy concentration of accommodations for visitors. Good camping sites, picnic areas, scenic vista points, parking locations and fishing spots are well spaced throughout the area. Hiking trails lead to points of interest and beauty through hardwood and pine forests.

At Keshena Falls the Menomonie Visitors Destination Center is located with a motel, restaurant, shop complex and museum. Side trips to the nearby lake areas just east of Keshena can be planned.

A listing of the river place names from north to south gives a graphic description of the river's character and activity throughout this 24-mile passage (The asterisk beside a name means that canoe portage is necessary; the dagger recommends portage for all but the most experienced). Gilmores Mistake*, Burnt Shanty Rapids*, Shotgun Eddy*, Pissmire Falls†, Wolf Rapids†, Otter Slide, The Trip Rapids†, Sullivan Falls*, Ducknest Falls*, Tea Kettle Rapids*, the Dalles*, Saturday Islands, Big Smokey Falls*, Pine Row, Fire Islands, Turtle Rapids†, White Rapids†, Big Eddy Falls*, Crow Rapids†, Soman Falls†, Slough Gurdy†, Wayka Rip†, Wayka Falls†, Spirit Rock and Keshena Falls*.

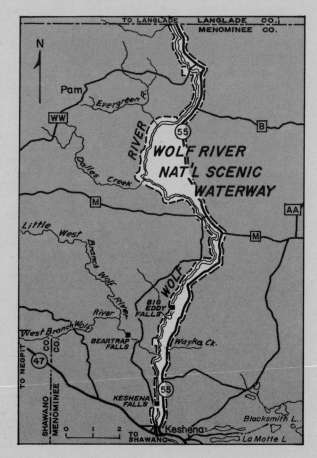

205

The Wolf is a trout fisherman's river. The areas around The Trip Rapids, Sullivan Falls and Ducknest Falls have been set aside for fly fishing only. Some walleye and white bass are also caught.

This 24-mile stretch of river is the shortest river segment to be included among the first nine Wild and Scenic Rivers, but it is extraordinarily beautiful and rich in scenic splendor.

Among the larger game, deer and black bear are common, and otter, beaver, muskrat, porcupine and the snowshoe hare frequent the area. The country is hilly; white pine forests and hardwood forests of ash, aspen, yellow birch and maple provide autumn colors.

This kind of boating takes a knowing oar, along with a cool head and scouting.

Index

INDEX

INDEX

A pack string rides into Eagle Cap Wilderness.

Wilderness Notes

_____   _____
_____   _____
_____   _____
_____   _____
_____   _____
_____   _____
_____   _____
_____   _____
_____   _____
_____   _____
_____   _____
_____   _____
_____   _____
_____   _____
_____   _____
_____   _____

Wilderness Notes

_____   _____

_____   _____

_____   _____

_____   _____

_____   _____

_____   _____

_____   _____

_____   _____

_____   _____

_____   _____

_____   _____

_____   _____

_____   _____

Wilderness Notes

Wilderness Notes

_____   _____

_____   _____

_____   _____

_____   _____

_____   _____

_____   _____

_____   _____

_____   _____

_____   _____

_____   _____

_____   _____

_____   _____

_____   _____

_____   _____

_____   _____

Wilderness Notes

_____   _____
_____   _____
_____   _____
_____   _____
_____   _____
_____   _____
_____   _____
_____   _____
_____   _____
_____   _____
_____   _____
_____   _____
_____   _____
_____   _____
_____   _____

Wilderness Notes

_____   _____

_____   _____

_____   _____

_____   _____

_____   _____

_____   _____

_____   _____

_____   _____

_____   _____

_____   _____

_____   _____

_____   _____

_____   _____

_____   _____

Other Goushā Publications

☐ **LOOK TO THE MOUNTAIN TOP**

Here is a much needed overview of American Indian cultures by storytellers and scholars such as Vine Deloria, Jr., Stewart Udall, Vincent Price and Theodora Kroeber Quinn. Full color used in 70 illustrations. Paperbound . . . . $ 3.95
Clothbound . . . . $ 6.95

☐ **EXPLORER'S GUIDE TO THE WEST**

The complete guide to the famous places, the offbeat adventures, the glorious sights of The American West. Six handsome HARD COVER volumes packed in a vinyl box and accompanied by two FREE bonuses—a Wilderness Escape Map and a Prospector's Treasure Map. $12.95

☐ **BICENTENNIAL BIKE TOURS**

Two hundred bicycle tours throughout the U.S., each touching on an important historical site or city. 100 maps. Paperbound . . . . $ 3.95

☐ **OUTDOOR ADVENTURES**

A collection of fishing tips, camping suggestions and anecdotes from the outdoor experiences of nationally known writer Herb Williams. Paperbound . . . . $ 1.95

☐ **AMERICAN CRAFTS GUIDE**

A big, nationwide, comprehensive directory lists thousands of craft shops, studios, museums, galleries, supply houses, places of instruction and sources of Indian and folk art . . . . . $ 3.95

☐ **BICENTENNIAL TOURGUIDE**

Beginning with 12 activities, such as Beach Exploring, Battlefield Tours and City Touring-all with a Bicentennial theme-this atlas contains maps of all 50 states and 25 American cities; with full color photographs and maps. Paperbound . . . . $ 1.00

☐ **WHERE ARE YOU?**

A map puzzle book for all ages. Paperbound . . . . $ 1.25

FAMILY FUN MAPS

Complete recreation and entertainment guides to major cities of the U.S. Detailed city maps, descriptive text, photographs.

☐ **Chicago** . . . . $ 1.25
☐ **Los Angeles** . . . . $ 1.25
☐ **Washington, D.C.** . . . . $ 1.25

Other descriptions and a handy order form appear on the next page

REC VEE TRAVELERS

A new concept in recreation maps—state guides for owners of trailers, pickup campers and motor homes. Where to go, where to camp, how to survive in cities, road hazards. Detailed state maps.

- ☐ **Northern California** . . . . $ 1.95
- ☐ **Southern California** . . . . $ 1.95
- ☐ **New York** . . . . $ 1.95
- ☐ **Vermont/New Hampshire** . . . . $ 1.95
- ☐ **Florida** . . . . $ 1.95
- ☐ **Texas** . . . . $ 1.95

TOURMAPS

☐ **Rodeos**

A tourmap of America's biggest and best. Descriptions of all events. U.S. road map showing location of major rodeos. . . . . $ 1.50

☐ **Landmarks of the Revolution**

A tourmap showing all the important historical sites you can visit during the 1973-1976 Bicentennial Celebration. Detailed maps, exciting descriptions. . . . . $ 1.50

☐ **The First Americans**

A tourmap of Indian lands. Where to visit the First Americans, where to see and buy arts and crafts, and maps of ancient and modern cultures. . . . . $ 1.50

TRAVEL PLANNERS

Practical and complete specialty maps that show travelers where to find the best attractions in the Northeastern, Southeastern, and Midwestern U.S.—and how to get there.

- ☐ **Northeastern U.S.** . . . . $ 1.25
- ☐ **Southeastern U.S.** . . . . $ 1.25
- ☐ **Midwestern States** . . . . $ 1.25

If you are unable to find any of these books locally, you can order directly from the publisher by using this handy order form.

GOUSHA PUBLICATIONS

P.O. Box 6227   San Jose, California 95150

Please send me the books and maps I have checked above. I am enclosing $_____ (check or money order—no currency or C.O.D.). Include list price plus 20¢ per book to cover shipping and handling. Add state and local taxes where applicable.

Name_____

Address_____

City_____ State _____ Zip_____

Allow three weeks for delivery.

Cut Here